DEMOCRACY AT THE EDGE OF CHAOS

Designing Institutions for Nonlinear Times

Lawrence R. Kunkel

ISBN: 979-8-9953857-0-7 (Hardcover print)
ISBN: 979-8-9953857-1-4 (Softcover print)
ISBN: 979-8-9953857-2-1 (Digital)

First Edition.

The Stable Democracy Press, New York City, printed and sent out
The design and typography were done by The Stable Democracy Press.

This book is dedicated to James Gleick, author of "Chaos: Making a New Science" (Viking Penguin Group, New York, 1987). His book introduced me to Chaos Theory, which was vital to my understanding of Complexity Economics and nonlinear dynamics. Independently, I connected these concepts to political economy, economic philosophy, moral ecology, systems humanism, and democratic instability.

About the Author

Lawrence R. Kunkel is a Game Theory and Complexity Economist. Kunkel's work embodies what might be called an interdisciplinary systems humanism: a fusion of economics, political philosophy, social psychology, chaos theory, and ethics into a unified framework for understanding and improving human freedom. Mr. Kunkel did his graduate work in the Division of Social Science at the University of Chicago (A.M., 1981), where he had matriculation privileges in the Graduate School of Economics, the Booth School of Business, the Law School, and the Committee on Social Thought. Mr. Kunkel served as the research assistant to George J. Stigler, the Charles R. Walgreen Distinguished Service Professor of Economics and the 1982 Nobel Laureate in Economics. He also studied under two other Nobel Prize Winners in Economics, Robert Lucas (1995) and Gary Becker (1992). Kunkel is the author of *The Moral Ecology of Collapse: Essays on Inequality, Complexity, and the Instability of Democratic Societies.*

Table of Contents

List of Figures

FOREWORD

Democracy is often described as a set of ideals—freedom, equality, representation, the rule of law—held together by civic virtue and sustained by a collective belief in fair play. That description is not wrong, but it is incomplete. In the twenty-first century, the most urgent truth about democracy is that it behaves less like a creed and more like a complex system: adaptive, nonlinear, sensitive to initial conditions, and prone to abrupt shifts when hidden thresholds are crossed. It can look stable for long periods, then, under accumulating stress, change state quickly. It can absorb shocks that seem existential and then stumble over disturbances that appear minor. It can survive bitter disagreement, yet fractures when trust and legitimacy quietly drain away.

This book begins from a sober premise: democratic life now sits closer to the edge of chaos than most of our inherited political language admits. That edge is not a metaphor for apocalypse. It is a technical description of a regime in which feedback loops become decisive and where governance (like any high-stakes system) can slip from control into volatility. When institutions operate near criticality, conflict becomes harder to contain, compromise becomes costlier, and small errors can propagate into large failures. The familiar symptoms—polarization, misinformation, corruption scandals, policy paralysis, declining faith in public authority—are not independent problems. They are signals that the system's parameters have shifted.

If democracy is a complex system, then the question we face is not simply, "Do we still believe?" It is: "What are the requirements and conditions that keep a pluralistic society governable?" That question pushes us away from performative nostalgia and toward design. It forces an engagement with incentives, constraints, information flows, and institutional capacity—the hard mechanics that convert values into lived reality. Democracies fail not only because someone violates a norm, but because the system begins rewarding violations; not only because citizens grow cynical, but because cynicism becomes rational under conditions of unequal power and unreliable rules; not only because leaders lie, but because the information environment becomes so disordered that truth loses its coordinating function.

To speak in systems terms is not to drain politics of meaning. It is to rescue meaning from illusion. It is to recognize that legitimacy is not a permanent asset but a fluctuating reserve; that rule consistency is not a rhetorical flourish but a stabilizer; that trust is not sentimentality but a form of social capital that reduces transaction costs and dampens conflict; that corruption is not merely moral failure but a stable equilibrium when detection is low and penalties are weak; and that polarization is not just disagreement but an affective state that changes the "physics" of collective decision-making.

The edge of chaos is where democracies often achieve their greatest dynamism—innovation, reform, creative coalition-building—because constraints loosen and new configurations become possible. But it is also where they become vulnerable to "bad attractors": stable patterns of governance that are corrosive yet self-sustaining. Emergency rule is one such attractor. When trust collapses and legitimacy weakens, the demand for decisive action intensifies; when institutions are captured or paralyzed, shortcuts become attractive; when the public feels humiliated or unseen, it becomes receptive to narratives of punishment and retribution. Under such conditions, exceptional powers can become the norm, and the temporary can become permanent.

The most important contribution of this book is its insistence that democratic repair is possible—but only if we treat it as a problem of sequencing in nonlinear times. Many reform agendas fail because they assume that good ideas, pursued with enough moral fervor, will produce good outcomes. Yet reforms are themselves shocks to the system. High-disruption reforms attempted below what this book calls "minimum viable legitimacy" can trigger backlash, deepen suspicion, and strengthen those who promise domination rather than fairness. The problem is not that reform is wrong; it is that reform has dynamics. In a fragile polity, every major change is interpreted through the lens of distrust. When the legitimacy reserve is low, even correct reforms can be read as factional warfare.

This is why the book advances an order of operations rather than a shopping list. It argues for keystone reforms that rebuild procedural trust: transparency, predictable rules, visible fairness, credible oversight, and clear constraints on discretionary power. These reforms do not solve everything—but they can raise the legitimacy floor enough to make bigger structural changes possible. From there, the agenda expands to capacity and delivery: the state's ability to execute, provide services reliably, enforce rules consistently, and learn from failure. A democracy that cannot deliver becomes a democracy that cannot persuade; promises become insults; policy becomes theater; cynicism becomes a rational response.

Only with legitimacy and capacity strengthened does the next rung become feasible: a prosperity architecture that reduces the stakes of conflict. Inequality and insecurity do more than offend our moral intuitions; they alter political incentives. When citizens experience politics as the only remaining instrument of survival—housing, healthcare, education, and dignity itself—compromise feels like surrender. When wealth concentrates, influence markets intensify; when influence markets intensify, capture becomes routine; when capture becomes routine, legitimacy collapses. The feedback loops tighten. A durable democratic system needs dampeners: institutions and policies that lower the temperature of conflict by making life less precarious and the rules more trustworthy.

In this framework, anti-capture reforms are not purely punitive. They are the engineering of incentives. The book's "payoff surface" logic makes a critical point: corruption and capture persist when they are profitable. Change the expected returns, raise the probability of detection, increase penalties, reduce discretionary opacity, build audit capacity, and the equilibrium shifts. The goal is not perfection. It is to cross the ridge, where capture becomes a bad bet. And when capture recedes, legitimacy can regenerate, because the public can again believe that rules apply to the powerful as well as the ordinary.

Perhaps the most distinctive aspect of this project is its insistence that democracy must also address meaning. Systems can be materially stable and still spiritually brittle. A society can achieve order without belonging, security without dignity, and growth without shared purpose. Such a society may not collapse immediately—but it will drift. People will search for identity substitutes in grievance, conspiracy, and punitive solidarity. The book, therefore, treats civic meaning as a practical program, not a sermon: the rituals, institutions, and public goods that help pluralistic people experience themselves as co-authors of a shared world.

Throughout these pages, readers will encounter diagrams: phase portraits, bifurcation forks, attractor metaphors—not as decoration, but as disciplined ways of thinking. In complex systems, the same event can have different effects depending on where the system sits. A shock during high trust can be absorbed; the same shock during low trust can trigger a cascade. The diagrams aim to make that logic visible. They offer a language for policymakers and citizens alike to ask better questions: Where is the system in its state space? What are the dominant feedback loops? Which dampeners are weakened? Which amplifiers are accelerating? Where are the thresholds? What would it take to move the system back into a safe operating space?

This book is written with urgency, but not with panic. It assumes that democratic repair will be contested, uneven, and imperfect. It assumes that political conflict cannot be eliminated—and should not be. The aim is not harmony. The aim is governability: the ability of a pluralistic society to sustain disagreement without sliding into mutual delegitimation and exceptionalism. That is what "democracy at the edge of chaos" ultimately means: a society able to live near complexity without being consumed by it.

If you read these chapters in one sitting, you may recognize patterns that feel uncomfortable. If you read them slowly, you may also sense something else: that the current moment, precisely because it is unstable, contains possibility. Near the edge, small changes can matter. The task is to make the right changes at the right time, in the right sequence—so that the system does not simply survive, but becomes capable again of producing fairness, dignity, and a future that citizens can inhabit without fear.

That is the promise of this book: not to predict collapse, but to show how to prevent it, by understanding democracy as a living system, and by designing institutions fit for nonlinear times.

Part I

Entering the Nonlinear Regime

Democracy is often described as fragile, but fragility is not a metaphor. In complex systems, fragility has a technical meaning: the system becomes highly sensitive to shocks, prone to cascades, and vulnerable to regime shifts that occur not by deliberate choice but by accumulated stress. Something small triggers something large. A rumor becomes a riot. A procedural dispute becomes a constitutional crisis. A financial tremor becomes a legitimate collapse. We tell ourselves that these are "political storms," anomalies in an otherwise stable climate. Yet what if the climate has changed?

Across the modern democratic world, public life increasingly feels like a society operating too close to its limits. The language of crisis has become normal, and normal politics has become a contest over reality itself. Institutions once treated as boring—courts, election administration, regulatory agencies, procurement rules—have become arenas of suspicion. The political bloodstream carries not only policy disagreements but existential fears. Even when elections proceed, legitimacy feels conditional; even when laws are passed, compliance feels negotiated; even when growth returns, resentment persists.

The standard stories compete for primacy. Some say the problem is misinformation, the attention economy, and a media ecosystem designed to provoke. Others point to polarization and the decay of civic norms. Others still claim democracy is being "attacked" by unscrupulous leaders and movements. These stories can be true at the same time. The question is whether they are sufficient.

This book begins from a different premise: democratic instability is not only a matter of bad actors or bad morals. It is also a matter of system dynamics. Democracies are complex adaptive systems: they are composed of many interacting agents (citizens, firms, media, parties, institutions), each adjusting to incentives and information. They rely on feedback loops—trust, legitimacy, shared norms, and rule-consistency—that stabilize conflict and keep competition within bounds. When those stabilizers weaken, the system does not simply become "worse." It behaves differently. It enters a new regime.

Complexity science provides us with a language for this: nonlinearity, thresholds, attractors, and phase transitions. In a nonlinear regime, small inputs can produce outsized outputs, not because the input is extraordinary but because the system's internal state has changed. The same spark behaves differently in dry brush than in wet soil. Likewise, the same political event behaves differently in a society with high trust than in one with exhausted legitimacy.

What changes a democracy's internal state? Many variables matter. But one variable is underappreciated because it is typically treated as a moral problem rather than a system parameter: inequality. When inequality exceeds certain thresholds, it alters the incentive landscape. It changes what citizens expect from institutions, what elites can buy from politics, and what mid-level actors learn about the rewards of opportunism. Over time, inequality can transform democratic life into a different game—one in which capture becomes rational, cynicism becomes adaptive, and civic cooperation becomes a losing strategy.

In that environment, polarization is not the root cause; it is an amplifier. The attention economy is not the sole culprit; it is an accelerant. The deeper issue is that the system's payoffs and feedback loops are being readjusted. If you change the payoffs, you change behavior. If you change behavior at scale, you change the regime.

This leads to the book's central metaphor: democracy at the edge of chaos. The edge of chaos is not mere disorder. In complexity theory, this region lies between rigid stability and total randomness, where systems can be innovative and adaptive yet vulnerable to cascades. A democracy that becomes too rigid toward rigidity becomes authoritarian and brittle; too far toward chaos becomes ungovernable. Healthy democracies are not perfectly stable; they are resilient. They absorb shocks without losing legitimacy. They correct without collapsing.

But resilience is not automatic. It depends on institutional design. It depends on the presence of "dampeners"—trust, legitimacy, and rule consistency—that reduce volatility. It depends on anti-capture defenses that prevent wealth and power from rewriting the rules to secure a permanent advantage. It depends on material and moral foundations, affordability, dignity, meaning—without which citizens withdraw consent and turn politics into tribal survival.

This book is therefore not an elegy for a collapsing republic. It is a design manual for stabilizing a nonlinear society. It treats democracy not as an inheritance that merely needs appreciation, but as an ecology that requires maintenance. It asks: What are the stabilizing feedback loops of democratic life? What breaks them? What design principles rebuild them? How do we prevent "bad attractors" in which corruption becomes stable, and reform becomes naive?

To speak of "design" is not to treat society as a machine. Complex systems cannot be controlled like clocks. Yet they can be shaped. Their incentive landscapes can be altered. Their feedback loops can be strengthened. Their thresholds can be respected. The goal is not utopia. The goal is governability with legitimacy, conflict without collapse.

If *The Moral Ecology of Collapse* examined how inequality, complexity, and moral drift produce fragility, this book takes the next step: it proposes an architecture for repair. It is written for citizens who sense that something has changed, for leaders who want to reduce volatility without reducing freedom, and for anyone who refuses the false choice between technocracy and nihilism.

Democracy is not dying because people forgot how to be virtuous. It is destabilizing because the system has entered a nonlinear regime—and because our institutions have not been redesigned for the physics of the new age. The edge of chaos is not a prophecy. It is a diagnosis. And diagnosis is where repair begins.

Chapter 1
The Edge of Chaos Republic

Democracies are often portrayed as moral projects or constitutional achievements: a people agree to govern themselves, constrain coercion through law, and settle conflict at the ballot box rather than with bullets. Those stories matter, but they leave out a crucial fact about the systems we inhabit: a republic is not merely a set of ideals, nor even a legal design; it is a living, nonlinear machine for converting conflict into legitimacy. It processes information, incentives, identities, fears, and aspirations. It routes the outputs of markets, media, courts, bureaucracies, movements, and geopolitical shocks back into the political bloodstream. And because these inputs interact—sometimes amplifying each other, sometimes canceling out—the republic behaves less like a clock and more like weather: patterned, sensitive, and occasionally stormy.

To call a democracy "at the edge of chaos" is not to indulge in drama. It is to borrow a precise intuition from complexity science: many adaptive systems do their best work in a narrow band between rigid order and incoherent disorder. Too much order and the system becomes brittle—stable until it shatters. Too much disorder and the system cannot coordinate—noise overwhelms signal, and collective action collapses into factionalism or paralysis. The edge-of-chaos region is where the system remains coherent enough to coordinate and legitimate enough to command obedience, yet flexible enough to learn, innovate, and survive shocks.

This chapter frames the republic as a complex adaptive system and argues that modern democracies are being pushed toward dangerous dynamics not because citizens suddenly became irrational, but because the underlying feedback loops—economic, informational, institutional, and geopolitical—have changed their coupling strength and speed. In nonlinear times, "normal politics" is not a safe assumption. The old equilibrium stories break down. The task of democratic design becomes less about perfecting static ideals and more about building institutions that can remain legitimate under turbulence: systems that can sense, absorb, adapt, and reform without lurching into breakdown.

1. The Republic as a Living System

A constitutional republic is often imagined as an arrangement of formal powers: legislature, executive, judiciary; federal and local authorities; rights and constraints. That description is accurate but incomplete. A republic is also an ecology—a set of interacting "species" of institutions, norms, and incentives that co-evolve. Courts depend on compliance; compliance depends on legitimacy; legitimacy depends on procedures, outcomes, and a sense of fairness; fairness depends on material distributions and cultural recognition; distributions depend on markets, technology, and policy; policy depends on elections and state capacity; elections depend on information; information depends on media architectures and trust; trust depends on experiences of governance and social cohesion. Each element is both a cause and an effect. That circularity is the signature of feedback.

Complex systems are characterized by:

- **Interdependence:** components affect each other in networks, not lines.
- **Nonlinearity:** small changes can produce large effects; large inputs can produce little.
- **Feedback:** outputs return as inputs, either stabilizing (negative feedback) or amplifying (positive feedback).
- **Adaptation:** agents learn; institutions respond; strategies evolve.
- **Emergence:** macro-behavior arises from micro-interactions without centralized control.
- **Path dependence:** history matters; early choices constrain later options.

A republic characterizes all of these. Elections are a learning mechanism. Laws are boundary conditions. Parties are coordination technologies. Norms are informal enforcement regimes. Civic trust is a shared resource. And legitimacy is the system's most precious form of energy: it reduces transaction costs, calms fear, and makes rule-following rational.

But legitimacy is also fragile. It can accumulate slowly and be lost quickly. It can be eroded not only by corruption or violence, but also by a prolonged mismatch between promised meaning and lived experience. When a democracy's story (equal dignity, fair opportunity, representation) diverges too far from material reality (exclusion, stagnation, capture), legitimacy begins to leak. The system then requires more coercion, more propaganda, more legal hardening, which further stresses legitimacy. That is a classic positive feedback loop.

2. What "Edge of Chaos" Actually Means for Politics

The phrase "edge of chaos" is sometimes used loosely to mean "a mess." In complexity research, it names a specific regime of behavior. Consider two extremes:

- **Over-ordered systems** (highly rigid): they produce consistent outputs, but they resist novelty. They excel in stable environments, then fail catastrophically when conditions change.
- **Over-chaotic systems** (highly disordered): they generate novelty but cannot preserve it. They fail to stabilize learning into reliable structures.

Between these extremes lies a region where systems can maintain **organized complexity**: enough structure to transmit information and coordinate action, enough flexibility to explore alternatives and adjust. In this regime, systems often show rich patterns, adaptive behavior, and high computational capacity.

Translated to governance, an edge-of-chaos republic is one in which:

- Conflict is real but **processable**.
- Competition exists but does not become **predatory**.
- Institutions are strong but not **frozen**.
- Norms are respected but not **sacred**.
- Reform is possible without revolution; **stability is possible without repression**.

The "edge" is not a single point. It is a band of tolerable turbulence—where a democracy can metabolize shocks, negotiate pluralism, and incorporate dissent. The danger is that modern conditions (rapid technological change, financialization, polarized media, geopolitical churn) can push democracies out of that band. When feedback loops become too fast, too amplified, or too tightly coupled, a system can pass a threshold and flip into a different attractor: chronic dysfunction, illiberalism, or fragmentation.

The essential question for institutional design is therefore not "How do we maximize stability?" but "How do we maintain *adaptive stability*—the kind that flexes under stress and reforms under pressure?"

3. Nonlinear Times and the Acceleration of Feedback

Why "nonlinear times"? Because the governance environment is increasingly defined by speed, connectivity, and cascading effects. Several developments have changed the operating conditions of democracy:

a) Information velocity and attention markets

Public opinion used to be shaped by slower cycles: newspapers, scheduled broadcasts, and local institutions. Today, attention is a high-frequency market. Content is ranked and replicated based on engagement metrics, and engagement is optimized through outrage, fear, and identity threat. This doesn't merely "misinform." It changes the dynamics of politics by tightening the coupling between emotional arousal and political behavior, accelerating rumor-to-action pipelines, and rewarding extreme signaling over measured deliberation.

b) Economic complexity and distributional stress

Modern economies are complex networks of global supply chains, concentrated platforms, and financial instruments. Small disruptions can ripple widely; concentrated power can extract rents; inequality can rise without a single identifiable villain. Economic frustration then becomes politically available: it is translated into resentment, scapegoating, or anti-institutional anger. When citizens experience stagnation or precarity, the moral authority of procedures erodes—especially if elites appear insulated.

c) Polarization as a network phenomenon

Polarization is not only ideology. It is also **assortment** (like-with-like sorting), **identity fusion**, and **negative partisanship**. As social and informational networks segregate, cross-cutting ties weaken; distrust becomes rational; compromise becomes betrayal. Polarization then behaves like a contagion in a network—spreading through homophily and reinforcement.

d) Geopolitical turbulence

External instability—wars, migration, supply shocks, great-power rivalry—feeds domestic stress. Democracies, which rely on consent and open debate, are especially vulnerable to disinformation and strategic manipulation. External pressure can tighten internal feedback loops, turning ordinary disagreement into existential fear.

In earlier eras, democratic institutions could rely on inertia—slow-moving assumptions about truth, status, work, and community. In nonlinear times, inertia becomes a liability. Systems must be designed to **sense** changes early, **dampen** destructive cascades, and **adapt** without delegitimizing themselves.

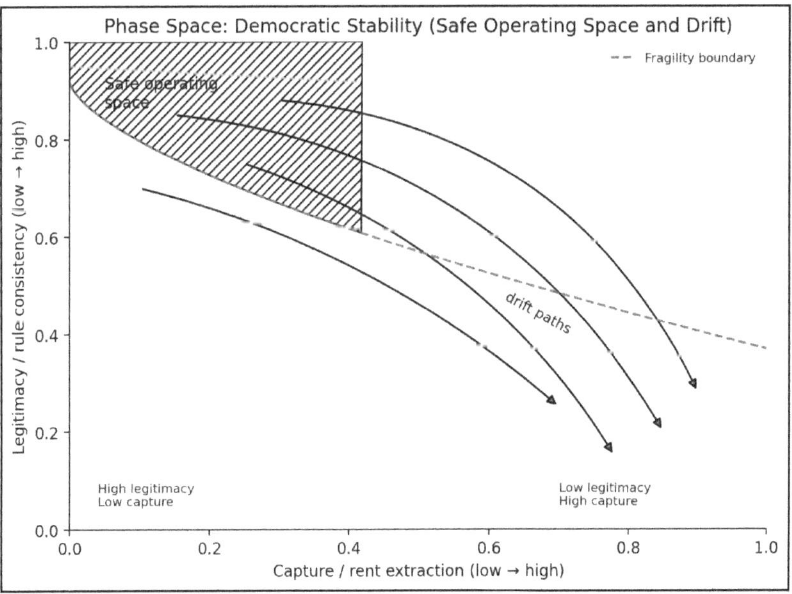

Figure 1.0: *Systems can remain stable within a bounded region of institutional performance. When capture rises and legitimacy erodes, trajectories tend to move toward a fragile zone where recovery becomes harder and instability becomes self-reinforcing.*

4. The Republic's Key State Variables

To treat democracy as a system is not to reduce it to numbers. It is to clarify which variables matter most for resilience. Several "state variables" determine whether a republic remains in the edge-of-chaos band:

1. **Legitimacy:** belief that rules are fair and binding even when one loses.

2. **State capacity:** ability to implement decisions competently and impartially.

3. **Social trust:** expectation that others will follow rules and reciprocate.

4. **Information integrity:** availability of shared facts and credible institutions.

5. **Distributional fairness:** not perfect equality, but tolerable injustice; the sense that the game is not rigged.

6. **Elite restraint:** willingness of powerful actors to accept limits and avoid zero-sum domination.

7. **Conflict-processing mechanisms:** courts, legislatures, mediators, federalism—channels that convert conflict into decisions.

8. **Adaptive pathways:** legitimate routes for reform—so pressure can become positive change without rupture.

These variables interact. For example, low state capacity worsens inequality (through poor service delivery), erodes legitimacy, increases polarization, undermines information integrity, and further weakens capacity. Once multiple variables deteriorate together, the system's behavior becomes nonlinear: decline accelerates, and the window for incremental repair narrows.

5. Attractors, Thresholds, and Democratic Phase Transitions

Complexity offers a useful metaphor: **attractors**—patterns toward which a system tends to move. A healthy democracy has a "good governance" attractor: competition produces alternation; alternation preserves legitimacy; legitimacy supports compliance; compliance enables policy; policy maintains welfare and security; welfare and security maintain legitimacy. This loop is never perfect, but it has restorative tendencies.

A stressed democracy can develop a different attractor: **mutual delegitimation**. Each side believes the other is not merely wrong but illegitimate. Elections become suspect. Courts become partisan. Media becomes tribal. Norms collapse. In this attractor, every conflict increases distrust, and every reform attempt is interpreted as a form of capture. The system becomes stuck in an escalation cycle.

Phase transitions occur when gradual changes in parameters produce sudden shifts in system behavior. For a republic, the "parameters" might include inequality, media fragmentation, institutional veto points, electoral incentives, or foreign interference. When they reach certain thresholds, politics can flip from compromise to rupture, from pluralism to hostility, from stability to chronic crisis.

This matters because it changes how we should interpret warning signs. In linear thinking, problems accumulate proportionally. In nonlinear thinking, the system can appear stable until it suddenly isn't. The question becomes: what are our early indicators of approaching thresholds? And how do we design institutions that either push thresholds farther away or soften the transitions?

6. The Central Paradox: Democracies Need Friction and Flow

A republic must do two contradictory things at once:

- **Provide friction** against impulsive majorities, demagogues, and transient passions.
- **Provide flow** for legitimate demands, reforms, and adaptive change.

Too much friction, and politics bottlenecks. Citizens experience impotence; governance seems captured; rage grows. Too much flow and politics becomes erratic; policy whiplash undermines planning; minorities fear domination; trust collapses. The art of constitutional design is balancing friction and flow.

Traditional democratic theory emphasized checks and balances—friction. Modern governance crises often reflect too little adaptive capacity, too much friction where it blocks reform and too little friction where it fails to stop bad-faith escalation. In nonlinear times, both errors are magnified.

An edge-of-chaos republic, therefore, requires **smart friction** (targeted constraints on destabilizing behavior) and **smart flow** (legitimate, efficient channels for adaptation). This is not a mere engineering problem; it is a moral problem. The goal is not to maximize efficiency but to preserve dignity, fairness, and self-government under stress.

7. Design Principles for an Edge-of-Chaos Republic

If this book is about "Designing Institutions for Nonlinear Times," we need design principles that correspond to nonlinear risks. Here are foundational ones:

Principle 1: Build for resilience, not just stability

Stability is the absence of visible change. Resilience is the ability to absorb disturbance and continue functioning. A stable system can be brittle; a resilient system can be noisy. Democracies should be evaluated not only by calmness but by their ability to survive shocks without abandoning rights or legitimacy.

Principle 2: Increase modularity and reduce cascade risk

When systems are tightly coupled, failures spread. Modularity—federalism, decentralization, and layered governance can prevent nationwide cascades. But modularity must be paired with coordination mechanisms, or it becomes fragmented. The goal is "containable failure": local errors do not become national breakdowns.

Principle 3: Create redundancy in democratic functions

Redundancy is often mocked as inefficiency, yet in complex systems, it is a form of insurance. Democracies need multiple pathways for representation, oversight, and accountability. When one channel is captured, others must still function.

Principle 4: Protect information integrity as critical infrastructure

If democracy is an information-processing system, then truthfulness and credibility are not luxuries; they are infrastructure. Institutions should incentivize verification, discourage manipulation, and increase transparency. This includes election administration, media norms, and digital platform accountability—without slipping into censorship or state propaganda.

Principle 5: Align incentives to reward cooperation, not just victory

Political systems that reward maximalist tactics will produce maximalist behavior. Electoral rules, primary systems, districting, legislative procedures, and campaign finance regimes shape incentives. A key aim is to make coalition-building more rewarding than annihilation politics.

Principle 6: Introduce adaptive governance and "stress tests"

Financial systems now undergo stress tests because policymakers learned that normal conditions are misleading. Democracies should similarly stress-test institutions for extreme polarization, disinformation shocks, abuse of emergency powers, and legitimacy crises. Adaptive governance means building mechanisms to revise rules responsibly, not only after a catastrophe.

Principle 7: Preserve moral legitimacy through fairness and restraint

No amount of technical design substitutes for moral credibility. If citizens believe the system is rigged, they will not cooperate. If elites break norms with impunity, others will follow. If justice seems selective, legitimacy evaporates. An edge-of-chaos republic requires visible commitments to fair play and shared dignity.

These principles are not partisan. They are systemic. They ask: how do we make a democracy robust to nonlinear disturbances while retaining liberal commitments?

8. The Danger of "Solutionism" and the Necessity of Humility

Complexity thinking also cautions against overconfidence. In nonlinear systems, interventions can have unintended consequences. Well-meant reforms can shift incentives in unexpected ways; new institutions can be gamed; transparency can become performative; decentralization can empower local tyrannies; centralization can become bureaucratic domination. The designer's posture must be humble: test, iterate, evaluate, adjust.

But humility cannot become paralysis. The republic cannot "wait for certainty." It must act under uncertainty. That is precisely why adaptive design matters: build institutions that can correct themselves without descending into crisis.

A useful metaphor here is steering. In calm water, you can set a course and relax. In rough seas, you must constantly adjust. The edge-of-chaos republic is not a utopia that eliminates turbulence; it is a vessel engineered to sail in turbulence—while keeping its crew committed to the voyage.

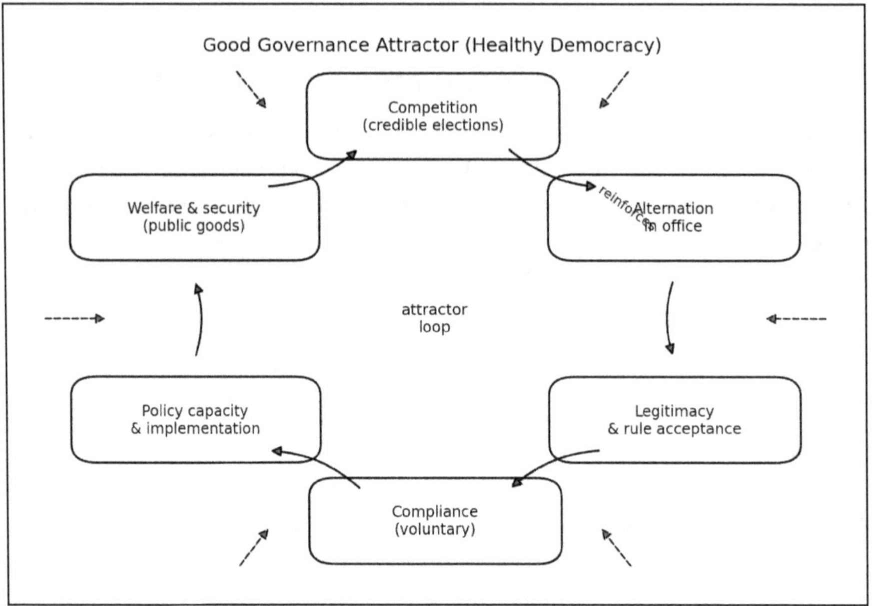

Figure 2.0: *Democratic Stabilizing Attractor Loop Diagram.*

This figure visualizes a **healthy democracy's stabilizing attractor**—a self-reinforcing pattern such that the system tends to return to after routine shocks:

1. **Competition** (credible elections) produces **alternation** in office rather than permanent rule.

2. **Alternation** preserves **legitimacy and rule acceptance** ("we can lose today and compete tomorrow").

3. **Legitimacy** supports **voluntary compliance** (people follow rules even when inconvenient).

4. **Compliance** enables **policy capacity and implementation** (institutions can execute).

5. Effective **policy** sustains **welfare and security** (public goods and risk reduction).

6. **Welfare and security** rebuild **legitimacy**, which stabilizes the whole cycle and keeps competition peaceful and productive.

In short: **institutions and performance create legitimacy; legitimacy creates cooperation; cooperation makes governance work; governance sustains legitimacy**, a virtuous loop that keeps the system in a stable basin.

9. A Diagnostic Map: Symptoms of an Edge-of-Chaos Crisis

What does it look like when a democracy is drifting out of the edge-of-chaos band?

- **Legitimacy wars:** routine processes (elections, courts, agencies) are treated as illegitimate when outcomes displease.
- **Norm collapse:** informal restraints (truthfulness, peaceful transfer, mutual toleration) erode.
- **Institutional capture narratives:** whether true or not, the perception that "the system is rigged" becomes widespread.
- **Policy volatility:** governance oscillates wildly, undermining long-term planning and credibility.
- **Constitutional hardball:** actors exploit loopholes and procedural weapons to maximize advantage.
- **Epistemic fragmentation:** citizens live in incompatible realities; shared facts vanish.
- **Scapegoat politics:** complex economic problems are simplified into demonized out-groups.
- **Emergency temptation:** leaders increasingly justify extraordinary powers as necessary.

These are not merely moral failures; they are dynamic markers—signs that feedback loops are amplifying rather than stabilizing.

10. The Chapter's Thesis and the Book's Promise

The thesis of "The Edge of Chaos Republic" is straightforward: democracy is most viable when it operates in a regime of organized complexity—stable enough to coordinate, flexible enough to adapt. Modern conditions are pushing democracies toward dangerous nonlinear dynamics by accelerating feedback loops, increasing cascade risks, and degrading shared informational and moral infrastructure. The appropriate response is not cynicism or authoritarian longing, but institutional redesign: a commitment to building systems that can absorb shocks, process conflict, and remain legitimate in turbulent times.

The book's promise is that institutional design can be reframed as resilience design. That includes constitutional rules, electoral incentives, administrative capacity, information ecosystems, and the cultural norms that enable self-government. The goal is not to freeze society into static harmony; it is to create a republic capable of enduring pluralism and change without breaking.

In the chapters that follow, we will develop a toolkit for nonlinear governance: how to recognize when a system is approaching thresholds; how to redesign incentives to promote coalition-building; how to protect information integrity without empowering censorship; how to strengthen state capacity without sacrificing accountability; how to build adaptive mechanisms for reform; and how to cultivate moral legitimacy in an age of distrust.

The edge of chaos is not where a democracy goes to die. It is where it must learn to live—by balancing the discipline of law with the creativity of reform, the dignity of rights with the necessity of shared reality, and the friction of constraint with the flow of adaptation. The republic's task is not to eliminate conflict, but to make conflict governable. In nonlinear times, that task becomes harder—and more urgent.

If democracy is to remain more than a memory or a slogan, it must become something like an "edge-of-chaos republic": a system designed not only for the world we hoped we lived in, but for the world we actually do—fast, networked, unequal, and turbulent. Designing institutions for that world is the work ahead.

Chapter 2

Inequality as a System Parameter

In political argument, inequality is usually treated as an outcome: a distribution of income, wealth, or opportunity that can be judged morally (fair or unfair), economically (efficient or wasteful), or politically (acceptable or destabilizing). That framing matters, but it is incomplete. In nonlinear times, inequality is better understood as a *system parameter*—a structural setting that changes how the entire democratic machine behaves. Like temperature in a chemical reaction or leverage in a financial system, inequality does not merely "sit there." It alters incentives, reshapes networks, modifies what information gets amplified, and changes the costs of coordination. Above certain thresholds, it can push a society across regime boundaries: from cooperative pluralism into adversarial factionalism; from reformable governance into capture; from trusted procedures into legitimacy crises.

This chapter develops that claim. It argues that inequality is not just a distributive condition but a control knob that adjusts the republic's dynamics: the strength of feedback loops, the speed of cascades, the topology of social networks, and the credibility of institutions. A democracy can endure many shocks, including economic downturns, security threats, and cultural conflicts, if its underlying parameters keep it within a stable, adaptive band. But when inequality rises beyond what the society's moral ecology can metabolize, the system's internal feedback becomes more amplifying than stabilizing. Polarization becomes stickier. Distrust becomes rational. Politics becomes more transactional and less legitimate. And the design problem shifts from "how to persuade voters" to "how to keep the democratic system from drifting into a different attractor."

To say that inequality is a system parameter is to say something stronger than "inequality causes problems." It is to say inequality changes the *rules of the game* by changing the environment in which all actors—citizens, parties, firms, media, courts—operate. It changes what strategies are rewarded and which are punished. It changes what institutions can realistically do. And it changes what the public can plausibly believe about fairness, merit, and representation.

1. What Is a System Parameter?

Complex systems have two kinds of variables. First, there are **state variables**: the things that move and fluctuate: public trust, unemployment, polarization, inflation, approval ratings, legislative productivity, protest intensity. Second, there are **parameters**: slower-moving conditions that shape the system's behavior: network connectivity, baseline inequality, demographic structure, institutional veto points, media architecture, campaign finance rules, levels of education, and the distribution of power across actors.

Parameters determine the system's "phase space," the landscape of possible behaviors. A system may appear stable under one set of parameters and become volatile under another—even with the same immediate shocks. The shock is not the whole story; the environment in which the shock hits is often the decisive factor.

In democratic societies, inequality functions as a parameter in several ways:

- It shapes **who has slack** and who lives on the margin—who can absorb risk and who cannot.
- It shapes **who can invest in influence**—in lobbying, media, philanthropy, think tanks, litigation, and political careers.
- It shapes **who feels represented** and who experiences politics as distant ritual.
- It shapes **the narrative plausibility** of democracy's moral claims ("equal citizenship," "fair opportunity," "one person, one vote").
- It shapes **how conflict is interpreted**: as manageable disagreement among equals or as predation by entrenched hierarchies.

Treating inequality as a parameter means we stop asking only "Is this distribution fair?" and start asking "What does this distribution do to the system's dynamics?" The moral question remains—but now it is joined by a stability question: what level and structure of inequality can a democracy tolerate before its feedback loops become pathological?

2. Inequality Is Not One Thing: Layers and Forms

Before we track mechanisms, we must clarify what "inequality" means in system terms. A democracy can sometimes tolerate inequality in one dimension if it compensates in another. Conversely, inequality can be destabilizing even at moderate levels if it is *experienced* as illegitimate or if it concentrates in the wrong places.

Key dimensions include:

1. **Income inequality** (flows): differences in earnings and yearly resources.
2. **Wealth inequality** (stocks): differences in accumulated assets, property, and capital ownership.
3. **Opportunity inequality** (mobility): differences in access to education, networks, health, and pathways into high-status positions.
4. **Spatial inequality** (geography): concentrated prosperity in certain regions and decay in others, often mirrored in political divides.
5. **Status inequality** (recognition): perceived dignity and social respect—who is treated as visible, competent, or disposable.
6. **Power inequality** (influence): differences in the capacity to shape rules, narratives, and enforcement.

A society can have relatively high income inequality yet maintain legitimacy if opportunity is robust, status is widely distributed, and political power remains broadly accountable. But when multiple inequalities align—when money becomes power, and power becomes immunity, and immunity becomes moral exemption—the democratic ecology changes qualitatively. That alignment is what makes inequality a control parameter: it changes the coupling between domains.

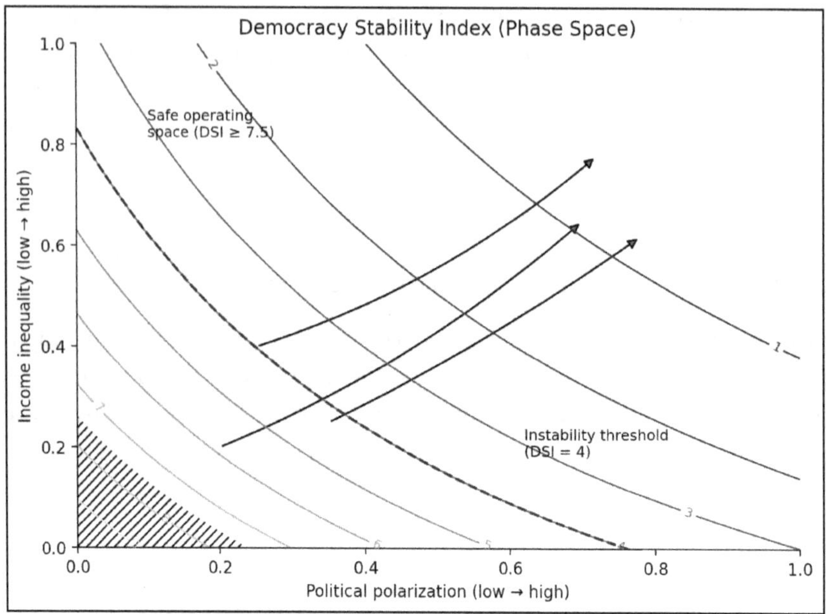

Figure 3.0: *Democratic Stability* is highest *in the lower-left:* **low polarization + low inequality** *(the hatched region).*

As either **polarization** or **inequality** increases, the system moves to **lower stability contours**, indicating declining governability and legitimacy reserves. The **dashed threshold contour** marks a tipping point: once crossed, small shocks (scandals, economic jolts, information cascades) are more likely to produce **discontinuous** political outcomes (crisis governance, institutional hardening, legitimacy collapse). The **drift arrows** visualize how compounding pressures can push the polity along a path in which each problem worsens the other (higher inequality raises the stakes; higher polarization reduces the capacity to correct inequality), accelerating movement toward instability.

3. Inequality Changes Incentives: The Strategic Landscape of Democracy

Democracy is a game with many players: voters, parties, donors, bureaucracies, firms, unions, media, courts, movements, and foreign actors. Each player responds to incentives. Inequality changes those incentives in predictable ways.

a) The rich face lower marginal costs of political investment

Influence is expensive. It requires time, expertise, access, and institutional knowledge. Wealth dramatically reduces the cost of these inputs. As inequality rises, the wealthy can invest in politics with low opportunity cost: funding campaigns, underwriting policy shops, financing lawsuits, building media ecosystems, and offering post-government employment. When influence becomes easier for a small class to purchase, the system begins to resemble an auction more than a deliberation.

This is not simply "corruption." It is structural. Even if every actor remains within legal bounds, unequal capacity produces unequal participation. Over time, rules evolve to serve those who can afford to participate at scale. The result is **policy drift**—governance that continues to function procedurally but slowly decouples from majority welfare.

b) The non-wealthy face higher participation costs and higher risk

For those living closer to the margin, politics competes with survival. Time off work, childcare, transportation, attention, these become scarce. Political participation becomes costly, and the perceived payoff declines when outcomes seem predetermined by donors or entrenched interests. This creates a feedback loop: low participation yields low responsiveness, which yields more cynicism, which yields even lower participation. The system then becomes less representative, further eroding its legitimacy.

c) Parties adapt by targeting funders and mobilizable identities

Parties are coordination machines. They seek resources to win elections. In highly unequal environments, parties become more dependent on wealthy donors, large industries, and "influence infrastructure." This dependency can subtly reshape platforms, candidate selection, and strategic emphasis. When material redistribution becomes constrained by donor influence, parties often pivot toward identity signaling, cultural conflict, and symbolic politics—areas where they can deliver "wins" without challenging the distribution of wealth and power.

The outcome is not necessarily a conspiracy; it is an equilibrium. Parties deliver what they can, and what the system rewards. In a high-inequality system, what is rewarded is often polarization-ready content and donor-safe policy.

4. Inequality Reshapes Networks: Topology, Segregation, and Cascades

Complex systems are built from networks. The structure of social networks affects what information spreads, which norms hold, and how quickly conflicts escalate. Inequality changes network topology in several ways.

a) Segregation and assortative clustering

As inequality grows, people sort. Neighborhoods, schools, workplaces, and online communities become more stratified. Cross-class interactions weaken, and so do cross-cutting identities. The society becomes a set of semi-separate worlds with different experiences of reality: different risk perceptions, different narratives of fairness, different norms of respect.

In network terms, inequality increases **modularity** (segmented clusters) without necessarily increasing **bridges** (ties across groups). High modularity can protect communities from some contagions, but it also reduces shared understanding and makes society more vulnerable to polarization cascades. When bridges weaken, disagreement becomes misinterpretation: the other side's choices look insane because the lived context is absent.

b) Elite network density and coordinated influence

At the top, inequality can increase the density of elite networks. Wealth concentrates in overlapping circles—finance, law, media, philanthropy, academia, and government. Dense networks coordinate more easily than dispersed networks. This makes elite influence more coherent, more resilient, and harder to counterbalance with diffuse public interests. Again, it's not necessarily malevolent; it's a structural advantage of concentrated coordination.

c) Contagion and amplification in stressed populations

At the bottom and middle, economic stress increases susceptibility to emotional contagion: fear, resentment, conspiracy, and scapegoating spread faster when people feel unprotected. Not because "the masses are irrational," but because insecurity increases the value of identity certainty and simple explanations. High inequality thus alters the gains from social emotions. Messages that promise dignity, blame, and belonging travel farther.

This creates a dangerous interaction with modern attention markets: inequality supplies psychological fuel; platforms supply high-speed distribution; politics supplies adversarial framing. The system's temperature rises.

5. Inequality Weakens Negative Feedback and Strengthens Positive Feedback

A stable democracy relies on **negative feedback loops**—mechanisms that dampen extremes and restore balance. Examples include credible courts, impartial administration, respected elections, shared media norms, and a political culture that tolerates losing. Inequality can weaken these stabilizers and strengthen destabilizing loops.

a) Legitimacy as negative feedback

Legitimacy is a stabilizer: when people believe institutions are fair, they accept outcomes they dislike. But legitimacy depends on a credible story about equal citizenship and fair opportunity. Severe inequality undermines that story. If the system consistently delivers prosperity and protection to some while exposing others to insecurity and humiliation, then "equal citizenship" becomes rhetorical. Compliance becomes conditional. Losing becomes intolerable because the stakes feel existential: when you lose, you are not merely outvoted, you are abandoned.

This is how inequality strengthens positive feedback: distrust leads to a refusal to cooperate; refusal increases dysfunction; dysfunction validates distrust.

b) State capacity and the delivery of service

When public services fail—health, education, infrastructure, safety—citizens experience the state as incompetent or biased. High inequality can drain state capacity through tax resistance, privatization pressures, and policy capture. It can also produce dual systems: high-quality private services for the affluent, deteriorating public services for everyone else. Dual systems corrode solidarity. People stop seeing public goods as "ours," and start seeing them as "theirs"—a cost imposed by outsiders.

That shift is dynamic: it makes it harder to reach redistributive compromises and increases the appeal of punitive politics.

c) Political capture as feedback

Inequality increases the returns to capture. When wealth is concentrated, the marginal value of shaping policy is enormous: small regulatory changes can yield huge private gains. This encourages firms and wealthy actors to invest heavily in influence. That investment changes policy, further increasing wealth concentration and the returns to capture. This is a classic positive feedback loop.

A democracy can survive some capture if countervailing forces—unions, watchdogs, courts, competitive markets, independent media—remain strong. But when inequality erodes those counterweights, capture becomes self-reinforcing.

6. Inequality and the Moral Ecology of Self-Government

The title of this book speaks of "designing institutions for nonlinear times," but institutions do not float above moral experience. Democracies require a moral ecology: shared expectations about fairness, dignity, reciprocity, and restraint. Inequality changes the ecology in two destabilizing ways.

a) It converts politics into a dignity struggle

When economic hierarchies harden, politics becomes less about policy and more about respect. People interpret events through the lens of status: who is seen, who is mocked, who is protected, who is punished. The result is a politics of humiliation and revenge—an environment where procedural arguments ("the law says…") lose persuasive power because the deeper grievance is moral: "the system does not treat us as equals."

b) It corrodes elite restraint and public trust

High inequality can produce a culture of exemption at the top: rules are for others. Even small, visible acts of elite impunity—insider deals, revolving-door enrichment, selective enforcement—have outsized legitimacy effects. In nonlinear systems, perception matters because it drives behavior. When citizens believe elites are unrestrained, they become less willing to restrain themselves. Norms decay simultaneously from the top down and the bottom up.

A republic cannot maintain the edge-of-chaos balance without elite restraint and popular trust. Inequality erodes both by making restraint costlier (more to lose) and trust less rational (more reasons to suspect rigging).

7. Inequality Pushes the System Toward Brittle Equilibria

One of the most dangerous features of high-inequality democracies is that they can look stable—until they don't. The system settles into brittle equilibria:

- Elections still occur, but participation becomes uneven and cynical.
- Institutions still function, but policy drifts toward donor priorities.
- Media still reports, but fragmentation accelerates tribal realities.
- Markets still produce growth, but gains concentrate.
- Courts still rule, but legitimacy becomes partisan.

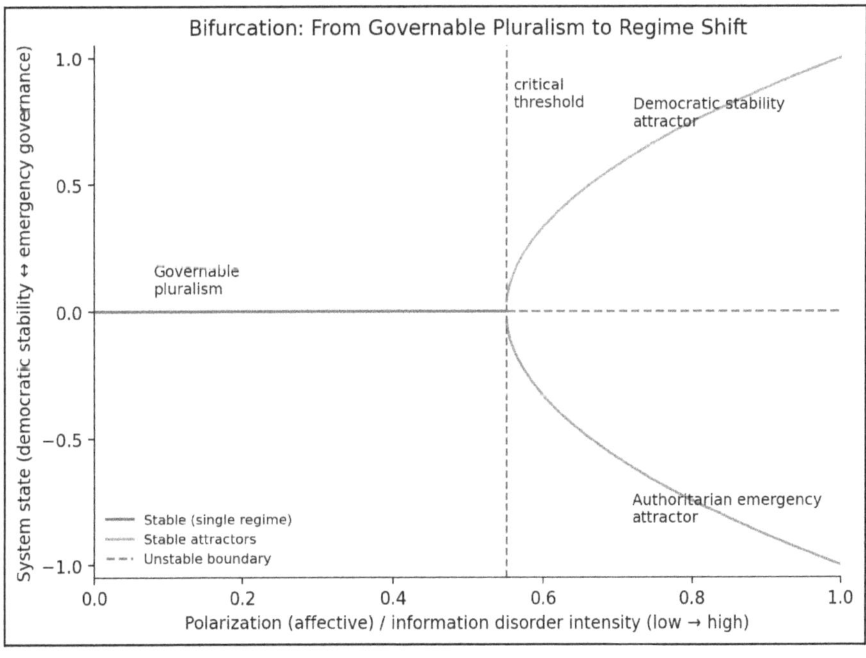

Figure 4.0: *Democratic Bifurcation.*

Brittle equilibria appear stable but are fragile in structure. A shock—financial crisis, pandemic, security event, migration surge, technological displacement—can push the system over a threshold into an open legitimacy crisis. People who tolerated injustice under normal times stop tolerating it under stress. Then politics becomes a scramble for control rather than a negotiation of interests.

The key insight is that inequality lowers the threshold at which shocks become existential. It narrows the safe operating space of democracy.

As affective polarization or information disorder intensifies beyond a critical point, the polity can lose its "single-regime" stability and become pulled toward competing equilibrium patterns, making outcomes highly sensitive to shocks and sequencing.

8. A Structural-Demographic Lens: Elites, Competition, and Instability

Another way to see inequality as a parameter is to consider elite dynamics. In many historical accounts of instability, crisis emerges not only from mass hardship but from elite conflict: too many aspirants chasing too few high-status positions, combined with a capacity to mobilize factions. Severe inequality often coexists with intensified elite competition because the rewards at the top are enormous. That can produce a political environment of constant escalation—constitutional hardball, information warfare, delegitimation—because the prize is not merely office but control over a system that distributes massive rents.

In such systems, elites have incentives to polarize the public as a resource: mobilizing identity groups to win control of institutions. The public becomes both participant and instrument. This intensifies factionalism and further reduces the possibility of broad-based reforms that might lower inequality, because reforms threaten the elite's prize.

Thus, inequality functions as a parameter not only by stressing the bottom but by inflaming competition at the top. The republic becomes squeezed between insecurity below and predation above.

9. Measuring Inequality as a Parameter: What to Watch

If inequality shapes system behavior, measurement should focus on *dynamics* rather than snapshots. Several metrics are especially relevant to democratic stability:

- **Wealth concentration and asset ownership:** who owns productive assets and housing; how concentrated is capital?
- **Income shares at the top:** not just overall inequality but extreme concentration that fuels capture.
- **Mobility and opportunity:** whether class position is sticky across generations.
- **Regional divergence:** whether prosperity and decline map onto political geography.
- **Market concentration:** the degree of monopoly power and rent extraction (often correlated with wealth concentration).
- **Cost burdens:** housing, healthcare, education, whether basic life inputs are becoming unaffordable.
- **Political money flows:** dependence of parties on large donors; the scale of influence infrastructure.
- **Trust and perceived fairness:** surveys of institutional trust, corruption perceptions, and procedural legitimacy.

The key is to treat these measures as signals of changing system parameters. Rising inequality is not just a moral alarm; it is a warning that the republic's dynamics may be shifting toward an unstable phase.

10. Inequality and Democratic Design: How to Lower Systemic Risk

If inequality is a parameter that pushes democracy toward bad attractors, the design challenge is not only redistribution after the fact but the redesign of the mechanisms that generate and translate inequality into power.

We can group design responses into four domains: **predistribution**, **redistribution**, **anti-capture architecture**, and **social cohesion infrastructure**.

a) Pre-distribution: shaping markets before taxes

Pre-distribution means structuring the economy so that market outcomes are less unequal and less politically corrosive:

- **Competitive markets and antitrust:** reduce rent extraction and monopoly-driven concentration.
- **Labor institutions:** collective bargaining frameworks, sectoral bargaining options, worker voice on governance.
- **Corporate governance reforms:** reduce short-term extraction; align incentives with long-term investment.
- **Broad-based asset ownership:** mechanisms for workers and citizens to accumulate stakes in productivity growth.
- **Public investment in capabilities:** education, training, childcare, infrastructure—expanding opportunity.

These are not merely "left" ideas; they are stability ideas. They reduce the coupling between wealth and domination and expand the number of people with a stake in the system's success.

b) Redistribution: taxes and transfers as stabilizers

Redistribution is negative feedback: it dampens extremes and preserves legitimacy. But it must be designed for political durability:

- **Progressive taxation that is intelligible and enforceable**
- **Universal or broadly inclusive benefits** that maintain cross-class buy-in
- **Automatic stabilizers** (unemployment insurance, countercyclical fiscal mechanisms) that respond quickly to shocks
- **Health and housing systems** that reduce existential insecurity

Redistribution is not only about equity; it is about keeping the system within its safe operating zone.

c) Anti-capture architecture: insulating governance from auctions

A high-inequality society must build stronger barriers between wealth and rule-making:

- **Campaign finance and transparency reforms**

- **Lobbying constraints and revolving-door limits**
- **Independent ethics enforcement**
- **Public financing options** that reduce donor dependence
- **Stronger conflict-of-interest rules** for officials and regulators

The aim is not purity but robustness: reducing the positive feedback loop where wealth buys policy, which buys more wealth.

d) Social cohesion infrastructure: rebuilding bridging ties

Because inequality fragments networks, democracies need institutions that rebuild cross-cutting identity and shared reality:

- **Civic education oriented toward systems thinking**
- **Local deliberative institutions** that build trust across lines
- **National service or shared projects** that create bridging experiences
- **Public media and information standards** that protect common facts without empowering censorship
- **Trustworthy administrative competence**—the daily experience of fair service

Cohesion is not propaganda; it is a network property. You cannot legislate trust directly, but you can build conditions in which trust becomes rational again.

11. The Core Claim: Inequality Narrows the Republic's Adaptive Range

We can now state the chapter's core claim with precision:

As inequality rises, it narrows the range of shocks and conflicts that democratic institutions can process without destabilizing legitimacy. It increases the returns to capture, accelerates polarization cascades, weakens cross-class solidarity, and transforms ordinary losses into existential threats. The system becomes more sensitive to perturbation—more nonlinear—because its stabilizing feedback is degraded and its amplifying feedback is strengthened.

This is why inequality is a parameter rather than merely an outcome. It sets the republic's sensitivity. It changes how hard it is to govern. It changes the amount of disagreement that can be tolerated. It changes how plausible procedural legitimacy feels. And it changes whether reform is experienced as credible or performative. A democracy does not need perfect equality to survive. But it does need a distribution of resources and power that preserves the moral meaning of equal citizenship and maintains the practical possibility of fair competition. When inequality becomes so large that citizenship feels graded—some with voice, some with noise—democracy begins to exit the edge-of-chaos band and drift toward a different regime: governance by faction, by oligarchy, or by cynical alternation without legitimacy.

12. Transition: Inequality and the "Nonlinear Times" Problem

The subtitle of the book—*Designing Institutions for Nonlinear Times*—is not rhetorical. Nonlinear times are precisely when parameter shifts matter most. In calm environments, a democracy can carry structural defects without immediate catastrophe. In turbulent environments, those defects become multipliers. Inequality is the multiplier of multipliers: it magnifies shocks, accelerates cascades, and turns policy failures into moral crises.

The next chapter will take this logic further by examining how inequality interacts with the information ecosystem—how it shapes not only material outcomes but the production of belief, narrative, and shared reality. Because in modern democracies, the stability of institutions depends as much on epistemic conditions—what citizens can plausibly know and trust—as on formal rules. Inequality destabilizes both the economy and the polity's mind. In nonlinear times, the republic cannot afford to treat it as an afterthought.

If Chapter 1 described the edge-of-chaos republic as a system that must balance coherence and adaptability, Chapter 2 identifies inequality as one of the most powerful settings on the control panel. Adjust it upward, and you do not merely redistribute money; you alter the republic's behavior: from cooperative learning to adversarial escalation, from legitimacy to suspicion, from reform to rupture. If we want democratic self-government to survive turbulence, we must treat inequality not as background scenery but as a central engineering constraint of the republic itself.

Chapter 3

The Epistemic Commons: Information Integrity in Networked Democracies

A democracy is not only a system for aggregating preferences; it is a system for producing *shared reality*. Elections, laws, courts, and bureaucracies do not function merely because they exist on paper, but because a sufficiently large portion of the population agrees—explicitly or implicitly—on what happened, what counts as evidence, what rules apply, and what outcomes are binding. When that epistemic substrate weakens, the republic loses the ability to metabolize conflict. Disagreement stops being a contest within a common frame and becomes a battle over the frame itself. At that point, institutional design faces a harder problem than representation: it must rebuild the informational conditions that make representation meaningful.

This chapter argues that in nonlinear times, *information integrity is a critical infrastructure*. It is not a "soft" cultural concern, nor merely a matter of media literacy. It is a core system variable that determines whether democratic feedback loops stabilize or explode. As information networks become faster, more segmented, and increasingly algorithmically optimized for engagement, the polity's epistemic commons—the shared space of facts, verification norms, and trusted arbiters—can fragment. That fragmentation interacts with inequality, polarization, and elite competition to produce dynamics that look increasingly like phase transitions: sudden legitimacy crises, cascades of distrust, and escalating constitutional hardball.

To design institutions for nonlinear times, we need to understand the republic's information ecology as a complex adaptive system: who produces information, how it spreads, what incentives drive amplification, how trust is earned or lost, and how governance can intervene without turning "information integrity" into a euphemism for censorship. The central challenge is to preserve a liberal democratic commitment to free inquiry while strengthening the epistemic conditions that allow free inquiry to inform self-government rather than dissolve into weaponized confusion.

1. The Epistemic Commons as a Public Good

In economics, a public good is typically defined as non-excludable and non-rivalrous: one person's use does not diminish another's, and it is hard to prevent anyone from using it. The epistemic commons is a public good in a different but parallel sense. It includes:

- shared factual baselines (what happened, how many, where, when),
- norms of evidence and argument (how we adjudicate claims),
- and institutional credibility (who is trusted to report or certify).

A functioning democracy does not require perfect consensus; it requires *bounded disagreement.* Citizens can deeply disagree about values and priorities if they share enough common information to argue coherently and accept outcomes.

But epistemic commons are also fragile. They are prone to free-riding (benefiting from trust while undermining it), to capture (turning credibility into a partisan asset), and to erosion (the slow loss of verification norms). And, crucially, they can collapse nonlinearly: trust can decline gradually, but once it crosses a threshold, it can fall quickly and become self-reinforcing. When "nobody believes anything," every claim becomes a power play, and the incentive shifts from persuasion to domination.

In earlier eras, the epistemic commons were sustained by a limited set of gatekeeping institutions: major newspapers, broadcast networks, universities, courts, and bureaucratic agencies. Those institutions were imperfectly biased, sometimes exclusionary—but their centrality created a kind of default coherence. Today, the information environment is more open and pluralistic, bringing genuine benefits. Yet the same openness has created new failure modes: high-velocity disinformation, algorithmic amplification of outrage, and the emergence of sealed "reality tunnels" that are socially reinforced and economically profitable.

If Chapter 2 treated inequality as a system parameter, we can treat information integrity as a *system constraint*: a condition that must be maintained for democratic coordination to remain possible. When that constraint is violated, other reforms—redistributive policy, electoral adjustments, administrative competence—struggle to regain legitimacy because citizens cannot agree on what is happening.

2. The Republic as an Information-Processing System

A useful way to conceptualize democracy is as a machine that converts dispersed signals into collective decisions. Markets do something similar: they aggregate information through prices. Democracies aggregate information through institutions: elections, hearings, courts, audits, investigative journalism, public comment, deliberation, and administrative expertise. In both cases, the system's performance depends on the quality of signals and the integrity of transmission.

Democratic information processing involves several steps:

1. **Sensing:** citizens and institutions observe problems and events.
2. **Encoding:** observations are translated into claims, stories, and data.
3. **Transmission:** claims spread through media, networks, and institutions.
4. **Verification:** claims are tested against evidence and counter-claims.
5. **Aggregation:** preferences and judgments are consolidated into decisions.
6. **Feedback:** outcomes shape future beliefs and behaviors.

Each step can fail. And because the system is nonlinear, small failures can propagate into large dysfunction if feedback loops amplify rather than correct.

Two kinds of feedback are especially important:

- **Negative feedback (stabilizing):** fact-checking, independent audits, courts, professional norms, correction mechanisms, and reputational penalties that dampen falsehoods.
- **Positive feedback (destabilizing):** viral outrage, identity reinforcement, echo chambers, and incentive structures that reward sensationalism and punish nuance.

A democracy remains within its adaptive band when negative feedback dominates. It drifts toward crisis when positive feedback overwhelms correction.

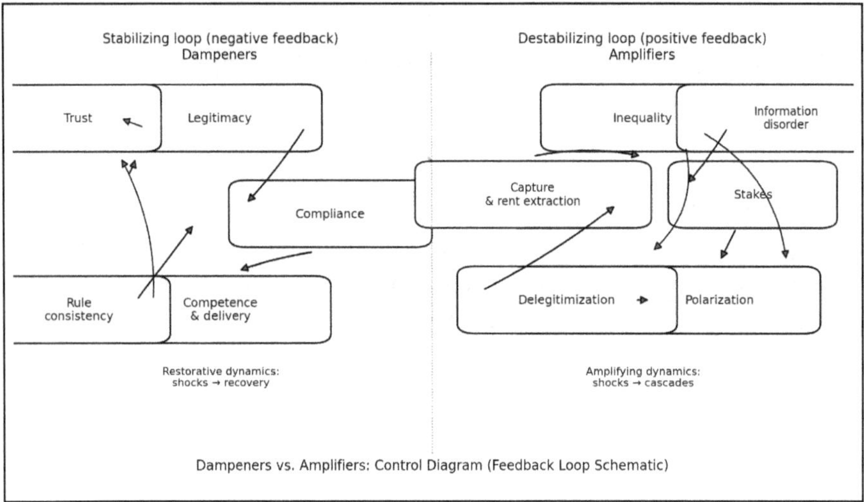

Figure 5.0: *Dampeners vs. Amplifiers Control Diagram*

Stabilization depends on dampeners that restore confidence and compliance after shocks, while amplifiers escalate conflict and extraction. This diagram clarifies where interventions can either strengthen stabilizing feedback or interrupt destabilizing cascades.

3. The New Information Regime: Why "Networked" Changes Everything

We are living through a structural change in the communication architecture of democracy. The shift is not just from print to digital; it is from *broadcast* to *networked amplification.*

In broadcast systems, a small number of institutions had high distribution power and were constrained by professional norms, legal liability, and reputational dependence on broad audiences. In networked systems, distribution power is fragmented and often mediated by algorithms optimized for engagement. The economic engine is attention, and attention is most reliably captured by novelty, outrage, fear, and identity threat.

Three features of the networked regime matter most for democratic stability:

a) Speed and compression

Information travels faster than deliberation. Viral claims outrun verification. The time between stimulus and response shrinks. In nonlinear systems, short feedback cycles increase volatility. Democracies require time to check facts, deliberate, and build coalitions. When the system's time constants are mismatched, when political response is demanded at social-media speed, institutions either appear unresponsive (eroding trust) or react impulsively (eroding competence and legitimacy).

b) Algorithmic gain and amplification

Algorithms function as "gain controls" that amplify some content and suppress others based on predicted engagement. Engagement is often driven by emotional arousal, not informational quality. This creates a structural bias toward content that polarizes and destabilizes. Importantly, this is not necessarily an ideological bias; it is a *dynamical bias* toward conflict.

When gain is high, small provocations can trigger large cascades. A minor incident can become a national moral panic. Misinterpretation can become a conspiracy movement. In such environments, governance becomes reactive, and political entrepreneurs learn to manipulate the system by manufacturing high-engagement controversies.

c) Identity-sorted epistemic communities

Networked media allows people to curate their information environment. In principle, this is empowering. In practice, it can intensify homophily: people cluster with those who share identities, grievances, and worldviews. Once a group becomes identity-sorted, information becomes less about truth and more about loyalty. Beliefs become badges. Correction becomes betrayal.

These features produce a new instability: *epistemic polarization*, where groups do not just disagree about values but inhabit incompatible realities. This is a severe threat because it disables the standard democratic mechanism for conflict resolution: persuasion. If your opponent's claims are not merely wrong but unintelligible or evil, and if your own information sources certify your worldview daily, then compromise becomes psychologically and politically costly.

4. The Misinformation Problem Is Not Only "False Content"—It Is Incentive Design

Public debate often frames the crisis as "misinformation," implying that the primary problem is inaccurate statements. But in system terms, misinformation is a symptom of deeper incentive structures. The more fundamental issue is that modern information markets reward *attention extraction*, and attention is often extracted through emotional activation.

This changes the behavior of multiple actors:

- **Content creators** are incentivized to be provocative and frequent rather than careful.
- **Politicians** are incentivized to perform for virality rather than legislate.
- **Platforms** are incentivized to maximize time-on-site, which correlates with arousal.
- **Audiences** are incentivized (psychologically) to seek identity-confirming narratives that reduce uncertainty and threat.

Under these incentives, misinformation is not an anomaly—it is an equilibrium. The system produces what it rewards. Therefore, solutions that focus only on policing individual falsehoods will be insufficient. The deeper design challenge is to adjust the incentive landscape so that verification and credibility are rewarded rather than punished.

5. Inequality and the Epistemic Commons: Coupling of Material and Informational Fragility

The previous chapter argued that inequality is a system parameter that increases instability. Here is one of the most important coupling effects: inequality intensifies epistemic fragmentation.

Why?

1. **Different lived realities produce different plausibility structures.** When people inhabit different economic worlds, they find different stories credible. A narrative of "opportunity and merit" sounds plausible to those who have benefited; to those who experience stagnation and precarity, it sounds like gaslighting. Conversely, narratives of "systemic rigging" sound plausible to those who have been excluded; they sound exaggerated to those whose lives seem stable.

2. **Economic stress increases cognitive vulnerability.** Insecurity increases the demand for meaning, blame, and belonging. It makes simplified explanations psychologically attractive. It increases the appeal of conspiracy narratives that turn chaos into intentionality.

3. **Wealth and power can shape information ecosystems.** Concentrated resources can finance media infrastructure, think tanks, advocacy networks, and litigation strategies that reshape what information is available and credible.

Thus, inequality not only produces political anger; it changes the informational environment in which anger is interpreted and mobilized. This is one reason modern democracies can look as if they are "losing their minds": the coupling of economic insecurity, identity conflict, and high-gain information networks generates dynamics akin to runaway feedback.

6. Trust as a System Variable: Why Institutions Become "Partisan" Even When They Don't

Trust is not a mood; it is a rational expectation under uncertainty. Citizens cannot personally verify everything. They rely on institutions, journalists, scientists, courts, and agencies to reduce uncertainty. When those institutions are trusted, the polity has a shared frame of reference. When they are not, every claim becomes contested.

Trust dynamics can become self-reinforcing. Once an institution is labeled partisan, any of its actions can be interpreted through that frame, and even neutral competence can be re-coded as bias. In polarized systems, actors have incentives to delegitimize neutral referees because eliminating referees increases the value of raw power. If no one is trusted, politics becomes coercion by other means.

This creates a strategic dilemma for democracies: impartial institutions are necessary for stability, yet they are increasingly targeted by factions precisely because they stabilize the system. The more an institution tries to correct misinformation or enforce norms, the more it can be accused of "bias," which further erodes trust.

This is not a reason to abandon impartiality; it is a reason to design **credibility architecture**—institutional arrangements that make trust more robust. Examples include transparency, bipartisan oversight, independent audits, and procedural constraints that limit discretionary power.

7. The Epistemic Commons and Legitimacy: From Persuasion to Mutual Delegitimation

Democratic legitimacy depends on losers' ability to accept outcomes. But losers accept outcomes only if they believe the process was fair and the facts were not manipulated. When epistemic fragmentation becomes extreme, elections themselves become informational battlegrounds. Claims of fraud, manipulation, or illegitimate administration can spread rapidly and become identity commitments. Once that happens, alternation in power—one of democracy's key stabilizers—becomes destabilizing. Every election becomes a potential legitimacy crisis.

In system terms, democracy shifts from a negative-feedback regime (elections correct governance) to a positive-feedback regime (elections amplify conflict). That is a profound phase change. It means the republic is no longer using elections to reduce error; it is using elections to intensify polarization.

An edge-of-chaos republic can tolerate passionate disagreement if the epistemic commons holds. Without it, the system approaches a brittle state: calm is temporary, and any shock can trigger a negative cascade.

8. Design Responses: How to Rebuild Information Integrity Without Censorship

The central policy challenge is to strengthen information integrity while preserving liberal commitments. Democracies cannot simply "ban bad ideas" without becoming the thing they fear. Nor can they ignore the problem and hope norms regenerate spontaneously. The design space is real, and it includes multiple layers:

Layer 1: Transparency and provenance—making origin and incentives visible

In a networked environment, citizens need tools to evaluate the credibility of sources. This is less about deciding what can be said and more about clarifying *who is speaking and why*. Design options include:

- Stronger disclosure for political advertising and sponsored content.
- Clear labeling of automated accounts and synthetic media.
- Auditable records of content amplification practices (platform transparency).
- Provenance standards for official information (cryptographic signatures, verifiable documents).

The goal is to reduce the asymmetry between manipulators and citizens by making manipulation more detectable.

Layer 2: Institutional redundancy—multiple trusted certifiers

A single "ministry of truth" is incompatible with liberal democracy. But *distributed credibility* is possible. Democracies can support multiple independent certification institutions that verify facts and processes, including:

- nonpartisan election audits,
- independent inspectors general,
- bipartisan oversight committees with real powers,
- professional standards bodies for journalism and science communication,
- and local civic institutions that validate information in context.

Redundancy reduces the risk that delegitimizing one institution collapses the entire epistemic structure.

Layer 3: Platform governance—adjusting incentive structures

The most difficult design arena is platform incentive. Democracies need not dictate specific viewpoints, but they can require:

- transparency about algorithmic ranking and major changes,
- research access for independent auditors,
- friction for high-velocity sharing (especially for unverified claims),
- stronger identity verification for certain high-reach accounts,
- and liability standards for demonstrably harmful, coordinated deception in specific domains (elections, public safety).

The aim is not to suppress dissent but to reduce high-gain amplification of deception.

A useful principle is **friction proportionality**: impose small, broadly applicable frictions that slow cascades without targeting ideology. For example, requiring users to open a link before sharing, or slowing the spread of content flagged as likely manipulated until verification occurs.

Layer 4: Civic capacity—building epistemic resilience in citizens

Education is often invoked vaguely, but there are concrete civic capacities democracies can cultivate:

- probabilistic thinking (comfort with uncertainty),
- understanding of incentives and manipulation,
- media literacy oriented toward provenance and verification,
- and civic norms of charitable interpretation and evidence-based disagreement.

These cannot be solved solely in schools; they require public institutions and cultural reinforcement.

Layer 5: Public-interest media and local journalism

Local journalism historically provided shared reference points and reduced the scale of conspiratorial thinking by anchoring reality in immediate institutions.

Its decline is an epistemic risk. Rebuilding public-interest media can provide stabilizing negative feedback. This can include funding mechanisms insulated from political control, local reporting infrastructure, and civic information hubs.

The key is independence and pluralism. The point is not propaganda, but reliable ground truth that can stand up to sensationalism.

9. Deliberation as a Corrective: Restoring Slow Feedback in a Fast System

One of the most underappreciated design tools is institutionalized deliberation—mechanisms that slow decision-making enough to allow learning and reduce polarization.

Organized assemblies, citizens' juries, and structured public consultations can:

- expose participants to cross-cutting perspectives,
- reduce caricature through real interaction,
- and produce recommendations that are harder to dismiss as partisan.

Deliberation does not replace elections. It supplements them by adding a slower feedback channel that stabilizes the system. Think of it as adding shock absorbers to a vehicle on rough terrain: you don't remove the engine; you reduce the oscillations.

In nonlinear times, democracies may need more "slow institutions" that can counterbalance fast attention cycles.

10. The Danger of Epistemic Authoritarianism—and How to Avoid It

Any attempt to strengthen information integrity risks sliding into coercive control. The line between verification and censorship can be abused. This is why design must emphasize:

- procedural constraints,
- transparency,
- independent oversight,
- and viewpoint-neutral mechanisms.

The principle should be to **govern processes, not opinions**. Democracies can regulate disclosure, provenance, and manipulation tactics while preserving free debate about values and contested claims.

Another principle: **separate certification from enforcement**. Fact-checkers can certify claims; citizens and institutions can decide how to weigh those certifications; enforcement should be limited to narrow domains where deception causes direct institutional harm (e.g., forged ballots, fake official documents, coordinated foreign interference in elections).

Finally: **trust is earned, not demanded**. Heavy-handed control often backfires by confirming suspicions of bias. The goal is to make trustworthy institutions so visibly fair and transparent that delegitimation becomes harder.

11. A Systems Diagnostic: Indicators of Epistemic Breakdown

Because epistemic collapse can be nonlinear, democracies should monitor early warning signals:

- rising belief in mutually exclusive realities across partisan groups,
- declining trust in neutral institutions (courts, election administrators),
- increased prevalence of conspiracy narratives that explain everything,
- rising rates of political violence or threats justified by "stolen reality,"
- and accelerated viral cycles around misinformation during crises.

These indicators should be treated as public health signals: warning signs of systemic vulnerability.

12. Toward an Epistemically Resilient Republic

We can now integrate this chapter's argument into the book's broader framework.

Chapter 1 argued that democracies must operate near the edge of chaos—stable enough to coordinate, flexible enough to adapt. Chapter 2 argued that inequality is a system parameter that narrows that region by increasing insecurity, capture risk, and polarization. Chapter 3 adds that democracy's adaptive stability depends on a functioning epistemic commons, and that modern networked communication threatens that commons by increasing speed, amplification, and identity-sorted realities.

The resulting picture is sobering; material inequality and informational fragility are coupled. As inequality rises, the informational environment becomes more vulnerable; as informational integrity collapses, redistributive and governance reforms become harder because no shared reality exists to legitimate them. The republic can become trapped in a vicious cycle: insecurity fuels outrage, outrage fuels misinformation, misinformation fuels distrust, distrust fuels institutional paralysis, and paralysis deepens insecurity.

Breaking that cycle requires institutional design that targets feedback loops:

- reduce high-gain amplification and manipulation incentives,
- rebuild credible certifiers and transparency mechanisms,
- strengthen civic capacities and deliberative structures,
- and restore public-interest media and local anchors of reality.

This is not a call for a return to old gatekeeping, and certainly not an argument for technocratic control. It is an argument for *epistemic engineering* in the best liberal sense: building systems that make truth-seeking viable, disagreement intelligible, and self-government possible under turbulence.

In nonlinear times, democracies cannot treat information as merely speech floating in the air. Speech is embedded in architectures, incentives, and networks. The design of those architectures is now part of democratic constitutionalism. If the republic is to remain at the edge of chaos rather than fall into it, it must treat the epistemic commons as a shared inheritance, one that requires stewardship, not nostalgia; design, not panic; and above all, institutions that can keep the pursuit of truth compatible with the practice of freedom.

Chapter 4

The Fragility Stack: Polarization and Information Disorder as a Nonlinear Contagion

A REPUBLIC RARELY collapses because one variable "gets worse." Democracies degrade when multiple vulnerabilities align—when stresses that were once separable become coupled, and when failures that were once containable begin to cascade. In nonlinear times, the most dangerous coupling is between **polarization** and **information disorder**. Each is destabilizing on its own; together they form a *fragility stack*: layered vulnerabilities that amplify one another, reduce the system's capacity to self-correct, and push the polity toward a new attractor—one characterized by mutual delegitimation, institutional corrosion, and episodic legitimacy crises.

This chapter argues that polarization and information disorder behave like a **nonlinear contagion** in networked democracies. They spread through social structures the way contagions spread through bodies—not via biology, but via incentives, identity, and attention. They exhibit threshold effects (slow drift followed by sudden escalation), super-spreader dynamics (high-reach actors and algorithmic amplification), and immune-system failure (breakdown of epistemic and civic defenses). Most importantly, they erode the republic's stabilizing feedback mechanisms—the very tools democracy uses to correct error and restore legitimacy.

Calling polarization and information disorder "contagion" is not a metaphor meant to alarm. It is a systems diagnosis meant to guide design. Contagions can be mitigated without eliminating freedom; the task is to identify transmission pathways, reduce amplification, build resilience, and create institutions that can dampen cascades rather than ride them into crisis.

1. The Fragility Stack: Why Modern Democracies Fail by Coupling

Complex systems fail through **coupling**. When subsystems are loosely connected, a shock can be absorbed locally. When subsystems become tightly connected—economy to identity, identity to media, media to elections, elections to legitimacy—small disturbances can propagate widely.

The fragility stack in many modern democracies looks like this:

1. **Material insecurity and inequality** increase grievance and reduce trust.
2. **Identity sorting** (geographic, cultural, online) turns political disagreement into tribal rivalry.
3. **Networked information systems** amplify emotionally arousing content and reward conflict.
4. **Polarization** makes truth a badge of loyalty rather than a shared resource.
5. **Information disorder** undermines shared reality and institutional credibility.
6. **Institutional performance declines** as governance becomes harder and legitimacy erodes.
7. **Cynicism intensifies**; conspiratorial narratives become plausible.
8. **Escalation becomes rational**; actors adopt hardball tactics to avoid being "destroyed."
9. The system enters a self-reinforcing cycle of **mutual delegitimation**.

Each layer adds vulnerability. Together, they produce a brittle system: it can appear stable for long periods and then destabilize rapidly after a trigger event: an election, a scandal, a crisis, a market crash, a security incident. The point is not that every democracy is doomed, but that the dynamics of failure are increasingly *nonlinear.*

The edge-of-chaos republic depends on a balance: enough contestation to remain free, enough coherence to remain governable. Polarization and information disorder shift the balance by increasing the "gain" on conflict and reducing the system's ability to dampen it.

2. Polarization Is Not Just Disagreement: It Is a Structural Shift in Incentives

Many societies have always had disagreements. Democracies are built for disagreement. The question is what kind. A healthy republic expects opponents to be wrong and sometimes even dangerous, but not fundamentally illegitimate. Polarization becomes system-threatening when it takes three forms simultaneously:

- **Affective polarization:** people dislike and distrust the other side, independent of policy differences.
- **Identity polarization:** political affiliation fuses with social identity (religion, region, lifestyle, class).
- **Institutional polarization:** neutral institutions (courts, agencies, universities, election administration) are viewed as captured or partisan.

In this regime, politics becomes existential. Losing is not a temporary inconvenience; it is perceived as long-term domination by an enemy. Under existential stakes, norms that depend on restraint collapse. The logic of escalation intensifies: if the other side is illegitimate, then any tactic becomes justified.

This is where polarization turns into a contagion. Not because emotions are infectious in a simplistic sense, but because polarization spreads through:

- **social imitation** (people copy the language and stance of their group),
- **status incentives** (extreme signals confer group status),

- **fear cascades** (threat perceptions amplify),
- **attention markets** (outrage content travels farther),
- and **institutional feedback** (each hardball move justifies the next).

Polarization becomes less an attitude and more an ecosystem of strategies.

3. Information Disorder Is Not Only "Misinformation": It Is a Degraded Epistemic Environment

Information disorder includes misinformation, disinformation, propaganda, and conspiratorial narratives, but the deeper problem is a shift in the polity's epistemic architecture:

- Verification loses to virality.
- Context loses to clip culture.
- Credibility loses to identity.
- Complexity loses to moral melodrama.
- Uncertainty loses to certainty performers.

In such an environment, truth becomes expensive. It requires time, attention, and institutional trust—resources increasingly scarce. Meanwhile, falsehood can be cheap and profitable. When systems reward cheap, confidence-saturated narratives, information disorder becomes an equilibrium rather than an exception.

Information disorder strengthens polarization because it supplies interpretive fuel: it allows each side to construct a reality in which the other is not merely wrong but monstrous. Polarization, in turn, exacerbates information disorder by punishing cross-cutting verification: correcting your own side feels like betrayal. The two variables become coupled.

4. The Contagion Model: Transmission, Amplification, and Threshold Effects

To treat polarization and information disorder as a nonlinear contagion, we can borrow three concepts: **transmission pathways**, **super-spreaders**, and **thresholds**.

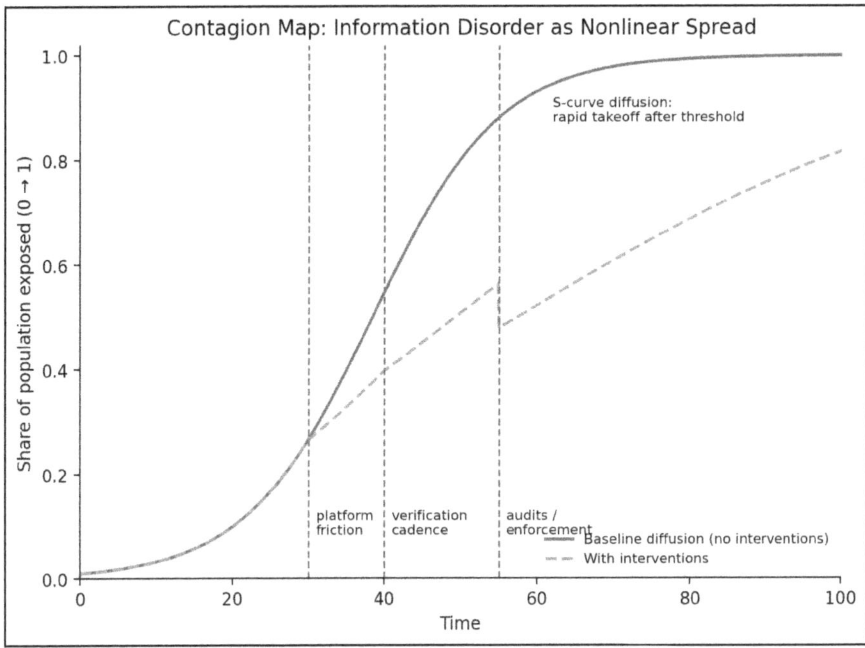

Figure 6.0: *Contagion Map: Information Disorder as Nonlinear Spread*

Misinformation behaves like an epidemic with threshold-driven takeoff and saturation. Interventions reduce the effective reproduction of false content and can flatten or delay the exposure curve, especially when implemented early and consistently.

a) Transmission pathways

Polarization and information disorder are transmitted through multiple channels:

1. **Interpersonal networks:** friends, families, workplaces, congregations.
2. **Media networks:** cable, talk radio, podcasts, online outlets.
3. **Platform networks:** algorithmic feeds that shape exposure.
4. **Institutional signals:** party leaders, public officials, courts, agencies.
5. **Cultural networks:** influencers, celebrities, community leaders.

Each channel has different "friction." Some are slow and intimate (family), some are fast and broadcast (platforms). In a high-gain environment, fast channels dominate the system's mood, while slow channels struggle to correct.

b) Super-spreaders

Not all nodes are equal. Certain actors and mechanisms function as super-spreaders:

- high-reach influencers and politicians,
- outrage-oriented media personalities,
- coordinated networks of accounts,
- algorithmic ranking systems optimized for engagement,
- crisis moments that spike attention and lower skepticism.

Super-spreader dynamics explain why a fringe idea can become mainstream rapidly. The network does not require many believers; it requires enough amplification to create the perception of ubiquity. Once people believe "everyone is talking about this," the idea gains legitimacy by volume.

c) Threshold effects and phase shifts

In nonlinear systems, change can be gradual until it isn't. A society can sustain rising polarization and still function until trust drops below a threshold, at which point a shock can trigger an abrupt legitimacy breakdown.

A classic example is election legitimacy. For decades, losing sides may accept outcomes grudgingly. But once the fraction of citizens who believe elections are fraudulent crosses a certain threshold, the losing side's incentive changes: acceptance becomes betrayal, and contestation becomes duty. At that point, the democratic stabilizer (elections) becomes a destabilizer (elections as legitimacy crises).

These thresholds are not fixed. Inequality, institutional performance, and external interference can lower them. That is the fragility stack in action.

5. Why Polarization Accelerates: The Mechanics of Identity Threat

Polarization intensifies when politics becomes a proxy for identity. Identity threat has special dynamical properties:

- It triggers **defensive cognition**: people seek information that confirms their group's virtue.
- It narrows **moral attention**: the other side's suffering becomes less visible.
- It justifies **preemptive aggression**: "if we don't win, they will destroy us."
- It increases **tolerance for lies**: lies that protect the group are seen as necessary.

Identity threat also compresses time. People under threat perceive urgency. That urgency interacts with social media's speed to produce rapid cycles of escalation: outrage, mobilization, retaliation, counter-outrage.

When identity drives politics, democracy begins to resemble a conflict between tribes rather than a contest among citizens. In this regime, the republic loses a crucial stabilizer: *mutual toleration*, the belief that opponents have a legitimate right to compete.

6. The Epistemic Immune System: How Democracies Normally Resist Contagion

Every society has an "epistemic immune system"—not a centralized authority, but a distributed set of norms and institutions that identify falsehood, reduce manipulation, and maintain shared reality. These include:

- professional journalistic standards,
- scientific and academic norms,
- legal standards of evidence,
- independent audits and inspectors,
- bipartisan election administration,

- civic norms of truth-telling and restraint,
- and reputational consequences for deception.

In healthy democracies, this immune system does not eliminate misinformation; it prevents it from becoming system-dominant. It provides negative feedback: correction, accountability, and credibility reinforcement.

In the fragility stack, the immune system fails for three reasons:

1. **Overload:** the volume and speed of claims exceed verification capacity.
2. **Capture narratives:** immune institutions are portrayed as partisan, reducing their ability to correct.
3. **Incentive inversion:** the system rewards the very content that immune institutions seek to dampen.

When the immune system fails, the polity becomes susceptible to "epistemic infections": conspiracies that metastasize, moral panics that drive policy, scapegoating cycles that normalize cruelty, and delegitimation campaigns that corrode institutions.

7. Feedback Loops That Turn Contagion into a Stable Attractor

Several feedback loops are especially powerful in converting polarization and information disorder into a stable, self-reinforcing regime.

Loop 1: Outrage → Attention → Incentives → More outrage

Outrage content yields attention; attention yields profit and status; profit and status attract more outrage producers; the ecosystem shifts toward maximalism.

Loop 2: Delegitimation → Distrust → Noncompliance → Dysfunction → More delegitimation

When institutions are distrusted, people comply less and cooperate less. That produces dysfunction (gridlock, bureaucratic failure, crisis mismanagement). Dysfunction then "proves" the institutions are illegitimate.

Loop 3: Identity threat → Selective exposure → Epistemic closure → Radicalization

Fear drives people into echo chambers; echo chambers increase certainty; certainty increases hostility; hostility increases fear.

Loop 4: Hardball tactics → Retaliation → Norm collapse → Permanent escalation

If one side uses extreme procedural tactics, the other side adapts. Over time, norms erode, and tactics become normalized. What once seemed shocking becomes the norm.

Loop 5: Inequality → Grievance → Populist storytelling → Distrust → Weakened reform capacity → More inequality

Economic insecurity increases receptivity to narratives of betrayal. Those narratives delegitimize institutions and make reform harder, thereby preserving inequality and deepening insecurity.

The point is not that one side is uniquely guilty. These loops can arise in many contexts. The system's incentives reward them. Once these loops dominate, the republic can fall into an attractor of chronic crisis: politics becomes less about solving problems and more about sustaining mobilization against an enemy.

8. Contagion Triggers: Why Crises Become Political Accelerants

Crises—pandemics, recessions, terrorist attacks, wars—are moments when uncertainty is high, and attention is concentrated. There are also moments when governments must act quickly, often under imperfect information. In such moments, polarization and information disorder become accelerants.

- Uncertainty increases demand for certainty.
- Fear increases willingness to scapegoat.
- Emergency measures increase suspicion of power abuse.
- Complex tradeoffs increase moral simplification.

In a low-polarization system, crises can increase solidarity. In a high-polarization system, crises become opportunities for blame and delegitimation. Each side interprets the crisis through its identity lens and information ecosystem. The crisis then becomes not a shared problem but a weapon.

This is why nonlinear times are so dangerous. The frequency of crises appears to be increasing—economic volatility, climate-related shocks, geopolitical tension, and technological disruption. If the fragility stack is already in place, repeated shocks can ratchet the system toward instability.

9. Institutional Consequences: From Governance to Performance Theater

When polarization and information disorder dominate, institutions shift function:

- **Legislatures** become stages for symbolic combat rather than bargaining arenas.
- **Courts** become perceived as partisan referees, reducing compliance.
- **Bureaucracies** become targets of suspicion, reducing capacity.
- **Elections** become legitimacy battlegrounds rather than corrective mechanisms.
- **Public administration** becomes a proxy war in which competence is interpreted as bias.

The republic's "learning mechanisms" degrade. Democracies learn through criticism, investigation, oversight, and policy iteration. But if criticism is interpreted as sabotage and oversight as persecution, learning becomes impossible. Institutions then ossify or lash out.

This is the tragedy of the fragility stack: it converts the system's corrective features into sources of conflict. The mechanisms that should restore stability instead amplify instability.

10. Breaking the Contagion: Design Principles for Dampening Cascades

If polarization and information disorder are a nonlinear contagion, the solution is not a single policy. It is a set of interventions aimed at transmission pathways, amplification mechanisms, and immune system resilience.

Principle 1: Reduce high-gain amplification without controlling viewpoints

Democracies can introduce **friction** that slows cascades without dictating ideology. Examples include:

- slowing the virality of unverified claims during elections or emergencies,
- requiring provenance signals for high-reach political content,
- increasing transparency about algorithmic ranking,
- limiting coordinated inauthentic behavior,
- and building independent audit access for researchers.

The goal is to lower the system's "gain"—to prevent small sparks from becoming infernos.

Principle 2: Rebuild credible referees through procedural robustness

Trust cannot be commanded. But institutions can be designed to be more visibly fair:

- bipartisan election administration with transparent audits,
- independent inspectors general with real authority,
- open-data standards for key governance metrics,
- clear conflict-of-interest rules and enforcement,
- and procedural constraints that reduce discretionary arbitrariness.

The aim is to make delegitimation harder by making fairness more observable.

Principle 3: Create cross-cutting civic infrastructures

Polarization thrives when society lacks bridging ties. Democracies need institutions that create cross-cutting interaction:

- civic service programs,
- local deliberative assemblies,
- cross-partisan community projects,
- shared public spaces and institutions,

- and educational structures that teach systems thinking and epistemic humility.

These are slow interventions, but they strengthen immune function.

Principle 4: Reduce existential stakes through institutional containment

When each election feels like total war, escalation becomes rational. Institutional design can reduce stakes:

- decentralization and federalism (with coordination),
- robust rights protections that cannot be easily reversed,
- independent courts that are procedurally credible,
- and policy mechanisms that reduce winner-take-all outcomes.

Containment does not eliminate conflict; it makes losing survivable.

Principle 5: Address inequality as the fuel source

The fragility stack is intensified by material insecurity and perceived rigging. Without addressing inequality, informational and civic reforms face headwinds. Economic reforms that reduce insecurity can lower receptivity to conspiratorial narratives and reduce the emotional temperature that drives contagion.

11. A Moral Warning: Contagion Politics Erodes the Soul of the Republic

It is tempting to treat polarization as a technical problem. But it has moral consequences. A republic at the edge of chaos is already a demanding moral achievement: it requires self-restraint, mutual toleration, and the willingness to lose without revenge. Polarization and information disorder corrode these virtues by making cruelty feel justified and deception feel necessary.

In a contagion regime, citizens begin to see each other not as neighbors but as threats. Politics becomes a theater of humiliation. The moral ecology shifts: dignity becomes scarce, and scarcity produces further conflict.

This is why design matters. Institutions shape incentives, and incentives shape character. A system that rewards outrage will produce outraged citizens. A system that rewards humiliation will produce humiliators. A system that rewards truth-telling and restraint can cultivate civic virtue—not perfectly, but meaningfully.

12. Conclusion: The Fragility Stack and The Edge-of-Chaos Test

The fragility stack is the modern republic's most urgent systems problem. Polarization and information disorder behave as nonlinear contagions because they spread through network dynamics, accelerate under high-gain attention systems, and erode the immune institutions that would normally contain them. They convert the democratic process from a stabilizing feedback mechanism into a destabilizing one, turning elections, courts, and media into battlegrounds over legitimacy itself.

The edge-of-chaos republic survives when it can process conflict without turning it into an existential threat—when it maintains a shared reality sufficient for persuasion and restraint sufficient for alternation in power. The fragility stack undermines both conditions. It narrows the safe operating space of democracy and increases the likelihood that shocks become regime-altering events.

The task, therefore, is not to eliminate disagreement, nor to yearn for a mythical past of consensus. The task is to design institutions and information architectures that reduce amplification of deception, strengthen the visibility of fairness, restore cross-cutting ties, and lower the existential stakes of political competition. In nonlinear times, we should treat polarization and information disorder the way we treat wildfire risk in a warming climate: as a predictable interaction of fuel, wind, and ignition. You cannot ban sparks, but you can reduce fuel, break up the landscape, and build systems that keep a fire from becoming a conflagration.

In the next chapter, we will turn from diagnosis to architecture: how to design institutions that create "smart friction" against escalation while preserving "smart flow" for adaptation, so a democracy can remain governable without becoming brittle, and free without becoming unmoored.

Part II

The Physics of Democratic Stability

Part I argued that democracy is not simply a moral ideal or a constitutional checklist. It is a living, nonlinear system, a complex adaptive republic that must continually convert conflict into legitimacy under conditions of uncertainty, pluralism, and change. We explored how modern democracies are being pushed toward dangerous dynamics by shifts in system parameters (especially inequality), by the degradation of shared informational infrastructure, and by the coupling of polarization with information disorder, which we called a fragility stack. The lesson was not fatalism or doom. The lesson was structural: if we want democracy to endure in nonlinear times, we must treat its stability as an *engineering and ecological problem* as much as a philosophical and political one.

Part II begins where that realization becomes operational. If Part I described the forces that push democracies toward instability, Part II asks the design question that follows: **what makes a democracy stable in the first place, and how do we build or restore those stabilizers under turbulence?** The title of this part of the book, *The Physics of Democratic Stability*, is not a metaphor meant to sound scientific. It is an attempt to discipline the conversation. "Physics," here, does not mean equations alone. It means the study of constraints, feedback, thresholds, and conserved quantities: the deep structure beneath surface events. It means asking what can and cannot be done with a given system, regardless of ideology. It means understanding how institutional architectures transform energy, fear, outrage, and aspiration into outcomes, and why certain designs dampen instability while others amplify it.

In ordinary civic discourse, stability is often mistaken for calm. But calm can be deceptive. A society can be calm because it is just, cohesive, and because its institutions work and citizens feel represented. But it can also be calm because it is suppressed, depoliticized, or numbed by resignation. Conversely, a society can be noisy and still be stable—if its noise is channeled into legitimate processes that resolve disputes and regenerate trust. Stability, in the systemic sense, is not the absence of chaos or discord. It is the ability to remain coherent under contestation: to sustain rule-following, peaceful alternation, and legitimate authority amid disagreement and shocks.

That is the core claim of Part II: **democratic stability is a dynamic achievement.** It depends on how institutions shape feedback loops, manage time and attention, distribute and constrain power, and maintain the epistemic and moral conditions necessary for cooperation. It depends on the *republic's physics*: the structural properties that determine whether perturbations are damped or amplified.

1. Why "Physics" Belongs in a Book About Democracy

Political science often analyzes democracy through categories: regime type, party system, constitutional design, civil liberties, and electoral rules. Philosophy often analyzes democracy through ideals: justice, equality, rights, dignity, and autonomy. Both approaches are essential, but both can overlook the key feature of modern democratic fragility: **nonlinearity.** In nonlinear systems, causes do not scale proportionally with effects. Small insults can trigger large cascades. Slow parameter drift can produce sudden phase transitions. And rational actors can generate collectively irrational outcomes due to incentive structures and feedback.

Complexity science, control theory, and network dynamics are not replacements for moral reasoning. They are complements. They force us to ask operational questions:

- What are the primary feedback loops that maintain democratic order?
- What conditions increase a democracy's sensitivity to shocks?
- Where are the thresholds—points at which behavior flips?
- Which institutional designs increase resilience, redundancy, and modularity?

- What stabilizers can restore negative feedback when positive feedback dominates?

In other words, what are the republic's *stability mechanisms*?

When engineers design a bridge, they do not merely ask whether the bridge is beautiful or whether it matches the architect's ideals. They ask whether it will withstand stress: wind, load, fatigue, and resonance. Democracies, like bridges, face stress. But unlike bridges, democracies are made of people—agents who learn, strategize, and adapt. That makes the "physics" more complicated, but the principle is the same: we must design for stress, not for perfect conditions.

Part II, therefore, proposes a different stance toward crisis in our democracy. Rather than treating each breakdown as a moral shock or partisan scandal, we treat it as a signal of underlying system strain. We ask what the breakdown reveals about the system's parameters and stabilizers. We adopt a diagnostic posture: *what is this telling us about the structure of the republic?* Then we move from diagnosis to design.

2. The Two Regimes of Democratic Failure: Brittle Order and Turbulent Collapse

A useful way to frame democratic stability is to distinguish between two failure regimes that lie on opposite sides of the edge-of-chaos band.

Brittle order occurs when institutions become rigid, unresponsive, and captured. The system may appear stable—elections occur, courts rule, budgets pass—but legitimacy leaks. Citizens feel unheard. Reforms are blocked. Inequality hardens. The result is resentment and latent instability. Brittle order is dangerous because it accumulates stress. It can endure for a long time, only to fail suddenly when a shock exposes the system's fragility.

Turbulent collapse occurs when institutions lose coherence. Trust disintegrates. Procedures no longer bind. Information disorder becomes system-dominant. Violence becomes thinkable. In this regime, the system is not merely unjust or captured; it is dynamically unstable. It cannot coordinate. It cannot credibly enforce rules. It cannot sustain a shared reality.

Part II concerns preventing both failure regimes. Stability is not simply the avoidance of chaos; it is the avoidance of brittleness as well. A democracy must be stable enough to enforce rules and preserve rights, but flexible enough to reform and adapt. The physics of democratic stability is therefore the physics of *adaptive stability*: resilience without repression, coherence without stagnation, authority without domination.

3. A Stability Vocabulary: Energy, Friction, Feedback, and Phase Transitions

To ground the discussion, Part II introduces a vocabulary that borrows from dynamical systems and translates it into political meaning. These terms are not meant to turn democracy into a math problem; they are meant to clarify the mechanisms beneath the narratives.

Energy: political intensity and mobilized emotion

In physical systems, energy is the capacity to do work. In democracies, "energy" appears as mobilized attention, anger, hope, fear, solidarity, and the willingness to act. Political energy is not bad; democracies need it. But energy must be channeled. If political energy is dissipated as nihilism, democracy becomes hollow. If political energy is concentrated as rage, democracy becomes violent. Stability involves converting energy into legitimate change through institutions.

Friction: constraints that slow cascades and prevent runaway escalation

Friction in politics includes constitutional checks, procedural rules, norms, and the time required for deliberation. Friction can be stabilizing: it prevents sudden shifts and protects rights. But too much friction produces paralysis and brittleness. Part II will develop the idea of **smart friction**: constraints that block destabilizing behavior without blocking necessary adaptation.

Feedback: mechanisms that correct errors or amplify dysfunction

Negative feedback stabilizes: elections that remove failed leaders, courts that correct abuses, audits that restore trust, and public services that reduce grievance. Positive feedback destabilizes: outrage cycles, capture loops, delegitimation spirals, and fear cascades. Stability requires strengthening negative feedback and weakening pathological positive feedback.

Phase transitions: regime shifts in democratic behavior

A democracy can suddenly move from "normal politics" to "existential politics". It can move from institutional legitimacy to legitimacy warfare. It can move from pluralism to civil conflict. These are phase transitions: abrupt shifts triggered by parameter drift and shocks. Part II will emphasize early-warning signals and stress testing—how to recognize when the system is nearing thresholds.

With this vocabulary, we can begin to treat democratic stability as something we can diagnose, design for, and protect.

4. WHAT PART II WILL DO: FROM DIAGNOSIS TO ARCHITECTURE

Part II is the book's architectural core. It will develop a framework for building democratic stabilizers under nonlinear conditions. The approach is intentionally interdisciplinary:

- From **control theory**, we borrow the idea that systems remain stable when they have adequate sensing, feedback, and damping—when they can detect deviations and correct them without overshooting.
- From **network science**, we borrow the idea that contagion and cascade depend on topology—how communities connect, how influence concentrates, how bridges form.
- From **institutional economics**, we borrow the idea that rules shape incentives and that incentive-compatible institutions are more stable than purely moral appeals.
- From **political theory**, we borrow the idea that legitimacy is a moral resource and that stability without dignity is not democratic stability at all.
- From **history**, we borrow pattern recognition: the recurrent pathways through which republics degrade—elite capture, polarization, economic shock, scapegoating, and emergency power.

The central commitment is to translate these perspectives into a practical design agenda: what to build, reinforce, and protect.

Part II will therefore focus on four categories of stabilizers:

1. **Legitimacy stabilizers**: procedural fairness, visible accountability, anti-corruption enforcement, and institutional credibility.

2. **Distributional stabilizers**: mechanisms that keep inequality within tolerable bounds and prevent extraction from becoming systemic.

3. **Epistemic stabilizers**: institutions that maintain shared reality and protect the information commons.

4. **Adaptive stabilizers**: pathways for reform, learning, and policy iteration that prevent brittleness.

The reader should expect a consistent pattern: we will identify a vulnerability, describe its dynamic behavior, show how it appears empirically in modern democracies, and propose design responses that modify feedback loops and reduce cascade risk.

5. The Democratic Stability Problem Is Not Partisan—It Is Structural

One of the greatest temptations in an era of polarization is to interpret stability as victory: "If our side wins, democracy will be stable." This is precisely backward. Democracies are stable when losing is survivable and legitimate. If stability depends on your side always winning, the system is already unstable.

Part II, therefore, treats democratic stability as a **nonpartisan systems constraint**. This does not mean moral neutrality. The book will take clear positions: democratic stability requires equal dignity, credible procedures, and constraints on domination. But the design goal is not to protect one coalition. It is to protect the republic as a conflict-processing system.

In practice, that means focusing on institutional incentives that make restraint rational. It means designing safeguards that apply regardless of who holds power. It means building legitimacy through fairness, competence, and transparency rather than through ideological conformity.

The reader should also expect a frank acknowledgment of tradeoffs. Some reforms increase resilience but reduce speed. Some reduce misinformation but risk overreach. Some increase representation but reduce decisiveness. The "physics" approach does not eliminate tradeoffs; it clarifies them and forces choices to be explicit.

6. The Stability Paradox: Democracies Must Remain Open to Challenge

A stable democracy must permit challenges to itself. This is the paradox at the heart of self-government: the system must allow dissent, opposition, and criticism—even criticism that undermines trust—because without freedom, democracy becomes a hollow ritual. Yet the system must also protect itself from strategies that exploit openness to destroy shared reality or seize power without restraint.

Part II will examine this paradox through the lens of **self-referential games**: actors can use democratic procedures to weaken democracy. They can delegitimize elections while running in them. They can demand free speech while flooding the public sphere with deception. They can invoke rights while hollowing out the institutions that protect rights.

To manage this paradox, democracies need not become authoritarian; they need to become **structurally intelligent**. They need rules that distinguish between legitimate dissent and destabilizing sabotage, not by judging ideology, but by judging tactics: manipulation, violence, corruption, and institutional capture.

This is one reason "physics" is helpful. It shifts attention from moralizing about motivations to analyzing the mechanics of harm: what behaviors generate cascades and which dampen them?

7. Stability as a Moral Ecology: Why Fairness Is a Stabilizer

A central claim of this book is that morality is not separate from stability; it is part of the stability mechanism. A republic is stable when citizens believe they are treated as equals in dignity and protected from domination. When people feel expendable, the republic's moral ecology fails, and stability becomes costly: it requires coercion, propaganda, or repression.

Fairness functions like a stabilizer in at least three ways:

1. **It sustains legitimacy.** People accept losses when they believe procedures are fair.
2. **It supports trust.** People cooperate when they believe others will reciprocate.

3. **It reduces existential politics.** When basic life conditions are secure, political defeat is less catastrophic.

Therefore, Part II will repeatedly return to an uncomfortable truth: a democracy cannot indefinitely "manage" severe inequality and widespread insecurity with procedural tweaks. If the moral ecology is degraded, stabilizers must include distributive and dignity-restoring reforms. Otherwise, the system remains parameter-shifted toward instability.

8. The Role of Institutions: Not to Perfect Humanity, But to Make Cooperation Rational

Democratic theory often assumes a citizenry capable of reasoned deliberation. Cynical theory often assumes citizens are tribal and manipulable. Both contain truths. But the institutional designer's task is not to win the argument about human nature; it is to build a system that works with human nature as it is: social, status-sensitive, prone to fear, capable of solidarity, capable of cruelty, and responsive to incentives.

Institutions can do three critical things:

- **Reduce the payoff to bad behavior.** If lying, corruption, or hardball tactics are rewarded, they will spread.
- **Increase the payoff to cooperation.** If compromise and competence yield political survival, they will be pursued.
- **Contain conflict.** If losing is survivable and rights are secure, zero-sum escalation becomes less rational.

This is why Part II will emphasize incentive design. Moral exhortation is insufficient in a high-stakes environment. Stability must be built into the game.

9. The Physics of Stability in Practice: Sensing, Damping, and Adaptation

When engineers build a stable system, they focus on three functions:

1. **Sensing:** detect problems early and accurately.
2. **Damping:** reduce oscillations and prevent runaway dynamics.
3. **Adaptation:** adjust structure when conditions change.

Democracies need the same functions.

- **Sensing** requires free inquiry, investigative journalism, audits, and statistical capacity. It also requires that sensed information be trusted and usable.
- **Damping** requires norms and procedures that slow escalation: cooling-off periods, independent referees, and constraints on violence and manipulation.
- **Adaptation** requires mechanisms for reform that are legitimate and achievable: constitutional amendments, institutional experimentation, policy pilots, and responsive governance.

Part II will ask how to strengthen these functions under modern conditions, where sensing is polluted by information disorder, damping is weakened by polarization, and adaptation is blocked by veto points and capture.

10. Preview of Part II's Arc

While the specific chapter titles may evolve, the arc of Part II will proceed according to a logical sequence:

- **From system dynamics to institutional stabilizers:** identifying the core feedback loops that keep democracies in an adaptive band.
- **From polarization and information disorder to governance design:** introducing smart friction, credibility architecture, and contagion dampeners.
- **From inequality and capture to anti-extractive institutional frameworks:** designing predistribution, anti-rent mechanisms, and anti-corruption safeguards.
- **From brittle institutions to adaptive governance:** creating pathways for reform, stress testing, and institutional learning.
- **From abstract design to actionable packages:** assembling reforms into coherent sets that can be adopted without requiring ideal political conditions.

In each case, the guiding question will remain: Does this reform strengthen negative feedback, reduce cascade risk, and preserve legitimacy under stress?

11. A Note on Tone: Analytic Urgency Without Apocalyptic Fatalism

Part II adopts a posture of urgency, but not apocalypse. It refuses two temptations:

- the temptation to treat the democratic crisis as mere spectacle or moral failure,
- and the temptation to treat it as destiny.

The "physics" framework does not guarantee success. It provides clarity. It helps us see which reforms are likely to stabilize the system and which are likely to backfire. It encourages humility and experimentation. And it demands seriousness about constraints: you cannot maintain democratic stability while ignoring inequality, while allowing information disorder to dominate, or while permitting unchecked political capture.

At the same time, the framework offers hope grounded in mechanism. Systems can be redesigned. Feedback loops can be altered. Incentives can be shifted. Institutions can be fortified. Cultures can change when structures reward different behaviors. Democracies have recovered before. But recovery requires that we stop treating each crisis as an isolated event and start treating the republic as a system with a stability problem.

12. The Thesis of Part II

We can state the thesis of Part II as follows:

> **Democratic stability is an emergent property produced by institutional architectures that maintain legitimacy, dampen destructive feedback, preserve shared reality, and enable adaptive reform under stress. In nonlinear times, stability requires a specific architecture, an engineering of incentives and feedback that keeps the republic within its safe operating space.**

Put differently: democracy is not stable because it is good; it is stable when it is built to be stable.

Part II will build the conceptual and practical toolkit required for that building. It will treat institutions as design objects, legitimacy as a measurable resource, and political conflict as a force that can be channeled rather than eliminated. It will show why some reforms are stabilizing, and others are destabilizing. It will insist that fairness, competence, and restraint are not sentimental virtues but structural necessities.

And it will do so with the central image of this book in mind: a republic near the edge of chaos—not doomed but dynamically challenged; not fragile by nature, but fragile by design choices; capable of resilience if it can learn to live within the constraints of its own physics.

In the chapters ahead, we will shift from describing the winds that buffet the republic to describing the architecture that can keep it upright. We will move from turbulence to stabilizers: the levers that matter most, the feedback loops that must be repaired, and the institutional designs that can make democratic self-government viable in nonlinear times.

That is the work of Part II: to treat democratic stability not as an abstract wish, but as a designable property of the republic, one that can be strengthened, stress-tested, and renewed.

Chapter 5

Dampeners: Trust, Legitimacy, and Rule Consistency

A democracy survives turbulence the way a physical structure survives vibration: not by eliminating shocks, but by converting destabilizing energy into manageable motion. In a bridge, dampeners absorb oscillation and prevent resonance. In a republic, the analogs are *trust, legitimacy, and rule consistency*, the "negative feedback" mechanisms that keep conflict from becoming a breakdown. When these dampeners are strong, politics can be loud without becoming lethal; institutions can be contested without becoming illegitimate; and crises can be endured without triggering permanent escalation. When these dampeners fail, the same shocks that once produced reforms begin to produce cascades: distrust spreads faster than verification, factional fear outruns restraint, and governance becomes a brittle contest for control rather than a stable process for collective decision-making.

This chapter argues that trust, legitimacy, and rule consistency are not soft cultural luxuries. They are the republic's most important *sources of stability*. They reduce the perceived stakes of political loss, lower the incentive to cheat, and make Nash equilibrium-type cooperation rational under uncertainty. They also operate nonlinearly. Trust can be accumulated slowly and lost suddenly; legitimacy can survive many policy disagreements but fail abruptly after a perceived procedural violation; rule consistency can be taken for granted until selective enforcement reveals that "rules" are merely weapons. Once these dampeners degrade below critical thresholds, a democracy does not merely become less pleasant; it becomes dynamically unstable. Conflict shifts from policy to regime. Disagreement becomes existential. And the system is drawn toward a new attractor: mutual delegitimation, in which every event is interpreted as proof that the other side is illegitimate and every tactic is justified as self-defense.

Part II is devoted to the physics of democratic stability: feedback loops, constraints, and institutional design for nonlinear times. Chapter 5 focuses on the stabilizing triad that keeps democratic oscillation from turning into democratic collapse. We will define these dampeners, explain how they function as negative feedback, show how they fail, and propose design principles and institutional reforms to restore them without drifting into repression or technocratic paternalism. The guiding question is simple: **what makes democratic rule binding even when citizens are angry, polarized, and uncertain?**

1. Dampeners as Negative Feedback in Political Systems

In a complex system, negative feedback mechanisms reduce deviation from a workable range. They don't eliminate variation; they keep variation bounded. In democracies, the core deviations that must be bounded are:

1. **Defection** (refusing to comply with shared rules),
2. **Escalation** (using increasingly extreme tactics to win or punish),
3. **Delegitimation** (denying the validity of institutions themselves),
4. **Capture** (transforming rules into instruments of extraction),
5. **Violence** (treating politics as war by other means).

Trust, legitimacy, and rule consistency dampen all five deviations. They do so by shaping expectations. A citizen complies not only because coercion exists, but because they believe compliance is reciprocated and meaningful. A losing faction accepts defeat not only because it must, but because it expects future fairness and future opportunity. Officials enforce laws not only because statutes exist, but because procedures are stable enough to protect them from arbitrary retaliation.

These dampeners are thus a *coordination architecture*. They allow millions of strangers to behave as if they are cooperating members of a shared project rather than rival tribes in a permanent contest. Without dampeners, the republic must substitute coercion for consent, propaganda for credibility, and emergency power for routine governance, which further degrades trust and legitimacy in a self-reinforcing spiral.

A crucial point: dampeners are not merely attitudes. They are produced by **structures**: repeatable procedures, transparent constraints, credible enforcement, and visible fairness. Culture matters, but culture is partly the downstream product of incentives. If a system rewards lying, lying spreads. If it rewards procedural cheating, cheating becomes normal. If it rewards restraint and competence, restraint becomes rational.

2. TRUST: THE INVISIBLE INFRASTRUCTURE OF COOPERATION

Trust is often treated as an emotion, something that rises and falls with scandals or charismatic leadership. In terms of stability, trust is a *public resource* that enables compliance, taxation, and peaceful exchange at a tolerable cost.

2.1 Three kinds of trust

- **Social trust** is trust in other people, an expectation that strangers will follow rules and reciprocate basic decency.
- **Institutional trust** is trust in systems, courts, agencies, election administrators, police, regulators, universities, and media.
- **Process trust** is the belief that decisions are made according to stable rules rather than arbitrary power.

These forms of trust reinforce each other. When institutions are fair and effective, social trust rises because people experience the world as predictable and cooperative behavior pays. When institutions are biased or incompetent, social trust falls because people infer that "others" are cheating or being favored. In a low-trust society, citizens retreat into narrower loyalties, family, tribe, faction—because broad cooperation no longer feels safe.

2.2 Trust as an economic and political stabilizer

Trust reduces transaction costs. People pay taxes more willingly, comply with regulations more readily, accept court outcomes more peacefully, and tolerate temporary losses more patiently. High-trust societies can govern with less force and less drama. Low-trust societies must govern by surveillance, punishment, or performative crackdowns, which further erode trust.

In nonlinear times, trust is even more valuable because it absorbs uncertainty. When shocks occur, pandemics, recessions, security threats—citizens cannot personally verify what is happening. They rely on institutions and on each other. If trust is high, the system coordinates rapidly. If trust is low, every shock becomes a legitimacy test, and coordination fails just when it is most needed.

2.3 Trust is rational—and therefore fragile

Trust is not naïveté. It is a rational bet under uncertainty. That means it depends on evidence. People update trust based on observed consistency, fairness, competence, and reciprocity. When citizens see selective enforcement, insider impunity, or arbitrary rule changes, distrust is rational. They infer that the system is rigged or unpredictable and adjust their behavior accordingly: they comply less, evade more, and invest in defensive politics.

This is why trust can collapse quickly. If people conclude that others will defect, or that institutions will not protect them, then defection becomes a dominant strategy. In a low-trust equilibrium, the rational move is to defect first (first-mover advantage).

3. Legitimacy: Why Rules Bind Beyond Coercion

Legitimacy is the republic's moral energy. It is the belief that political authority is justified and that the system's decisions are binding, even when one disagrees. Legitimacy is not the same as popularity. A government can be unpopular yet legitimate. Legitimacy is deeper: it is about whether people accept the *right* of institutions to rule.

3.1 The three dimensions of legitimacy

A useful way to evaluate legitimacy is:

1. **Input legitimacy**: Are people represented? Are elections fair? Is participation meaningful?

2. **Throughput legitimacy**: Are processes transparent, impartial, and consistent? Are decisions made with integrity?

3. **Output legitimacy**: Does governance work? Does it protect basic welfare, rights, and security?

A democracy can survive shortfalls in one dimension if the others remain strong. For example, a period of poor performance (output) can be tolerated if procedures are trusted (throughput) and representation remains credible (input). But when legitimacy declines across all three dimensions, the system enters a dangerous and unstable state.

3.2 Legitimacy as a stabilizing feedback loop

Legitimacy creates compliance. Compliance enables governance. Governance success reinforces legitimacy. That is the stabilizing loop at the heart of a democratic order.

When legitimacy erodes, compliance declines. Declining compliance undermines governance effectiveness. Poor performance further erodes legitimacy. That is the destabilizing loop, a classic positive feedback that can push the system toward crisis.

3.3 Procedural justice: the hidden engine of legitimacy

One of the strongest predictors of legitimacy is not outcomes but **procedural justice**, the perception that the rules are applied fairly, that people are heard, and that authorities act with neutral principles. Citizens are often willing to accept unfavorable outcomes when they believe the process was honest and consistent.

This matters because democracy cannot guarantee everyone will win on substance. It can only guarantee that everyone is treated as an equal citizen in the procedure. When procedural justice fails, when outcomes appear bought, manipulated, or arbitrarily imposed, legitimacy collapses faster than any policy failure could cause.

3.4 The legitimacy of restraint

Democracies require *self-binding*. Winners restrain themselves because they anticipate being losers later. Legitimacy grows when winners show restraint: protecting minority rights, respecting norms, refusing to weaponize institutions for vengeance. Restraint signals that the system is not merely a power structure; it is law.

When restraint collapses, when every victory is used to entrench advantage, the system teaches losers that the only rational strategy is preemptive escalation. Legitimacy then becomes factional: each side believes legitimacy exists only when it wins. When legitimacy fractures, democracy collapses under its own weight.

4. Rule Consistency: Credible Commitment in a Contested Polity

Rule consistency is the most technical of the dampeners, and arguably the most decisive in nonlinear times. It refers to the stability and predictability of rules over time, and the impartiality of their enforcement across people and factions.

Rule consistency includes:

- stable election rules and credible administration,
- predictable legal standards and due process,
- consistent regulatory enforcement,
- transparent budgeting and procurement norms,
- and a general expectation that officials cannot rewrite rules opportunistically.

4.1 Consistency is not rigidity

Rule consistency does not mean rules never change. Democracies must adapt. Consistency means changes occur **through legitimate pathways** (legislative processes, judicial review, constitutional procedures) and are applied **universally**, not selectively.

A democracy must find the balance between:

- **Credible commitment** (rules stable enough to be trusted), and
- **Adaptive capacity** (rules flexible enough to respond to new conditions).

This balance is the heart of "physics of stability" design: too much rigidity produces brittleness; too much volatility produces chaos.

4.2 Why rule inconsistency is a contagion accelerator

Inconsistent enforcement is corrosive because it turns law into a signal of factional dominance rather than a neutral constraint. Once citizens believe rules are applied selectively, they stop seeing compliance as a civic duty and begin to see it as surrender. They then search for ways to evade, resist, or retaliate.

Rule inconsistency also fuels conspiracy thinking. If rules change suddenly or enforcement seems arbitrary, people infer hidden motives. In an information-disordered environment (especially in hyper-connected information networks), those motives become stories that spread rapidly. Thus, inconsistent rules don't just create injustice; they create *epistemic volatility*.

4.3 Rule-of-law credibility as a stabilizer

The rule of law is not merely the existence of laws. It is the **credibility** of law as a system of constraints that applies to the powerful and the weak alike. When high-status actors appear immune, through wealth, networks, or political influence, rule consistency collapses. Nothing destroys legitimacy faster than the perception that law is for some but not for others.

5. THE FAILURE MODES: HOW DAMPENERS DEGRADE INTO FRAGILITY

Because these dampeners are interdependent, they often fail together (cascade). The fragility stack described earlier can be restated in the language of dampeners:

- inequality and insecurity corrode trust,
- polarized information ecosystems corrode legitimacy,
- opportunistic pressure corrodes rule consistency,
- corruption and impunity corrode all three at once.

Let's name the major failure modes.

5.1 Selective enforcement and the politics of impunity

When citizens believe enforcement is selective, the system moves from legal constraint to factional warfare. People interpret prosecutions as persecution and non-prosecutions as favoritism. This is a catastrophic failure mode because it turns accountability, normally a stabilizer, into a destabilizer.

The solution is not "less enforcement." The solution is **credible, procedurally constrained enforcement** with transparent standards, independent oversight, and consistent universal application.

5.2 Rule volatility and governance whiplash

Rapid policy reversals and chaotic rule changes can occur in highly polarized systems or in systems with weak procedural constraints. Whiplash creates uncertainty, undermining investment, planning, and civic confidence. Citizens begin to see institutions as unstable and politics as arbitrary. This increases the incentive to seize power permanently "before the rules change again."

5.3 Legitimacy warfare: when institutions become contested objects

Institutions, courts, electoral bodies, and agencies become targets rather than referees. Each side seeks not merely to win policy but to delegitimize the arbiters. Once that becomes normal, the republic loses the capacity to resolve disputes peacefully.

5.4 Emergency power normalization

Crises tempt leaders to bypass procedures. Sometimes emergency powers are necessary, but they are systemically dangerous because they train citizens to expect rule-bending and train leaders to exploit exceptions. If emergency governance becomes routine, rule consistency collapses, and legitimacy becomes conditional.

5.5 Narrative substitution: when politics becomes performance

In low-trust environments, performance becomes more valuable than competence because citizens cannot easily verify competence. Leaders then invest in spectacle, scapegoating, and symbolic conflict. Governance quality declines, further eroding trust and creating another positive feedback loop.

6. Building Dampeners: Design Principles for Trust, Legitimacy, and Consistency

Dampeners cannot be built by a political narrative alone. They are designed through institutions and reinforced by norms. The following design principles are central to democratic stability.

Principle 1: Make fairness visible

People do not trust what they cannot observe. Fairness must be *legible*. That means transparent processes, clear standards, public reporting, and understandable explanations, not bureaucratic opacity.

Principle 2: Constrain discretion where stakes are high

High-discretion systems invite accusations of bias and invite real abuse. The higher the stakes (elections, prosecutions, emergency powers), the more the system needs rule-bound procedures, independent oversight, and auditability.

Principle 3: Build independent referees with redundant credibility

No single institution can hold trust in a polarized environment. Democracies need multiple overlapping referees: inspectors general, independent auditors, bipartisan commissions, professionalized civil services, and courts with credible ethical constraints. Redundancy prevents single-point legitimacy failure.

Principle 4: Align incentives so restraint is rational

If the system rewards hardball, it will spread. Reforms must reduce the payoff to escalation and increase the payoff to cooperation, through electoral incentives, procedural rules, and enforcement norms.

Principle 5: Reduce the existential stakes of losing

When losing feels existential, escalation becomes rational. Rights protections, decentralized governance, and credible constraints reduce the perceived stakes and, in turn, the incentive to burn institutions down.

Principle 6: Build "credible flexibility"

Rules must adapt, but adaptation must be predictable. Mechanisms like sunset clauses, scheduled reviews, independent commissions, and transparent rule-making processes allow change without chaos.

7. Practical Architecture: What Dampeners Look Like in Institutional Form

This section turns principles into design objects, structures that can actually be built.

7.1 Election integrity as a trust and legitimacy damper

Elections are democracy's primary negative feedback mechanism: the system corrects errors by replacing leaders. When election legitimacy is contested, the stabilizer becomes a destabilizer.

Stability-oriented election administration includes:

- professional, insulated election management bodies,
- transparent chain-of-custody and ballot handling procedures,
- routine post-election audits as standard practice (not ad hoc),
- clear, uniform rules applied across jurisdictions,
- bipartisan or multi-stakeholder oversight with limited discretion,
- and public-facing communication protocols that explain processes in plain language.

Crucially, election integrity must be **procedural** rather than partisan. The goal is not to ensure one outcome; it is to make the process so visibly fair that fraud narratives have less traction and citizens have a shared basis for acceptance.

7.2 Anti-corruption and ethics enforcement as rule-consistency devices

Corruption is not only theft. It is an attack on rule consistency: it signals that the system is for sale. Even small corruption scandals can have outsized systemic effects by contaminating legitimacy across institutions.

Stability-focused ethics design includes:

- strong conflict-of-interest rules with teeth,
- transparent financial disclosure for public officials,
- independent ethics bodies with prosecutorial referral authority,
- procurement transparency and open contracting data,

- revolving-door limitations and cooling-off periods,
- and credible penalties applied consistently regardless of status.

The key is **symmetry**: rules must bind the powerful. Nothing else restores trust more efficiently than visible accountability at the top that constrains "bad actors."

7.3 Administrative competence as legitimacy reinforcement

Output legitimacy matters. When the government cannot deliver basic services, citizens infer incompetence or bias. Competence is therefore a stabilizing asset.

Competence-enhancing architecture includes:

- protected professional civil service, insulated from political purges
- performance measurement and continuous improvement frameworks
- streamlined service delivery with transparent standards
- robust inspector-general functions to detect failure early
- and emergency response structures that are rehearsed and audited.

Competence must also be communicated carefully. In low-trust environments, messaging can backfire if it sounds self-congratulatory. The most persuasive competence is *experienced*: reliable services, fair processes, and predictable outcomes.

7.4 Judicial legitimacy and the discipline of neutrality

Courts are stabilizers when they are trusted. They become destabilizers when perceived as partisan weapons. Courts cannot control perceptions entirely, but they can control procedures and ethics.

Legitimacy supports include:

- transparent reasoning and accessible explanations of rulings,
- strict ethics and recusal standards,
- predictable jurisprudential methods rather than opportunistic shifts,
- limits on forum shopping where possible,
- and institutional humility, recognizing when political questions require democratic resolution.

A critical point: judicial power must be paired with judicial credibility. When credibility falls, judicial intervention can accelerate instability even if it is legally correct.

7.5 Legislative process reforms as "smart friction"

Legislatures are where conflict is supposed to be processed into compromise. When legislatures become performative or paralyzed, politics migrates to executive orders, courts, and street conflict, often less stable arenas.

Smart friction reforms can include:

- procedures that reward cross-coalition bargaining,
- committee transparency and genuine deliberation time,
- clearer budget processes that reduce last-minute hostage dynamics,
- rules that reduce incentives for symbolic sabotage,
- and structured negotiation mechanisms during major crises.

The goal is not to force consensus, but to make bargaining possible and to reduce the payoff to theatrical obstruction while promoting a "win-win" compromise.

7.6 Credible communication institutions: rebuilding epistemic trust

Trust collapses when citizens cannot comprehend what to believe. Democratic stability, therefore, requires credible information infrastructure, not propaganda, but verification capacity.

Institutional supports include:

- independent statistical agencies with protected autonomy,
- open data standards for key metrics,
- regular, transparent reporting during crises,
- independent audit access for researchers,
- and public-interest media support that is insulated from partisan control.

This chapter's theme is dampening. In information terms, dampening means slowing viral cascades and strengthening verification feedback.

8. Trust Repair Is Path Dependent: How to Rebuild After Breakdown

A hard reality: once trust collapses, it cannot be restored by appeals to unity. It must be restored by *repeated evidence of fairness and consistency.*

8.1 The sequencing problem

In fragile democracies, reform sequencing matters. If you attempt ambitious redistributive reforms before restoring procedural trust, reforms may be interpreted as capture. If you attempt to enforce anti-disinformation measures before establishing impartial credibility, it may be interpreted as censorship. If you attempt aggressive anti-corruption efforts without transparent standards, it may be interpreted as persecution.

A stability sequencing often follows this logic:

1. Restore rule consistency and procedural fairness (visible, credible reforms).
2. Reinforce impartial referees and audit mechanisms (reducing delegitimation incentives).
3. Improve service delivery and reduce insecurity (rebuilding output legitimacy).
4. Introduce longer-horizon structural reforms once trust has regained its footing.

This is not a moral hierarchy; it is a dynamical one. The goal is to rebuild the negative feedback loops that make reform seem legitimate rather than domination.

8.2 Symbolic repair versus structural repair

Symbolic gestures can help, apologies, commissions, truth-telling, but they are not substitutes for structural changes. Citizens trust what they can verify repeatedly: consistent enforcement, fair processes, and reliable services.

8.3 Local trust as a foundation

National trust is abstract. Local trust is experienced. Often, the most effective trust repair begins with local institutions: schools, health systems, municipal services, community courts, and local media. When people see fair governance close to home, generalized trust can slowly expand upward to the national level.

9. The Tradeoffs: Dampeners can Become Suppressors if Mis-designed

Dampeners stabilize, but they can also be abused. A system can "stabilize" itself through repression, censorship, or elite entrenchment, forms of brittle order. The challenge is to build democratic dampeners that preserve freedom. In engineering, too much damping can make a system sluggish. In politics, over-damping can look like:

- excessive veto points that block reform,
- bureaucratic opacity that prevents accountability,
- legalism that substitutes procedure for justice,
- and a culture of deference that suppresses dissent.

This produces brittleness: calm on the surface, stress and instability underneath.

9.2 The discipline of liberal dampening

Democratic dampening must be:

- **procedural**, not ideological,
- **transparent**, not secretive,
- **accountable**, not insulated from scrutiny,
- **general**, not selectively targeted.

Stability that depends on silencing opponents is not democratic stability. It is merely quiet domination, and it eventually produces backlash.

10. Measuring Dampeners: Indicators and Stress Tests for Stability

Part II emphasizes "physics," which implies measurement, not perfect quantification, but systematic indicators that reveal whether stabilizers are weakening.

Potential indicators of weakness include:

- trends in institutional trust across groups,
- perceived fairness of courts and elections,
- compliance measures (tax compliance, regulatory compliance),
- frequency of constitutional hardball tactics,
- volatility of key rules (election laws, regulatory standards),
- corruption perception and enforcement credibility,
- and frequency of legitimacy disputes (routine outcomes framed as illegitimate).

Democracies should also conduct **institutional stress tests** that are structured exercises that ask:

- What happens if a close election is contested?
- What happens if a major disinformation campaign hits during a crisis?
- What happens if emergency powers are invoked repeatedly?
- What happens if courts are widely perceived as partisan?
- What happens if public services fail during a shock?

Stress tests are not paranoia. They are basic resilience planning in a nonlinear environment.

11. The Chapter's Central Claim: Dampeners Preserve the Edge-of-Chaos Republic

An edge-of-chaos republic lives in a narrow band: enough conflict to remain free, enough coherence to remain governable. Trust, legitimacy, and rule consistency are the dampeners that keep the republic in that band of safety. They do not eliminate anger, ideology, or conflict. They make it *processable.* They reduce the likelihood that disputes become existential and that shocks become regime crises.

When these dampeners are strong:

- losers accept outcomes because future fairness is plausible,
- winners restrain themselves because legitimacy matters more than domination,

- citizens comply because rules feel reciprocal and consistent,
- institutions can adapt because change occurs through credible pathways.

When these dampeners fail:

- politics becomes a fight over the referee,
- enforcement becomes interpreted as persecution,
- rule changes become interpreted as capture,
- and the system enters a self-reinforcing cycle of distrust and escalation.

That is the physics: dampeners determine whether the system's oscillations decay or grow.

12. Conclusion: Stability Is Built, Then Defended

Democratic stability is not a natural condition; it is an institutional achievement. Trust is built from repeated reciprocity and visible fairness. Legitimacy is built on procedural justice, restraint, and competence. Rule consistency is built from credible commitment, rules that bind the powerful and change only through legitimate pathways. Together, they form the republic's stabilizing triad, the dampeners that keep democracy from tearing itself apart under stress.

In nonlinear times, this triad becomes even more important because the environment is faster, more networked, and more prone to cascades. That means dampeners must be designed deliberately. Democracies must protect election integrity as a public trust mechanism, enforce ethics symmetrically to prevent rule-of-law collapse, strengthen administrative competence to preserve output legitimacy, and build transparent, constrained procedures to reduce the incentive to engage in delegitimation warfare. The payoff is not utopia. The payoff is governability: a republic capable of disagreement without breakdown, reform without rupture, and conflict without civil war.

In the next chapter, we will extend this stabilizer framework into a more explicitly architectural question: how to design "smart friction" and adaptive pathways so that the system can change without destabilizing itself. How to build institutions that are not only fair and consistent, but capable of learning under turbulence.

Chapter 6

Bad Attractors: Why Corruption Becomes Stable

Corruption is usually discussed as a moral failure: greedy officials, cynical donors, weak enforcement, decaying norms. Those are real, but they are not the whole story, especially in nonlinear times. The deeper puzzle is not that corruption exists. The deeper puzzle is that corruption so often becomes *self-sustaining*. It persists across elections. It survives scandals. It adapts to reforms. It becomes normalized. It becomes "how things work." In system terms, corruption often behaves like a **bad attractor**—a stable pattern of behavior that the political economy repeatedly falls into, even when most people dislike it and even when it measurably weakens the state.

This chapter explains why. It treats corruption not as isolated wrongdoing but as a **dynamic equilibrium** produced by incentives, networks, and feedback loops. Corruption becomes stable when it (1) pays individuals, (2) coordinates elites, (3) substitutes for missing institutional reliability, and (4) disables the very dampeners: trust, legitimacy, and rule consistency that would otherwise contain it. Once those conditions are in place, corruption is not a stain on the system; it becomes part of the system's operating system. It is, in effect, an alternative governance regime: rule by rent rather than rule by law.

To understand "why corruption becomes stable," we need to shift from moral indictment to structural diagnosis. We need to see how corruption becomes rational, contagious, and insulated from accountability, and why anti-corruption efforts often fail or backfire. Most importantly, we need to understand how a democracy escapes a bad attractor without sliding into repression or factional persecution, because corruption is often fought with tools that can themselves destabilize legitimacy.

1. What Is a "Bad Attractor" in Democratic Life?

In dynamical systems, an attractor is a region of behavior toward which a system tends to move. The system can be bumped around by shocks, but it repeatedly returns to the attractor steady state unless the underlying parameters change. A "bad attractor" is simply an attractor with undesirable properties: it is stable, persistent, and costly to exit, because the system's local incentives keep pushing it back.

Corruption becomes a bad attractor when the following are true:

1. **Local rationality, global ruin:** Individual actors benefit from corrupt behavior even as society suffers overall (a negative externality).

2. **Coordination of complicity:** Corruption becomes a network, not an isolated act; participants protect one another.

3. **Institutional hollowing:** The enforcement and oversight mechanisms that would punish corruption are captured, intimidated, or discredited.

4. **Normative normalization:** Citizens come to expect corruption, adapt to it, and stop believing reform is possible.

5. **Positive feedback dominance:** Each act of corruption increases the conditions for more corruption by weakening trust, increasing inequality, and degrading rule consistency.

Once these elements align, corruption has a basin of attraction. You can elect a new leader, pass new rules, or expose scandals, and the system still slides back into the same pattern because the underlying incentive landscape has not changed. The scandal becomes theater. The reforms become paperwork. The media attention span moves on, and the attractor remains.

This is not an exercise in despair. It is a call for precision. If corruption is a stable equilibrium, it must be disrupted, as equilibria are, by changing payoffs, breaking networks, restoring credible enforcement, and rebuilding the dampeners discussed in Chapter 5. Without altering the dynamics, moral condemnation does little. It may even strengthen corruption by feeding cynicism and collective resignation.

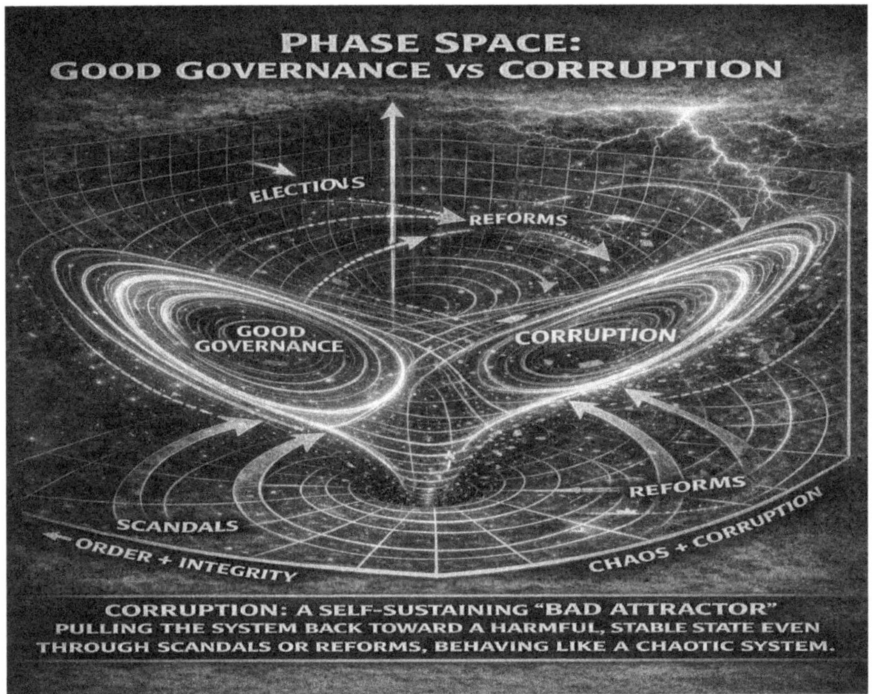

Figure 7.0: *Phase Space Model: Good Governance vs. Corruption*

2. Corruption Is Not One Thing: A Taxonomy of Corrupt Equilibria

Corruption is often treated as a single phenomenon, but different forms have distinct mechanisms of stability.

2.1 Petty corruption: bribery as lubrication in a low-trust state

Petty corruption emerges where bureaucracy is slow, rules are arbitrary, and officials are underpaid or unaccountable. Bribes become a parallel pricing system: citizens pay to get what should be routine. Petty corruption can become stable because it substitutes for reliability: people prefer paying a bribe to waiting indefinitely. The bribe becomes a predictable, if unjust, mechanism for coordination in a dysfunctional or inefficient system.

2.2 Grand corruption: extraction at scale

Grand corruption involves high-level officials steering contracts, privatizations, licenses, land deals, and regulatory decisions for massive private gain. This form becomes stable because it finances political survival: money buys influence, influence buys policy, policy buys more money.

2.3 Systemic corruption: corruption as the governing logic

Systemic corruption is not "bad apples." It is when the system's incentives push most actors toward corruption and punish those who resist. In systemic corruption, honest officials become liabilities; whistleblowers become threats; integrity becomes career suicide. This is the most stable bad attractor because it creates an internal immune system: it defends itself.

2.4 State capture: when private power writes the rules

State capture is the deepest version. It is when powerful actors shape laws, enforcement priorities, regulatory standards, judicial appointments, and media narratives to legalize or normalize extraction. It is "corruption with paperwork," less a violation of the rules than the rewriting of rules to permit domination.

2.5 "Legal corruption": influence markets inside democratic procedures

Even where outright bribery is rare, democracies can develop legalized channels of disproportionate influence: campaign finance regimes, revolving doors, lobbying ecosystems, think tank funding, litigation strategies, and privatized policy expertise. This is often not illegal, but it can be destabilizing because it decouples the government from broader public welfare needs and undermines trust.

Different corrupt equilibria can coexist. Petty corruption can be widespread while grand corruption is concentrated. Legal corruption can flourish alongside periodic prosecutions. The stability question is the same: what feedback loops keep the equilibrium in place?

3. The Micro-Foundations: Why Corruption Becomes Rational

To understand stability, begin at the individual decision point. Why does an official take a bribe? Why does a firm pay it? Why does a politician accept donor influence? In a stable corruption equilibrium, each actor has plausible reasons for his actions.

3.1 Expected value and the probability of punishment

Corruption becomes rational when the expected payoff exceeds the expected cost:

- Payoff: money, power, career advantages, protection.
- Cost: legal punishment, job loss, reputational damage.

If enforcement is weak, selective, or slow, the expected cost is low. If corruption is common, reputational cost is low because the act is normalized. If networks protect participants, legal risk is low. Under those conditions, corruption becomes not reckless but rational.

3.2 The coordination game: "If everyone does it, I must"

Corruption often resembles a coordination equilibrium. Imagine a firm bidding for contracts in a system where competitors pay bribes. Even if the firm prefers integrity, it believes it will lose contracts unless it participates. A public official believes they will be punished or excluded if they refuse to distribute favors within the network. Citizens believe they must pay to access services.

This is not a simple prisoner's dilemma where cooperation is always better. It is closer to a **zero-sum game**: if everyone cooperates on honesty, the system is better, but if many defect into corruption, honesty becomes individually dangerous. The "honest equilibrium" exists only if enough others are honest. Once the system tips into a "corrupt equilibrium," individuals rationally adapt.

3.3 Corruption as insurance in uncertain institutions

In low-trust states, legal protection is unreliable. Contracts are not enforced impartially. Courts are slow or politicized. In that environment, relationships and favors become insurance. Corruption provides predictability: you pay to ensure the outcomes you want. You cultivate patrons. You embed yourself in networks that can protect you.

This reveals a dark truth: corruption can be *functional* in the short run. It helps individuals navigate an unreliable system. That short-run function is precisely what makes it stable. People don't defend corruption because they love it; they defend it because it reduces uncertainty when the rule of law is not credible.

4. The Meso-Level: Networks, Patronage, and the Ecology of Complicity

Corruption becomes stable when it becomes networked. The central shift is from isolated wrongdoing to **organized protection**.

4.1 Patronage as a political technology

Patronage networks distribute benefits, jobs, contracts, permits, and exemptions in exchange for loyalty. This can be overt or subtle. Patronage stabilizes power by creating a dependency structure. Those who benefit become invested in the system's survival. Those who refuse become excluded.

Patronage also solves an elite coordination problem by binding factions together through shared rents. When politics is uncertain, shared extraction can be the glue that holds coalitions in place. The coalition may fight publicly, but it cooperates privately on rent distribution.

4.2 The "mutual hostage" mechanism

Corruption networks often function through mutual exposure. Participants accumulate secrets on one another. That creates mutual hostages: if one person defects and reports, others can retaliate or reveal. This makes corruption stable by raising the cost of whistleblowing and increasing the benefits of silence.

4.3 Selective transparency and controlled scandal

In stable, corrupt systems, information is not absent; it is managed. Scandals occur, but they are strategically released to eliminate rivals rather than to purify the system. The public sees corruption exposed, yet nothing changes. This produces cynicism and demobilization, two of corruption's strongest allies.

4.4 The laundering of legitimacy through philanthropy and symbolism

As corruption becomes sophisticated, it often develops legitimacy buffers: charitable foundations, public works, cultural patronage, and branded "reform" initiatives. These can be genuine in part, but they also serve as moral camouflage. The system learns to manage public anger by producing symbolic goods while preserving extractive structures.

5. Corruption as a Feedback Machine: The Loops That Make It Stable

Now we can state the core mechanism: corruption becomes stable because it produces **positive feedback loops** that reinforce its own conditions.

Loop 1: Corruption → inequality → political capture → more corruption

Corruption concentrates wealth. Concentrated wealth buys influence. Influence shapes policy and enforcement. Policy and enforcement enable further corruption and rent extraction. The loop tightens.

Loop 2: Corruption → institutional decay → citizen distrust → lower compliance → weaker state → more corruption

Corruption degrades service delivery and fairness. Citizens lose trust and comply less, tax evasion rises, and civic cooperation falls. The state becomes less capable and more dependent on informal networks. Weak capacity increases opportunities for corruption. Again, the loop tightens.

Loop 3: Corruption → selective enforcement → perception of injustice → norm collapse → more corruption

When people believe the powerful are immune, they stop treating the law as legitimate. Small-scale dishonesty spreads: cheating, evasion, fraud. The moral ecology shifts toward opportunism. That social norm shift makes corruption even easier and less shameful.

Loop 4: Corruption → information control → epistemic fragmentation → accountability failure → more corruption

Corruption incentivizes control of narratives: media influence, disinformation, intimidation of journalists, and capture of regulators. As shared reality fragments, accountability collapses. Citizens cannot coordinate around truth. Corruption thrives in that collective fog.

Loop 5: Anti-corruption as weapon → legitimacy loss → public cynicism → resignation → corruption stability

When anti-corruption is selectively applied as a factional weapon, it paradoxically stabilizes corruption overall. Citizens conclude that "everyone is corrupt" and that enforcement is mere persecution. That cynicism reduces reform energy and makes corruption safer.

These loops explain why corruption persists even after elections and reforms. The system is not merely tolerating corruption; it is converting corruption into structural advantage.

6. THE CORRUPTION–LEGITIMACY PARADOX: WHY REFORM BECOMES HARDER THE LONGER CORRUPTION LASTS

There is a cruel paradox at the heart of the bad attractor. The longer corruption persists, the harder it becomes to remove because corruption erodes the very conditions necessary for successful reform.

Recall Chapter 5's dampeners: trust, legitimacy, and rule consistency. Anti-corruption requires all three:

- **Trust** so that citizens believe enforcement is fair and worth supporting.
- **Legitimacy** so institutions can act without being dismissed as partisan weapons.
- **Rule consistency** so enforcement is predictable and symmetric, reducing retaliation and fear.

Corruption destroys these dampeners. It lowers trust through visible unfairness. It lowers legitimacy by making institutions appear captured. It lowers rule consistency by making enforcement selective. Thus, the system becomes trapped: to remove corruption, you need legitimacy, but corruption has already hollowed out legitimacy. This is why corruption is an attractor. It increases the energy barrier to escape. Reforms that would be credible in a healthy system become suspect in a corrupt one. Citizens interpret them through the lens of betrayal and inevitability.

7. Why Democracies Are Not Immune: The Subtler Stability of "Influence Corruption"

Modern democracies often pride themselves on low levels of bribery. But corruption evolves. It seeks legal cover. It hides in complexity. It becomes professionalized.

7.1 The influence market and the "policy supply chain"

Policy is produced through a supply chain: research, drafting, lobbying, litigation, regulation, enforcement, media framing, and bureaucratic implementation. Wealth can insert itself at every stage. It funds expertise. It shapes the narratives. It staffs agencies via revolving doors. It litigates to set precedents. It lobbies for exemptions. It writes "technical" rules whose distributional consequences are opaque but are deliberately designed to benefit the regime's benefactors.

This can become stable corruption because it does not appear to be corruption. It looks like normal politics. Yet it produces the same systemic effect: rule inconsistency, capture, and loss of trust.

7.2 Complexity as camouflage

As governance becomes more complex, financial regulation, tax codes, procurement rules, and public oversight become harder. Complexity creates opacity. Opacity reduces accountability. Reduced accountability increases corruption. Corrupt systems often *prefer* complexity because it makes extraction less visible. The tax code is a good example; the more complex it is, the easier it is to camouflage tax avoidance and outright tax evasion.

7.3 The legitimizing story: "This is just expertise"

Influence corruption is often justified as expertise: "policy is complicated; experts must guide it." Expertise is real and necessary, but when it is funded and filtered by concentrated interests, it becomes a channel for capture. The story of expertise becomes a legitimacy shield.

The result is a dangerous stability: citizens sense that the system is rigged but cannot prove it in a simple narrative. That uncertainty is fertile ground for populist delegitimation and conspiracy theories. Thus, "legal corruption" becomes a seed of epistemic and political instability even when it remains within formal rules.

8. Corruption as a Stable Equilibrium in Game-Theoretic Terms

To deepen the stability argument, consider corruption as a strategic equilibrium.

8.1 Repeated games and the reward of loyalty

Corruption networks operate in repeated games. Participants reward loyalty and punish defection. Over time, the expected future benefits of remaining in the network exceed the one-time benefit of exposing it. This is especially true when law enforcement is unreliable or politicized.

8.2 Asymmetric punishment

A key feature of corrupt equilibria is asymmetric punishment: the system punishes honesty more consistently than it punishes corruption. An honest official is excluded, threatened, demoted, or isolated. The corrupt official is protected. This flips the moral incentive structure. Once that inversion occurs, corruption becomes stable because it is enforced socially even when law enforcement is weak.

8.3 Information asymmetry and citizen coordination failure

Even if most citizens dislike corruption, they may fail to coordinate against it because information is fragmented and the individual costs of activism are high. Each person assumes reform is unlikely and therefore rationally becomes a free rider. Corruption persists not because it is popular, but because opposition is dispersed and unrewarded.

This is one reason anti-corruption often requires "coordination entrepreneurs"—leaders, movements, investigative journalists, or institutions that can focus public attention and reduce the coordination costs of reform. Without that focal point, the corrupt equilibrium remains.

9. The Escape Problem: Why "Just Prosecute Them" Often Fails

If corruption is stable, why not simply punish it? Because enforcement is embedded in the system.

9.1 The enforcement credibility constraint

Prosecution only deters if it is credible, consistent, and perceived as fair. In polarized environments, prosecutions can be interpreted as factional warfare, thereby reducing deterrence and increasing retaliation.

9.2 Corruption adapts

When enforcement increases, corruption often evolves. It shifts from overt bribery to subtler influence. It moves money through intermediaries. It hides in procurement complexity. It uses legal loopholes. It captures auditors. It launders reputations. Stable corruption is adaptive.

9.3 The authoritarian temptation

Anti-corruption campaigns can become tools of authoritarian consolidation: eliminate rivals under the banner of cleansing. That can reduce visible corruption in the short term while increasing fear and reducing accountability, thereby creating a different bad attractor: brittle order with selective punishment. The "physics" lesson is that stability achieved through coercion can be unstable in the long run because it destroys legitimacy. Therefore, the question is not "How do we punish?" but "How do we design enforcement that restores dampeners rather than destroying them?"

10. Designing Exits: How to Destabilize the Bad Attractor Without Destabilizing Democracy

Escaping a bad attractor requires changing the system's incentive landscape, breaking corruption networks, and restoring trust and consistency with the rules. The following are design strategies for a better functioning, more just democracy.

10.1 Reduce rents: shrink the payoff structure that fuels capture

Corruption thrives where rents are large: monopolies, licensing choke points, opaque procurement, concentrated market power, and discretionary regulation. Lowering rents reduces incentives for corruption:

- simplify overly discretionary rules,
- increase competitive bidding and open contracting,

- strengthen antitrust and reduce monopoly privileges,
- eliminate loopholes that create private windfalls,
- standardize procedures to reduce gatekeeper power and reduce regulatory friction.

This is "predistribution" applied to corruption: change the structure to make extraction harder.

10.2 Reduce discretion and increase auditability

Where discretion is unavoidable, it must be constrained and audited.

- clear written standards for decisions,
- random audits and routine oversight,
- public disclosure of procurement and permitting data,
- digital systems that reduce cash and face-to-face bargaining,
- strong paper trails and tamper-resistant records.

The goal is not to eliminate judgment, but to make judgment accountable and legible, turning potential points of corruption into verifiable processes.

10.3 Build independent accountability institutions with redundant credibility

Because legitimacy is fragile, anti-corruption needs institutions that are insulated from factional control yet accountable to the law.

- independent inspectors general,
- professional civil services protected from purge,
- independent audit agencies with publication duties,
- ethics bodies with real enforcement capacity,
- whistleblower protections with credible follow-through.

Redundancy matters: if one institution is attacked, others remain.

10.4 Protect the epistemic commons: investigative capacity as a stabilizer

Corruption thrives in informational fog. Democracies need robust investigative journalism, public-interest reporting, and transparency laws—not as cultural niceties but as stabilizers.

- freedom-of-information mechanisms with enforceable timelines,
- legal protections for journalists and sources,
- open data portals for budgets, contracts, and enforcement actions,
- independent research access to detect patterns.

This is not about "trusting the media." It is about building verification capacity into the system.

10.5 Campaign finance and influence architecture: drying the channels of legal corruption

Where markets are influenced, reforms must reduce dependence on concentrated money.

- transparency of political spending,
- limits on revolving doors and conflicts of interest,
- public financing mechanisms where feasible,
- disclosure of lobbying and policy drafting roles,
- ethics enforcement that binds elites.

The aim is not purity; it is **rule consistency**, making governance less responsive to wealth and more responsive to public interest.

10.6 Sequencing: restore dampeners before maximal enforcement

In low-trust systems, sweeping crackdowns can backfire. A stable exit often requires sequencing:

1. **Create credibility**: establish independent oversight and transparent standards.
2. **Signal symmetry**: enforce rules across factions and status levels.

3. **Target keystone nodes**: dismantle network coordinators (procurement rings, gatekeepers) rather than chasing every petty act.

4. **Institutionalize reforms**: embed transparency, audits, and rule constraints so corruption cannot simply mutate.

The goal is to shift expectations. Once people believe enforcement is real and fair, behavior changes rapidly. That is a nonlinear benefit: credibility can produce cascade improvements.

11. Early Warning Signals: Detecting Drift Toward the Bad Attractor

Because corruption often becomes stable gradually, democracies should monitor warning signals:

- rising perception that "the system is rigged,"
- increasing reliance on informal networks to solve basic problems,
- deterioration of procurement integrity and contract competition,
- normalization of revolving-door practices and conflict-of-interest exceptions,
- selective enforcement patterns visible to the public,
- weakening of investigative capacity and transparency,
- and a gap between formal rules and lived outcomes.

These signals indicate not only moral decline but dynamical drift: the basin of attraction is deepening.

12. Conclusion: Corruption Becomes Stable Because It Rewires the Republic's Physics

Corruption is stable when it is self-reinforcing. It becomes a bad attractor when it reshapes incentives, organizes protective networks, and hollows out the dampeners of trust, legitimacy, and rule consistency. In that state, corruption is not merely rule-breaking. It becomes rule-making. It converts the republic from a system that processes conflict into legitimacy into a system that processes power into rent.

The physics of democratic stability, therefore, demands a hard recognition: **anti-corruption is not a moral campaign; it is a systems redesign project.** It must reduce rents, constrain discretion, build auditability, strengthen independent oversight, and restore credibility through symmetric enforcement. Above all, it must rebuild the dampeners that make law bind beyond coercion. Without that, anti-corruption becomes either theater (which stabilizes corruption through cynicism) or persecution (which destabilizes democracy through delegitimation).

A republic escapes bad attractors the way systems escape deep basins: by changing parameters, reshaping incentives, and building new pathways for stable behavior. The hopeful truth is that stable equilibria can flip. When credible enforcement returns, when transparency becomes routine, when impunity is punctured at high levels, and when citizens experience fair service delivery, expectations can shift quickly. Trust can regrow. Legitimacy can be repaired. Rule consistency can be restored.

The bad attractor is stable—but not eternal. Its stability is maintained by structures, and structures can be redesigned.

In the next chapter, we will examine the complementary danger: when attempts to restore stability through excessive control produce brittleness, how "overcorrection" can create another bad attractor, one that appears stable but stores stress until rupture.

Chapter 7

Tipping Points: When Small Shocks Become Regime Shifts

Democracies do not usually die the way they are described in headlines. They rarely collapse because "one election happened," or "one leader was elected," or "one protest turned violent." Those events matter, but they are almost never the whole story. In the physics of complex systems, collapses are typically **threshold events**: long periods of gradual parameter drift followed by a sudden phase transition once a tipping point is crossed. What appears to be an abrupt rupture is often the visible crest of an invisible, accumulating wave.

This chapter is about that wave. It asks why modern democracies increasingly behave like systems near criticality, where small shocks can trigger disproportionate outcomes, and what institutional designers can do about it. If the previous chapters identified the republic's dampeners (trust, legitimacy, rule consistency) and the way corruption can become a stable bad attractor, this chapter adds a core stability insight: **regime shifts often occur not because shocks are unusually large, but because the system has become unusually sensitive.**

When a polity approaches a tipping point, its ability to absorb disturbance weakens. The same shock that would have produced a news cycle in a resilient democracy can produce a constitutional crisis in a fragile one. The same scandal that would have led to resignations in a high-trust system can produce a legitimacy collapse in a low-trust system. The same policy failure that would have triggered reform in a flexible system can trigger radicalization in a brittle system.

In nonlinear times, the central design challenge is no longer merely the moral problem of governance ("what should we do?") but the dynamical problem of stability ("what can the system endure without becoming chaotic?"). That is what tipping points reveal: the distance between ordinary politics and systemic rupture can be smaller than we assume.

1. What a Tipping Point Is—and What It Is Not

A tipping point is often described as the moment "everything changed." In systems terms, it is the moment when **small perturbations push the system into a different stable pattern of behavior**, a different attractor. Crucially, the tipping point is not just an event. It is a structural condition.

1.1 The standard structure: slow drift, then sudden change

Most tipping points share a recognizable structure:

1. **Parameter drift:** slow changes accumulate (inequality, polarization, institutional capture, media fragmentation, demographic sorting, declining trust).

2. **Dampener erosion:** stabilizing feedback weakens (courts lose credibility, elections are contested, rule consistency breaks, and enforcement looks selective).

3. **Critical sensitivity:** the system becomes "high gain" (outrage spreads faster, coalition-building becomes harder, compromise becomes betrayal).

4. **Trigger shock:** a discrete event hits (crisis, scandal, contested election, security incident).

5. **Cascade:** feedback loops amplify the shock into a broader breakdown (mass protest, institutional defection, elite splits, violence, emergency powers).

6. **Regime shift:** the system settles into a new attractor (illiberal consolidation, chronic dysfunction, fragmentation, or a reformist reset).

The public usually sees steps 4–6. Designers and analysts must track steps 1–3.

1.2 Tipping points are <u>conditional</u>, not mystical

A tipping point does not mean "democracy is fragile by nature." It means the system's stabilizers have been weakened and its coupling has increased. In a healthy democracy, shocks are localized; in a fragile democracy, shocks cascade.

This re-framing matters, both morally and analytically. When democracies treat tipping points as fate, "people are crazy," "society is doomed," they surrender the possibility of design. But tipping points are, by definition, structural. Structures can be modified.

1.3 A simple model: the potential well

Imagine democratic stability as a ball sitting in a valley. The valley is the **basin of attraction**: the set of conditions under which the system returns to stability after disturbance. As parameters drift, rising inequality and eroding legitimacy make the valley shallower. The ball sits higher. Now, a small movement (a shock event) can push it over the ridge into another valley: authoritarianism, fragmentation, or chronic dysfunction.

The designer's job is to deepen the valley (strengthen dampeners), widen it (increase tolerance for disagreement and shock), and lower the ridge (create safe pathways for reform so pressure doesn't build catastrophically).

2. The Core Mechanisms That Turn Small Shocks into Cascades

Why do small shocks sometimes cause regime shifts? In complex democracies, there are several mechanisms.

2.1 Positive feedback overwhelms negative feedback

In stable democracies, negative feedback dominates:

- elections correct failures,

- courts constrain abuses,
- oversight exposes wrongdoing,
- professional administration stabilizes service delivery,
- social trust dampens rumors and panic.

Near tipping points, these stabilizers weaken. Meanwhile, positive feedback grows:

- outrage feeds attention feeds outrage,
- delegitimation feeds distrust feeds noncompliance,
- polarization feeds identity, fear feeds polarization,
- corruption feeds inequality, which feeds capture, which feeds corruption.

At the tipping point, positive feedback becomes the system's dominant behavior. Once that happens, "normal" corrective institutions can become accelerants. A court ruling becomes a partisan trigger; an investigation becomes persecution; an audit becomes a conspiracy.

2.2 Coupling: failures no longer stay in their lane

Modern democracies are increasingly tightly coupled across domains:

- the economy is coupled to identity (status loss interpreted as cultural humiliation),
- identity is coupled to media (algorithmic segmentation),
- media is coupled to elections (legitimacy narratives),
- elections are coupled to courts (judicialized politics),
- courts are coupled to executive power (emergency claims),
- executive power is coupled to the security apparatus (order vs chaos framing).

In loosely coupled systems, a scandal in one institution doesn't delegitimize all institutions. In tightly coupled systems, it can. Tipping points occur when coupling makes cross-domain cascades easy.

2.3 Threshold models of collective behavior

Many social behaviors follow threshold dynamics: people participate if enough others participate. Protest, compliance, civil disobedience, and even acceptance of election outcomes can behave this way.

When trust is high, most citizens' threshold for defection is high: they tolerate imperfection. When trust is low, thresholds drop: it takes less to trigger refusal, protest, or belief in illegitimacy. The same shock can therefore mobilize vastly more people in a low-trust system.

The tipping point can be conceptualized as a moment when enough thresholds are crossed simultaneously, producing a cascade.

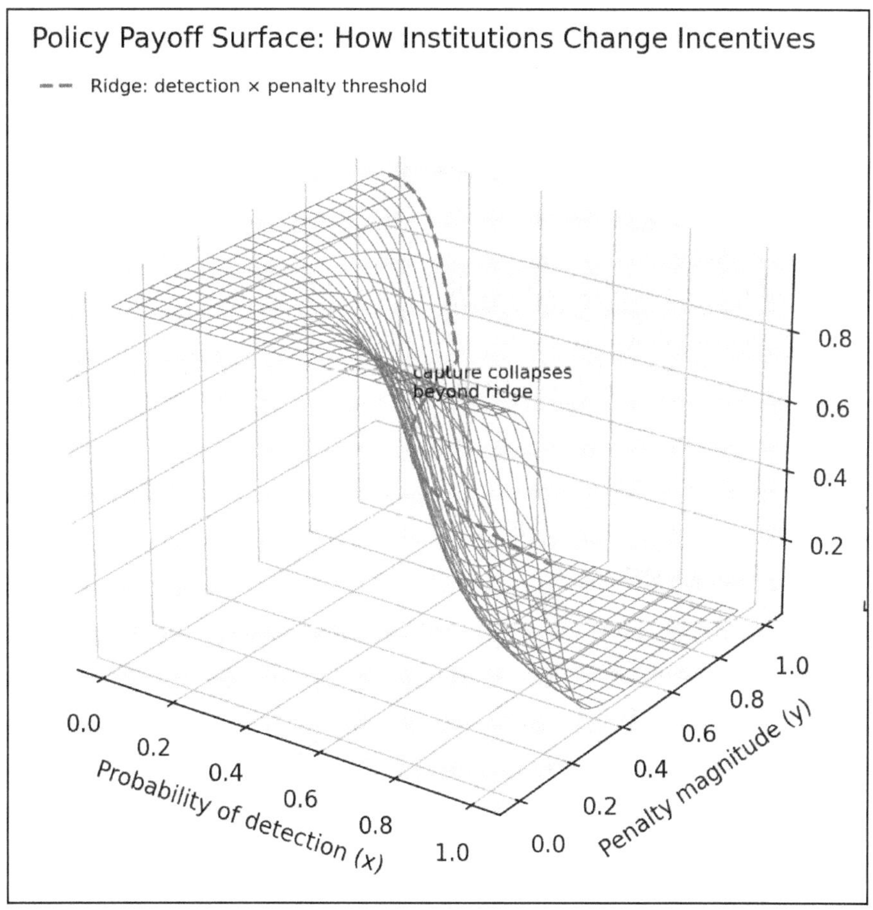

Figure 8.0: *Policy Capture Cascade*

2.4 Elite splits: the hidden pivot of regime change

Regime shifts often hinge on **elite coordination**. Democracies survive because elites, political, economic, military, and judicial, accept rules and restrain themselves. When elites split on legitimacy or strategy, a tipping point approaches.

Elite splits can occur when:

- the costs of restraint rise (stakes become existential),
- corruption networks fracture into rival factions,
- external shocks reduce resource flows (recession, sanctions),
- institutions are weaponized unevenly (fear of persecution),
- or the public becomes ungovernable, forcing elites to choose repression or reform.

A key insight: **mass polarization becomes system-threatening when it aligns with elite polarization.** When elites remain committed to procedural rules, mass conflict can be contained. When elites resort to coercion, the system can flip rapidly.

2.5 Information disorder as an ignition accelerator

In Chapter 4, we described polarization and information disorder as nonlinear contagion. Near tipping points, informational dynamics become especially dangerous:

- rumors spread faster than correction,
- identity-sorted communities reinforce conflicting realities,
- and manipulative actors can ignite conflict cheaply.

Information disorder does not need to persuade everyone; it only needs to push a critical mass across thresholds, enough to delegitimize institutions or justify emergency measures.

3. The "Tipping Point Stack": When Multiple Vulnerabilities Align

A democracy approaches tipping points not because a single factor breaks, but because multiple stabilizers weaken simultaneously. A useful diagnostic is the tipping point stack:

1. **Distributional stress** (inequality, affordability crises, stagnation)
2. **Epistemic fragmentation** (no shared facts, distrust in referees)
3. **Institutional coercion** (procedural cheating normalized)
4. **Selective enforcement** (rule consistency collapses)
5. **Elite competition for rents** (capture and corruption escalate)
6. **External shock exposure** (geopolitical pressure, migration, war, cyber operations)
7. **Identity threat saturation** (politics becomes existential)

Any one of these episodes is manageable. Several together are dangerous. When most are present, the system becomes poised, with high potential energy and low damping.

This is the physics of democratic fragility: **as dampeners degrade, the republic becomes an amplifier.**

4. Types of Democratic Regime Shifts

A "Tipping point" is not a single outcome. Democracies can flip into different regimes depending on which feedback loops dominate after the cascade.

4.1 Illiberal consolidation: democracy hollowed from within

In this regime shift, elections continue, but liberal constraints weaken: courts are captured or delegitimized, the media is pressured, the civil service is politicized, the opposition is harassed, and rules are altered to entrench incumbents. The system maintains procedural shells but loses substantive competition and rights protections.

This shift often occurs when:

- polarization makes "winning" feel existential,
- emergency narratives justify extraordinary powers,
- and institutional constraints are weakened incrementally.

The tipping point is often a moment when opposition is no longer treated as legitimate, and the machinery of rule consistency is repurposed for entrenchment.

4.2 Chronic legitimacy warfare: stable dysfunction as an attractor

Here, no side achieves consolidation, but legitimacy is permanently contested. Elections are continually disputed, courts are seen as partisan, and the governance regime oscillates between paralysis and executive improvisation. The system becomes stuck in a high-conflict attractor—no longer able to deliver reforms but not fully collapsing.

This outcome is common when:

- institutions are strong enough to block consolidation,
- but too weak to produce trusted decisions.

It is "stable instability": the system remains democratic in form but unstable in function, with chronic crisis as the baseline.

4.3 Fragmentation and local sovereignty: the republic becomes modular by force

In some cases, tipping points produce decentralization, not as planned federalism, but as fragmentation. Localities refuse to enforce national rules; regions drift into incompatible governance; informal power centers proliferate.

This can occur when:

- central legitimacy collapses,
- enforcement capacity weakens,
- and identity divisions map onto geography.

Fragmentation can be violent or bureaucratic. Either way, it reduces the system's coherence and increases the risk of further conflict or soft succession.

4.4 Emergency authoritarianism: order as the organizing principle

In severe cascades like mass violence, economic collapse, or war, executive power can expand rapidly. Emergencies become normal. Rights are suspended. Opposition is framed as a security threat.

This shift is often triggered by a genuine crisis but sustained by the incentive structures created afterward. Once emergency powers exist, actors learn to use them for political advantage.

4.5 Reformist resets: tipping points toward renewal

Not all tipping points are downward. Systems can also flip toward reform if the shock produces:

- broad coalitions across identity lines,
- credible accountability that restores trust,
- and institutional redesign that strengthens dampeners.

Reformist resets are rarer because they require coordination, credible leadership, and institutional pathways for change. But they are possible, especially when a crisis is severe enough to discredit existing elites and open space for new rules.

The essential question is: **what determines which basin the system falls into after crossing the ridge?** Much depends on elite behavior, institutional redundancy, and whether legitimacy can be restored quickly.

5. Early Warning Signals: How to Detect the Approach to Criticality

In physical systems, approaching a tipping point often produces measurable phenomena like **critical slowing down**: the system takes longer to recover from disturbances. Democracies show analogous signals.

5.1 Slower recovery from political shocks

In resilient democracies, scandals fade, and institutions reassert normalcy. Near tipping points, shocks linger, metastasize, and become permanent narratives of identity. A telling sign is that each new controversy does not replace the old one but stacks on top of it, reinforcing the same distrust.

5.2 Escalating volatility in legitimacy beliefs

Watch not only what people believe, but how quickly beliefs flip and polarize. When legitimacy beliefs (trust in elections, courts, and agencies) become highly volatile and strongly sorted by identity, the system is losing its common frame of reference.

5.3 Norm collapse and "constitutional hardball" normalization

When tactics once considered unacceptable become normal, refusal to concede, routine delegitimating of referees, aggressive use of procedural loopholes, expect the ridge to be closer. Hardball is not just ugliness; it is parameter drift toward instability.

5.4 Institutional response asymmetry

In stable systems, institutions respond consistently across cases. Near tipping points, responses become erratic: overreaction in some cases, paralysis in others. This erratic pattern signals that rule consistency is weakening and that discretion is being politicized.

5.5 Rising "existential framing" in politics

When political rhetoric increasingly frames opponents as enemies, traitors, or existential threats, it lowers thresholds for violence and rule inconsistency. Existential framing is a contagion accelerant.

5.6 Declining willingness to accept loss

A key stability indicator is whether losing is survivable. When large shares of the population express unwillingness to accept election outcomes or categorical distrust of the process, the stabilizing function of elections is failing.

5.7 Elite hedging behavior

Elites often sense instability earlier than the public. Indicators include:

- capital flight or unusual financial hedging (gold prices rising is a good example),
- intensified private security,
- aggressive media acquisitions,
- rapid reshuffling of institutional leadership,
- and open talk of "extraordinary measures."

These behaviors can be self-fulfilling: elite hedging signals danger, which, in turn, increases public anxiety, further increasing instability.

6. CASE PATTERNS: HOW TIPPING POINTS OFTEN UNFOLD

Rather than offering a single historical narrative, we can identify recurring patterns across many democratic societies.

Pattern A: The contested election cascade

- **Parameter drift:** rising polarization, distrust in referees, media fragmentation.
- **Shock:** a close election with procedural confusion or contested counting.
- **Cascade:** fraud claims spread; protests escalate; institutions are pressured; violence becomes thinkable.
- **Outcome:** legitimacy warfare or illiberal consolidation, depending on elite restraint.

In this pattern, the election, normally a negative feedback loop, becomes a positive feedback loop. The system's correction mechanism turns into its ignition source.

Pattern B: The corruption scandal that breaks the bargain

- **Parameter drift:** corruption normalized, inequality rising, enforcement selective, cynicism widespread.
- **Shock:** a high-profile scandal reveals elite impunity or systemic theft.
- **Cascade:** protest waves; elite splits; institutional paralysis; emergency measures; or reformist reset.
- **Outcome:** either a new corrupt coalition (bad attractor persists) or a reset if enforcement becomes credible and symmetric.

Here, the tipping point emerges when citizens realize the implicit bargain ("we tolerate some corruption because the system functions") has been violated. If governance no longer delivers, tolerance collapses.

Pattern C: Policing or violence trigger in a saturated identity environment

- **Parameter drift:** status inequality, distrust in law enforcement, identity polarization, and misinformation.
- **Shock:** a violent incident interpreted as emblematic injustice.

- **Cascade:** protests, counter-protests, rumor escalation, political exploitation, and possible vigilantism.
- **Outcome:** either reforms that rebuild legitimacy or intensified factional fear and security escalation.

The key mechanism is interpretive saturation: in polarized systems, incidents are not local; they are symbolic. Symbolic events travel faster than facts and can quickly push thresholds to the breaking point.

Pattern D: The economic shock that turns grievance into regime crisis

- **Parameter drift:** affordability strain, debt burdens, labor precarity, perceived rigging.
- **Shock:** recession, inflation spike, surge in unemployment, financial crisis.
- **Cascade:** scapegoating, anti-institutional mobilization, demand for strongman solutions, elite panic.
- **Outcome:** an illiberal turn or an unstable alternation, depending on institutional dampeners and welfare stabilizers.

Economic shocks become political regime shocks when legitimacy is already brittle and when safety nets are weak.

Pattern E: External conflict as an internal legitimacy test

- **Parameter drift:** distrust, polarization, declining state capacity.
- **Shock:** war, major attack, migration surge, foreign interference.
- **Cascade:** emergency powers, suspicion of internal enemies, information warfare, and temptations of repression.
- **Outcome:** emergency authoritarianism, fragmentation, or rally-around-the-flag cohesion.

External threats can unify high-trust democracies but fracture low-trust ones. The difference lies in the dampeners' strength.

7. Why Tipping Points Are More Likely Now: Nonlinear Times as a Criticality Machine

Modern conditions increase the likelihood of tipping points through three structural shifts.

7.1 Speed: feedback cycles are shorter than deliberation cycles

Attention markets demand instant response, but institutions require time. This mismatch creates a perception of unresponsiveness ("they don't care") and impulsive governance ("they're panicking"), both of which erode legitimacy.

7.2 Connectivity: cascades travel farther

Highly networked societies transmit emotions, rumors, and mobilization rapidly across geography. Local events become national crises within hours. This increases the probability that a shock crosses enough thresholds to trigger a regime shift.

7.3 Complexity: more opaque systems invite conspiratorial explanation

When economic and political systems are complex and outcomes feel arbitrary, citizens become vulnerable to simplistic narratives. In a low-trust environment, complexity becomes a legitimacy liability. People prefer "someone is controlling this" to "this is complicated." That preference increases susceptibility to disinformation and accelerates cascades. In short, nonlinear times push democracies closer to criticality by tightening coupling, increasing gain, and shortening feedback loops.

8. Hysteresis: Why Recovery Is Harder Than Collapse

One of the most important "physics" insights is hysteresis: in many systems, the path down is not the same as the path up. Once trust and legitimacy collapse, restoring them requires more than reversing the initial conditions.

A democracy can lose trust quickly through:

- a perceived stolen election,
- selective enforcement scandal,
- emergency power abuse,
- or visible elite impunity.

But restoring trust requires repeated, consistent evidence over time:

- credible audits,
- symmetric accountability,
- fair service delivery,
- transparent rule-making,
- and visible restraint by winners.

This asymmetry is why tipping points are so dangerous. A single shock can push the system into a new basin of attraction, and climbing back out can take years, even if reforms begin immediately.

Design implication: **Preventing a fall is often cheaper than rebuilding after one.** That is not pessimism; it is the basic dynamic of legitimacy.

9. Designing for Tipping Points: Widening the Safe Operating Space

If tipping points occur when the system becomes overly sensitive, then democratic design should aim to **reduce sensitivity** and **increase damping** while preserving freedom and adaptability.

9.1 Strengthen dampeners (Chapter 5's triad)

- **Trust:** build through competence, transparency, and fair treatment; reduce everyday experiences of arbitrariness.
- **Legitimacy:** protect procedural justice; emphasize visible restraint; ensure losers believe the system remains theirs too.
- **Rule consistency:** constrain discretion; enforce ethics symmetrically; standardize high-stakes procedures like election administration.

These dampeners deepen the basin of attraction and therefore system stability.

9.2 Reduce coupling: keep failures from cascading

Design strategies include:

- **Institutional modularity:** federalism and decentralization with coordination, so local failures don't become national legitimacy crises.

- **Redundant oversight:** multiple independent auditors and referees, so delegitimizing one institution doesn't collapse accountability.
- **Firebreaks in information systems:** friction proportionality, slowing viral spread of unverified claims during elections and crises without policing viewpoints.

Coupling reduction does not eliminate conflict; it prevents total-system cascades.

9.3 Lower the stakes of losing: make alternation survivable

Winner-take-all dynamics intensify tipping risk. Stabilizing reforms can include:

- robust rights protections that cannot be easily reversed,
- credible limits on executive discretion,
- neutral civil service protections,
- and policy designs that reduce catastrophic swings.

From a game-theoretic standpoint, when losing is survivable, actors have less incentive to push the system over the edge.

9.4 Build credible pathways for reform: vent pressure before rupture

Brittleness creates tipping points because pressure builds up behind blocked reform channels. Democracies need legitimate adaptation pathways:

- independent commissions with real authority in specific domains (districting, ethics, election administration),
- deliberative mechanisms (citizens' assemblies) to reduce polarization and increase perceived fairness,
- scheduled policy reviews, sunset clauses, and iterative experimentation,
- and constitutional amendment pathways that are difficult but not impossible.

When reform is plausible, citizens are less tempted by rupture.

9.5 Stress testing: treat democracy like critical infrastructure

Democracies should routinely stress test and game out:

- contested elections,

- major misinformation waves,
- emergency power scenarios,
- corruption scandals involving top officials,
- and simultaneous crises (economic + security + health).

Stress testing is not paranoia; it is resilience engineering and stability architecture. It reveals single points of failure before real shocks exploit them.

9.6 Crisis protocols that preserve legitimacy

When tipping points are near, crisis response must prioritize legitimacy over order. This includes:

- transparent communication with verifiable data,
- independent audits and public reporting,
- restraint in the use of force,
- clear legal standards for emergency measures,
- and bipartisan or multi-stakeholder oversight where possible.

The goal is to prevent crisis response from becoming the trigger for regime shift.

10. The "Tipping Point Playbook": A Stability Checklist for Designers

To make the chapter operational, here is a condensed playbook of questions institutional designers should ask.

1. **Where are our single points of legitimacy failure?**
   (election administration, courts, policing, emergency powers, procurement)

2. **Which institutions are expected to act as referees, and are they trusted across factions?**
   If not, what redundancies exist?

3. **Where is discretion highest and auditability lowest?**
   Those are corruption and legitimacy risk nodes.

4. **What are our early warning indicators of criticality?**
   (declining acceptance of outcomes, escalation of hardball, trust collapse)

5. **What firebreaks exist to prevent informational cascades?**
   (verification infrastructure, transparency, friction mechanisms)

6. **Is losing survivable for major factions?**
   If not, reduce winner-take-all stakes through rights, constraints, and decentralization.

7. **Do citizens believe reform is possible without rupture?**
   If not, create credible reform channels.

8. **Can the state deliver basic competence under stress?**
   If not, invest in capacity and reliability because output legitimacy is a stabilizer.

9. **Is accountability symmetric and visible?**
   If not, anti-corruption will be interpreted as persecution, accelerating the crisis.

10. **Are emergency powers constrained, time-limited, and overseen?**
    If not, crises become opportunities for consolidation.

A republic that can answer these questions convincingly is less likely to be surprised by tipping points.

11. A Final Caution: "Tipping Point Thinking" Must Not Become Fatalism

Understanding tipping points can backfire if it produces either panic ("we are doomed") or cynical acceleration ("let it burn"). Both reactions are destabilizing. The purpose of tipping point analysis is not to dramatize. It is to clarify what stabilizers do and where the thresholds lie.

A democracy near criticality has two urgent tasks:

1. **Stop destabilizing responses:** cease behaviors that degrade dampeners like selective enforcement, institutional hardball, legitimacy warfare, and normalization of corruption.

2. **Start damping:** build visible fairness, restore rule consistency, reduce coupling, and make reform plausible.

The hopeful truth of nonlinear systems is that they can also improve rapidly once feedback shifts. When legitimacy returns, trust can grow faster than expected. When enforcement becomes symmetric, norms can rebound. When reform becomes plausible, citizens can choose patience over rupture.

But the timeframe matters. Near tipping points, delays are costly because the basin of attraction is shallow. Preventive design is the best form of democratic preservation.

12. Conclusion: Regime Shifts Are the Price of Ignored Parameters

Tipping points are not accidents. They are structural consequences of parameter drift: rising inequality, weakening trust, eroding rule consistency, growing corruption, tightening informational contagion, escalating polarization, and increasing existential stakes. Small shocks become regime shifts when stabilizers no longer stabilize, when the republic becomes an amplifier rather than a processor.

The physics lesson is clear: **democratic stability must be designed for criticality.** In nonlinear times, you cannot assume that tomorrow will behave like yesterday. You must build institutions that can absorb shocks without triggering regime change, and you must maintain dampeners so that conflict remains governable.

In the next chapter, we will move from tipping points to *stability engineering*: how to design adaptive institutions that can learn under turbulence, how to build "smart friction" and "credible flexibility," so the republic remains resilient without becoming brittle, and flexible without becoming chaotic.

Part III

Designing Institutions for Nonlinear Times

Part I of this book argued that democratic life is not best understood as a stable equilibrium punctuated by occasional crises. It is better understood as a complex adaptive system, forever balancing between brittle order and incoherent disorder—an edge-of-chaos republic that must continuously convert conflict into legitimacy. Part II then shifted into the "physics" of stability: the dampeners that absorb oscillation (trust, legitimacy, rule consistency), the bad attractors that trap systems in self-reinforcing corruption, and the tipping points where small shocks become regime shifts. Taken together, Parts I and II supplied a diagnosis of democratic fragility under modern conditions and a vocabulary for understanding why "normal politics" no longer guarantees normal outcomes.

Part III begins where diagnosis must become design. If democracies now operate in nonlinear environments—where feedback loops are faster, coupling is tighter, and institutional errors can cascade—then the central civic task is institutional engineering: **how do we design political systems that remain legitimate and governable under turbulence?** Not merely under ideal conditions, but under conditions of polarization, inequality, information disorder, geopolitical stress, technological disruption, and recurring crisis.

This part of the book adopts a designer's stance. It treats institutions as *devices* that shape incentives, constrain harmful strategies, and channel collective energy into cooperation rather than escalation. It recognizes that constitutions and laws are not only moral declarations; they are control systems. They are arrangements of friction, flow, sensing, feedback, and adaptation. And like all control systems, they can be well-tuned or poorly tuned for the environment in which they operate.

To "design institutions for nonlinear times" is to accept three uncomfortable truths:

1. **Democracies cannot rely on virtue alone.** They must make cooperation rational and hardball costly, even when actors are polarized and opportunistic.

2. **Democracies cannot rely on slow feedback in a fast environment.** They must build new ways to sense problems early and dampen high-velocity cascades without sacrificing freedom.

3. **Democracies cannot rely on static rules for dynamic conditions.** They must incorporate adaptive governance mechanisms that revise policies and procedures in a legitimate, transparent, and iterative manner.

Part III is therefore not a utopian manifesto. It is a practical blueprint for resilience: a set of design principles and institutional modules meant to keep democracies within their safe operating space. Where Part II explained the mechanics of breakdown, Part III explores the mechanics of durability.

1. What Changes When We Admit We Live in Nonlinear Times?

In linear politics, incremental reforms produce incremental outcomes. Institutions are assumed to behave predictably. Trust can be repaired by rhetorical appeals. Crises are treated as anomalies. This is the mental model that quietly underwrites much civic debate: if a problem is large, the response should be proportionate; if a policy fails, another policy will replace it; if polarization rises, leaders should call for unity; if trust declines, institutions should communicate better.

Nonlinear times shatter these assumptions. They are characterized by:

- **Thresholds:** systems can tolerate stress until they suddenly cannot.
- **Cascades:** failures propagate across domains and networks.

- **Hysteresis:** collapse can be quick while recovery is slow.
- **Amplification:** media and identity dynamics increase the gain on conflict.
- **Parameter drift:** long-run structural changes reshape everything else—inequality, market concentration, platform architecture, and geopolitical instability.
- **Strategic adaptation:** actors learn to exploit loopholes, incentives, and attention systems faster than rules can be updated.

In nonlinear times, the naive reform agenda—add a rule here, punish a bad actor there—often fails because it does not change the system's feedback loops. Worse, it can backfire. A crackdown can become a legitimacy crisis. A new rule can become a new weapon. A transparency measure can become performative. A reform that assumes goodwill can be exploited by bad faith.

Designing for nonlinear times requires a shift in how we think about institutions. Institutions are not merely containers for politics; they are *active shapers of dynamics.* The designer must think in terms of:

- **incentive compatibility:** do rules reward the behavior we need?
- **robustness to adversaries:** do rules survive strategic exploitation?
- **damping and stability:** do institutions reduce oscillations or amplify them?
- **adaptive capacity:** can rules update without regime crisis?
- **redundancy and modularity:** can the system tolerate failures without cascading?

These are engineering questions—but they are also moral questions, because the goal is not merely stability, but stable freedom: a democracy that remains open, pluralistic, and just under stress.

2. Institutions as "Control Systems" Rather Than Ideals on Paper

Every democracy has ideals: rights, equality, representation, and the rule of law. Those ideals are not optional; they are the republic's moral justification. But ideals must be embodied in mechanisms. A right is only as real as the institutions that enforce it. Representation is only as meaningful as the rules that translate voices into decisions. The rule of law is only as credible as the consistency of enforcement and the constraint on discretion.

From a control-system perspective, institutions perform five critical functions:

1. **Sensing:** detecting problems, measuring conditions, revealing corruption, and gathering feedback from society.

2. **Filtering:** distinguishing signal from noise, especially in an information-disordered environment.

3. **Decision-making:** converting information into policy through legitimate procedures.

4. **Actuation:** implementing decisions through capable administration.

5. **Feedback and correction:** learning from outcomes and adjusting rules, budgets, and strategies.

In a stable environment, deficiencies in one function can be masked by the others. In a turbulent environment, deficiencies compound. Weak sensing produces blind governance; weak filtering produces panic governance; weak actuation produces cynicism; weak feedback produces brittleness. The result is a republic that cannot learn. And a republic that cannot learn is a republic near the edge of chaos.

Part III will therefore treat institutional design as the construction of *learning capacity under pressure*. The key question is not "what policy do we prefer?" but "what institutional architecture allows us to implement policies competently, revise them legitimately, and maintain trust even when outcomes are contested?"

3. The Design Problem: Balancing Friction and Flow

Part I introduced the central paradox: democracies need both friction and flow.

- **Friction** protects rights and prevents impulsive majorities and demagogues from rapidly transforming the system.
- **Flow** allows legitimate demands and reforms to move through institutions without rupture.

Too much friction leads to paralysis and brittle order—reform becomes impossible, grievances accumulate, and shocks trigger rupture. Too much flow leads to volatility and chaos—policy whiplash, instability, and fear.

Nonlinear times increase the difficulty of balancing friction and flow because:

- attention cycles pressure institutions to respond instantly,
- polarization increases the temptation to use power maximally,
- and inequality increases the stakes of losing.

Part III will repeatedly return to a design principle we can call **smart friction and smart flow**:

- **Smart friction** blocks destabilizing tactics (corruption, capture, violence, delegitimation, emergency-power abuse) while preserving legitimate dissent and reform.
- **Smart flow** accelerates problem-solving, service delivery, and legitimate policy revision without surrendering accountability.

The goal is not to engineer consensus; it is to engineer *processable conflict.*

4. Robustness to Bad Faith: Designing for Adversarial Politics

One of the defining features of nonlinear times is that institutional vulnerabilities are exploited at scale and at speed. Bad faith is not new in politics, but modern conditions magnify it. A loophole can be weaponized instantly and replicated widely. A procedural exploit can become a permanent tactic. A false narrative can be amplified to millions within hours. A captured agency can quickly reshape rules. An institution that relies on informal norms can be overwhelmed.

This changes design priorities. In earlier eras, systems could rely more heavily on norms: mutual toleration, restraint, and good-faith interpretation. In a more adversarial environment, institutions must assume:

- actors will seek asymmetric advantage,
- attention incentives will reward escalation,
- and informational manipulation will become common.

Designing for adversarial politics does not mean becoming cynical. It means building **anti-fragile constraints**: structures that do not collapse under stress and make cheating costly.

Examples include:

- procedures that reduce discretionary power and increase auditability,
- independent oversight with real teeth,
- election administration that is transparent and routinely audited,
- anti-corruption enforcement insulated from factional control,
- and rules that prevent entrenchment strategies from quietly succeeding.

These are not partisan measures. They are the democratic equivalent of safety standards: they protect the system regardless of who holds power.

5. Legitimacy as the Non-Negotiable Design Constraint

Every institution in Part III will be evaluated against a central constraint: **legitimacy**. Stability achieved through repression, censorship, or selective punishment is not democratic stability. It is a brittle order that stores stress until rupture.

Therefore, Part III insists on "liberal dampening": stabilizers that are:

- transparent,
- procedurally constrained,
- accountable,
- and generally applicable across factions.

This is especially important in domains such as information integrity and anti-corruption, where the temptation to use heavy-handed measures is strong and the risk of delegitimation is high. A democracy can defeat misinformation by becoming a censorial state, but then it defeats itself. It can reduce corruption through factional purges, but then it builds an authoritarian attractor. The designer's challenge is to preserve legitimacy while enforcing boundaries—an inherently difficult but unavoidable task.

6. Designing for Learning: Adaptive Governance Without Improvisational Chaos

One of the most important implications of nonlinear times is that we cannot design one perfect set of rules and assume it will remain optimal. Technology changes. Markets shift. Geopolitical pressures evolve. Social norms mutate. A democracy must therefore become capable of **iterative adaptation**.

But "adaptation" can mean two opposite things:

- **Adaptive governance:** rule changes through transparent, legitimate processes; experiments; evaluation; revision; institutional learning.
- **Improvisational chaos:** rule changes through executive whim, emergency decrees, or opportunistic manipulation; policy whiplash; diminished trust.

Part III will propose mechanisms that enable adaptive governance while preventing improvisational chaos:

- sunset clauses and scheduled policy reviews,
- independent commissions for technical domains (districting, ethics, election administration) with strong transparency and oversight,
- policy experimentation with evaluation and scaling,
- and institutional stress tests and after-action reviews.

The goal is to create **credible flexibility**: the ability to change rules without making them feel arbitrary. In a fragile democracy, credible flexibility is one of the strongest stabilizers because it prevents pressure from accumulating behind blocked reforms.

7. The Institutional Modules of Part III

Part III will present a set of design modules, interlocking reforms that can be assembled into a resilience architecture. These modules fall into five broad categories:

1. **Representation and coalition design**
   Reforms that reduce winner-take-all incentives, reward coalition-building, and ensure the broad legitimacy of outcomes.

2. **Accountability and anti-capture architecture**
   Reforms that constrain corruption, reduce the influence of concentrated wealth, and make enforcement symmetric and credible.

3. **Information integrity and epistemic resilience**
   Reforms that protect the epistemic commons by increasing provenance, transparency, verification capacity, and appropriate friction against high-velocity manipulation.

4. **Administrative capacity and service legitimacy**
   Reforms that make government competent, reliable, and fair in daily life because competence is not technocratic vanity but a legitimacy foundation.

5. **Adaptive and crisis governance**
   Reforms that prepare institutions to handle shocks without triggering regime shifts: emergency-power constraints, crisis protocols, and learning systems.

Throughout, the emphasis will be on *system behavior*. Each module will be evaluated according to whether it strengthens negative feedback, reduces cascade risk, and expands the safe operating space of democracy.

8. The "Safe Operating Space" of Democratic Governance

Borrowing language from ecological resilience, we can think of democracies as having a safe operating space: a range of conditions under which self-government remains legitimate and effective. When key parameters drift—inequality rises, information disorder spreads, institutional trust collapses—the safe operating space narrows. Shocks that once were tolerable become dangerous.

Part III is, in effect, a project to enlarge that safe operating space. It does so by:

- lowering the gain on outrage and manipulation,
- increasing the visibility of fairness,
- strengthening enforcement credibility,
- improving service delivery,
- and building adaptation pathways that prevent brittleness.

In short, it aims to redesign the republic so that it can live at the edge of chaos without falling over it.

9. A Candid Note About Constraints: Design Cannot Substitute for Politics

Institutional design is powerful, but it is not magic. Reforms must be adopted by political actors with interests. They must be implemented by institutions that may be partially captured. They must be communicated in an information environment that rewards conflict. And they must operate amid inequality and global turbulence.

Part III, therefore, treats design not as a one-time constitutional convention but as a strategy of incremental yet coherent building. The idea is not to wait for perfect conditions. It is to build reforms that are:

- politically feasible in stages,
- mutually reinforcing,
- and legitimacy-preserving across coalitions.

This is why modularity matters. A democracy may not be able to implement everything at once, but it can implement keystone reforms that improve the credibility of enforcement, reduce disinformation cascades, and restore basic competence, thereby widening the window for deeper reforms.

Part III will also address sequencing: what reforms should come first in fragile conditions. As argued in Part II, restoring trust and rule consistency often must precede maximal redistributive or confrontational reforms. Otherwise, reform is interpreted as capture. Sequencing is not a moral compromise; it is systems realism.

10. The Moral Center: Designing for Dignity Under Turbulence

The phrase "designing institutions" can sound cold. But the purpose is human. Institutions exist to protect dignity, prevent domination, and enable people to live meaningful lives in a shared society. In nonlinear times, the greatest threat is not only that the system breaks, but that it breaks in ways that degrade humanity, turning politics into humiliation, turning neighbors into enemies, turning truth into a weapon, turning public life into a theater of fear.

Part III holds that dignity is not merely a value; it is a stabilizing resource. When people feel seen, protected, and treated fairly, they are more likely to cooperate, tolerate losses, and resist demagogic escalation. When people feel disposable, they become vulnerable to factional rage and radicalization. Thus, the design goal is not merely to preserve procedures but to preserve the lived experience of equal citizenship.

To design institutions for nonlinear times is therefore to design for:

- **predictability without rigidity,**
- **accountability without persecution,**
- **truth-seeking without censorship,**
- **security without repression,**
- **reform without rupture,**
- **pluralism without fragmentation.**

This is the moral and technical challenge of modern democracy.

11. What to Expect in the Chapters Ahead

Part III will proceed from foundational design principles to specific institutional architectures. The reader can expect:

- a chapter on **smart friction**—how to constrain destabilizing tactics while preserving democratic contestation;
- a chapter on **coalition incentives**—how electoral and legislative rules can reward cooperation rather than maximalism;
- a chapter on **anti-capture and anti-rent design**—how to reduce the profitability of corruption and influence markets;
- a chapter on **epistemic resilience**—how to protect information integrity through transparency, provenance, and friction proportionality;
- a chapter on **administrative legitimacy**—how competence and fairness in service delivery sustain trust;

- and a chapter on **adaptive governance and crisis protocols**—how to learn, stress test, and revise rules without legitimating improvisational power grabs.

Each chapter will treat institutions as interacting modules rather than isolated fixes. The emphasis will be on coherent packages that change system behavior rather than symbolic reforms that look good but do little.

12. THE THESIS OF PART III

We can state Part III's thesis plainly:

> **In nonlinear times, democratic survival depends on institutional designs that reduce cascade risk, strengthen negative feedback, and preserve legitimacy under high polarization and high uncertainty.**

Or, in the language of this book's title: the physics of democratic stability demands architecture. It demands institutions tuned for turbulent environments that can absorb shocks, process conflict, and adapt without losing the moral meaning of self-government.

Part III attempts to sketch that architecture. It is offered not as a final blueprint but as a framework: a way to think about democratic reform as resilience engineering, grounded in incentives and feedback rather than in slogans. It asks us to see democracy as a system that must be maintained, repaired, and redesigned because the environment has changed and because the costs of complacency are nonlinear.

If Parts I and II told the story of how democracies approach the edge of chaos and what happens when dampeners fail, Part III is the constructive response: a design approach to keeping democracies within their safe operating space. It is a guide to building institutions that can remain free under pressure, legitimate under contestation, and governable under turbulence.

The question is no longer whether democracies will face shocks. They will. The question is whether they will have institutions capable of absorbing those shocks without converting them into regime shifts. Designing institutions for nonlinear times is the work of answering that question—practically, morally, and urgently.

Chapter 8

The Anti-Capture State: Rules That Change Payoffs

A democracy can survive disagreement. It can survive noisy elections, bitter policy fights, and even periodic scandals. What cannot survive indefinitely is a state that ceases to serve as a neutral instrument of public purpose and becomes a rentable machine, an engine of extraction. When that happens, politics stops being a contest about the common good and becomes a contest about who gets to control the tollbooth. In such a system, corruption is not a deviation; it is the operating logic. Inequality is not an unfortunate outcome; it is the business model. And legitimacy erodes because citizens experience law as selective, procedure as theater, and public life as a rigged game.

Chapter 6 described corruption as a bad attractor: a self-reinforcing equilibrium that persists even when citizens despise it. This chapter asks the next design question: **How do you build an "anti-capture state"—a set of rules and institutions that change the payoffs so capture becomes difficult, expensive, and strategically unattractive?** Not through moral exhortation or episodic prosecutions alone, but through structural changes that alter incentives across the political economy.

The key claim of this chapter is that anti-capture design is fundamentally about **payoffs**. If capture is profitable, it will be pursued. If rents can be extracted quietly, they will be. If influence can be purchased cheaply relative to its returns, it will be. If enforcement is selective, capture will be interpreted as factional dominance and will escalate. The anti-capture state, therefore, does not rely on saintly politicians. It relies on institutional architecture that makes capture harder to execute, easier to detect, and more costly to sustain.

This is "physics" applied to governance: we do not ask whether elites will behave well; we assume they will behave strategically. We then design a system where strategic behavior is more likely to produce public-serving outcomes than extractive ones.

1. What Capture Is—and Why It Is Rational

"Capture" can sound like a moral category ("corrupt elites take over"), but analytically it is a structural phenomenon: **a durable shift in the alignment of state action from public purpose toward concentrated private advantage**.

Capture can take many forms:

- **Regulatory capture:** agencies serve the industries they regulate.
- **Legislative capture:** laws are written to favor donors, incumbents, or concentrated interests.
- **Judicial capture:** courts are shaped to protect certain factions or economic interests.
- **Administrative capture:** civil service and procurement are turned into patronage networks.
- **Information capture:** media ecosystems and expertise pipelines are shaped to legitimate extraction.
- **Enforcement capture:** prosecutors and inspectors are politicized or constrained; impunity becomes structural.

Capture is rational because the returns are enormous. A single regulatory exemption can be worth billions. A favorable tax provision can persist for decades. A contracting rule can create an oligopoly. A licensing regime can exclude competitors. A judicial precedent can reshape whole markets. Compared to these returns, the cost of influence—campaign finance, lobbying, litigation, revolving-door career paths—can be small. In classic economic terms, capture is a high-return investment.

The anti-capture state begins with this realism: **if the payoff to capture exceeds the payoff to productive investment, rational actors will prefer capture**. Worse, capture can crowd out productive investment, because why innovate when you can rent? Over time, the political economy becomes an extraction game.

2. The Capture Equilibrium: How It Becomes Self-Reinforcing

Capture becomes stable—an attractor—when it reproduces its own conditions. Several feedback loops matter.

2.1 Capture → rents → political money → more capture

Capture generates rents. Rents finance political influence. Political influence deepens capture.

2.2 Capture → inequality → dependency → lower resistance

As capture concentrates wealth, the median citizen's bargaining power weakens. People become more economically insecure, more time-poor, and less able to monitor politics. This reduces resistance and increases susceptibility to demagogic narratives. The field is cleared for further capture.

2.3 Capture → distrust → low compliance → weak state → more capture

When citizens perceive the government as captured, they comply less (e.g., tax evasion, regulatory resistance, civic withdrawal). Lower compliance weakens state capacity. A weaker state relies more on private actors and contractors, increasing capture channels.

2.4 Capture → information disorder → accountability collapse → more capture

Captured actors invest in narrative control: think tanks, PR, media acquisitions, litigation, and online influence. This clouds accountability and fragments shared reality, making it harder for citizens to coordinate on reform.

2.5 Anti-capture as factional weapon → delegitimation → stalemate → capture persists

In polarized societies, anti-capture actions can be interpreted as partisan persecution. When legitimacy is low, even real enforcement can backfire. This creates a stalemate, which favors the already-captured system.

These loops imply a design requirement: **anti-capture must be symmetric, procedurally constrained, and visibly fair**, or it will be politically unsustainable and may worsen delegitimation.

3. What an "Anti-Capture State" Is

The anti-capture state is neither a larger nor a smaller state. It is a **state with rules that prevent the conversion of public authority into private rent**. It has three core characteristics:

1. **Low-rent structure:** fewer choke points that can be monetized.
2. **High auditability:** decisions are transparent, traceable, and reviewable.
3. **Credible enforcement:** violations are punished consistently, including among elites.

In short, it is a state designed to keep the payoff to capture below the payoff to productive economic and political participation.

This is a design project, not merely a policy preference. It requires changes in:

- campaign finance and political money,
- lobbying and revolving-door incentives,
- procurement and contracting,
- regulatory procedure and transparency,
- antitrust and market structure,
- ethics and conflicts of interest,
- and the epistemic infrastructure of democracy (data, audits, investigative capacity).

The anti-capture state is a stability architecture. It strengthens trust and legitimacy by making governance visibly fairer, and it reduces tipping-point risk by cutting off the fuel supply—rents—that intensify polarization and corruption.

4. Rules That Change Payoffs: The Four Levers

Anti-capture design is fundamentally about altering incentives. We can group the most powerful payoff-changing rules into four levers:

1. **Rent reduction:** reduce the size and accessibility of extractable rents.
2. **Transaction cost increase:** make capture attempts more expensive and risky.
3. **Detection probability increase:** make capture more visible and auditable.
4. **Penalty credibility increase:** ensure meaningful, consistent consequences.

Each lever alone helps. Together, they can shift equilibria.

4.1 Rent reduction: shrinking the capture prize

Rent arises when rules create scarcity, monopoly, or discretionary privilege. The anti-capture state attacks rents at their source:

- **Antitrust enforcement** to reduce market concentration and monopoly pricing power.
- **Competitive procurement** to prevent contracting oligopolies.
- **Licensing reform** where licensing creates unnecessary choke points.
- **Tax simplification** to reduce loophole engineering.
- **Standardized regulatory pathways** to reduce discretionary exemptions.
- **Sunset clauses** for targeted tax expenditures and subsidies.

Rent reduction is not anti-business; it is pro-competition and pro-productivity. It shifts investment from political engineering back to economic creation.

4.2 Transaction cost increase: making capture harder to execute

Even if rents exist, capture becomes less attractive when it is difficult to organize.

- limit stealth political spending and dark money,
- require real-time transparency for lobbying and political ads,
- restrict revolving-door pathways,
- increase procedural hurdles for last-minute legislative riders,
- mandate public comment and response-to-comments for major rule changes,
- and require rigorous conflict-of-interest disclosures.

The goal is to increase the effort and risk required to buy outcomes.

4.3 Detection probability increase: visibility as deterrence

Corruption thrives in opacity. Anti-capture states build "auditability by default":

- open contracting data (who bid, who won, why),
- public beneficial ownership registries for companies,
- machine-readable budgets and spending,
- published enforcement statistics,
- randomized audits and inspector-general reporting,
- and protected access for independent researchers.

Detection is deterrence. If capture cannot hide, it becomes less profitable and riskier.

4.4 Penalty credibility increase: consequences that bind the powerful

The final lever is enforcement credibility. Penalties deter only if they are real and symmetric.

- independent ethics enforcement,
- prosecutorial independence with oversight,
- meaningful civil and criminal penalties for bribery, fraud, and procurement abuse,
- clawbacks and debarment from contracting,
- and professional sanctions (licenses, bar discipline) for enablers.

This is crucial: **elite impunity is the death of rule consistency**. When the powerful are seen as immune, trust collapses and capture becomes normal.

5. The Anti-Capture Toolkit: Institutional Modules

We now translate levers into modules—design objects that can be implemented.

Module A: Transparent political money and influence pathways

If political survival depends on money, and money can be concentrated, then capture is structurally incentivized. Anti-capture design does not require banning political spending, but it does require making influence legible and reducing dependency on concentrated donors.

Key elements:

- **Real-time disclosure** of major donations and spending, with accessible databases.
- **Beneficial ownership transparency** for donor entities and shell organizations.
- **Stronger coordination rules** to prevent laundering political spending through intermediaries.
- **Public matching funds** or vouchers to amplify small donors and reduce elite leverage.
- **Clear, enforceable limits** on gifts, travel, and perks to officials.
- **Disclosure of policy drafting**: when legislation or regulatory text is provided by outside entities, it must be declared.

The purpose is to reduce hidden influence and alter the payoff structure: influence becomes harder to buy quietly, and the returns to stealth decrease.

Module B: Revolving-door and conflict-of-interest constraints

Capture is often executed through personnel pipelines. Officials regulate industries and then join them, or arrive from them. Expertise is real, but conflicts can be structural.

Anti-capture design includes:

- robust sideline periods for senior officials entering regulated industries,

- restrictions on lobbying by former officials for defined periods,
- mandatory recusal rules with public disclosure,
- blind trust or divestment requirements for certain roles,
- and transparency about meetings with industry actors.

This module changes payoffs by reducing the private career returns from public decisions. It is one of the most effective ways to reduce capture without expanding bureaucracy.

Module C: Procurement and contracting as a capture firewall

Modern states spend vast sums through contracts. Procurement is a prime capture node.

Anti-capture procurement includes:

- open competitive bidding as the default,
- clear scoring criteria published in advance,
- public disclosure of bids, evaluation, and awards (with limited, justified redactions),
- randomized audits of contracts,
- debarment for fraud and collusion,
- and anti-collusion enforcement coordination with antitrust authorities.

This module simultaneously reduces rents and increases detection. It also strengthens legitimacy because citizens can see where the money goes.

Module D: Regulatory procedure—reduce discretion, increase auditability

Regulatory capture thrives where agencies have high discretion and low transparency.

Key designs include:

- mandatory publication of evidence used in rule-making,
- clear cost-benefit and distributional impact analysis,
- response-to-comments requirements (not just collecting comments),
- public logs of meetings between regulators and affected industries,

- independent review units for major rules,
- and sunset/review schedules for complex regulations.

The goal is not to paralyze regulation. It is to make it less rentable.

Module E: Antitrust and market-structure reform as anti-capture policy

Market concentration increases capture risk because large firms have more resources to influence policy and more ability to extract rents. Competitive markets reduce the payoff to capture because rents are harder to sustain.

Anti-capture states treat competition policy as democracy policy:

- robust merger review with political economy considerations,
- enforcement against anti-competitive conduct,
- scrutiny of platform monopolies and gatekeepers,
- and policies that reduce switching costs and lock-in.

Competition is a democratic stabilizer: it reduces both economic and political concentration.

Module F: Independent auditing and inspectors general with real power

To raise detection probability and credibility of penalties, democracies need independent oversight.

Core features:

- legally protected independence for inspectors general,
- guaranteed budgets or protected funding mechanisms,
- subpoena power and access to records,
- mandatory public reporting timelines,
- and structured referral pathways for prosecution.

Oversight institutions must also be protected from politicization: their procedures should be transparent, their standards clear, and their enforcement symmetric.

Module G: Whistleblower protection and reward mechanisms

Because corruption is often hidden, insiders are key sources of detection. But whistleblowing is personally dangerous.

Anti-capture states protect and incentivize disclosure:

- strong anti-retaliation laws with enforcement,
- confidential reporting channels outside agency chains of command,
- legal aid for whistleblowers,
- and (where appropriate) financial rewards for evidence leading to recoveries.

This module changes payoffs by making defection from corruption networks less costly and more attractive.

Module H: Transparency of ownership and money flows

Capture often hides behind shell companies and opaque ownership.

Anti-capture design includes:

- beneficial ownership registries,
- transparency in real estate ownership where relevant,
- stricter anti-money laundering enforcement in key nodes,
- and cooperation among agencies to track flows.

Even in advanced democracies, opaque ownership can undermine enforcement. Visibility is the precondition of rule consistency.

6. The Anti-Capture State and Legitimacy: Enforcement Without Persecution

The central danger of anti-capture efforts is legitimacy collapse. In polarized environments, enforcement can be interpreted as factional weaponry. The anti-capture state must therefore be designed to preserve procedural credibility.

6.1 The symmetry principle

If anti-capture is perceived as selectively targeting one faction, it becomes a destabilizer. The anti-capture state must enforce rules across parties, regions, and status groups. Symmetry is not only moral; it is stabilizing. It prevents retaliation spirals and keeps enforcement within the dampeners of trust and rule consistency.

6.2 Procedural constraints and transparency

Enforcement must follow transparent standards:

- published criteria for investigations,
- clear chains of responsibility,
- independent review of enforcement decisions,
- and public reporting that explains actions without grandstanding.

The goal is to prevent "rule by accusation" and to build credibility that enforcement is lawful rather than political.

6.3 Avoiding the "purge equilibrium"

A republic can eliminate certain corrupt actors by empowering a strong executive to purge rivals. But that often produces a new attractor: authoritarian control justified by anti-corruption rhetoric. The anti-capture state must avoid concentrating discretionary power in a single leader. It should distribute enforcement across independent institutions with checks and oversight.

7. Sequencing and Political Feasibility: How to Build An Anti-Capture State in the Real World

Institutional design must face political constraints. Capture is not an accident; it is defended by those who benefit. Therefore, sequencing matters. The anti-capture state is often built through a strategy of **keystone reforms**, changes that increase transparency and the credibility of enforcement first, thereby making deeper reforms possible later.

7.1 Keystone reforms

Examples of keystone reforms include:

- real-time transparency of political spending and lobbying,
- procurement transparency and open contracting,
- empowered inspectors general and audit bodies,
- conflict-of-interest enforcement,
- and whistleblower protections.

These reforms are keystone because they raise detection probability and credibility, which quickly change behavior.

7.2 Build coalitions around fairness, not ideology

Anti-capture reforms can be framed as protecting taxpayers, competition, and equal citizenship, values that can bridge partisan divides. When framed as a factional weapon, they fail.

7.3 Use modular implementation

Rather than a single "grand anti-corruption bill," implement modules:

- transparency module,
- procurement module,
- ethics module,
- oversight module,
- competition module.

Modularity reduces resistance, allows learning, and avoids the perception of revolutionary overhaul.

8. A Design Lens: Anti-Capture as "Payoff Inversion"

We can now state the core conceptual move of this chapter. Capture persists because it is a profitable strategy. The anti-capture state aims to invert payoffs:

- **Make influence more expensive and more visible.**
- **Make rent extraction less durable and less scalable.**
- **Make enforcement more credible and more symmetric.**
- **Make productive investment more rewarding than political engineering.**

This is not naïve. It is practical. Systems change when incentives change.

The highest ambition of the anti-capture state is not merely fewer scandals. It is the restoration of democratic equilibrium: a polity where public authority is not routinely monetized and where citizens experience law as consistent rather than rentable. In that equilibrium, trust can regrow, legitimacy can stabilize, and the republic's safe operating space can widen.

9. The Anti-Capture State as a Resilience Architecture

Why does this belong in Part III, "*Designing Institutions for Nonlinear Times*"? Because capture is not only unjust but also destabilizing. Capture narrows the safe operating space by:

- increasing inequality and insecurity,
- degrading trust and rule consistency,
- and intensifying polarization through perceived rigging.

An anti-capture state is therefore a resilience architecture. It is a way to lower the system's baseline stress, reduce the probability of tipping points, and prevent the system from sliding into bad attractors.

In nonlinear times, resilience cannot be built only through crisis response. It must be built through structural re-design, reducing the incentives for extraction that make crises more likely and more explosive.

10. Conclusion: Democracy Must Make Extraction a Losing Strategy

Democracy is not guaranteed by elections alone. It is guaranteed, when it is guaranteed—by a credible rule of law, by institutions that treat citizens as equals, and by an economy where prosperity is not systematically converted into political domination. When capture becomes stable, those guarantees fade. The state becomes a rentable machine. Citizens stop believing in fairness. Politics becomes existential. The republic becomes sensitive to shocks.

The anti-capture state is the democratic answer to that danger. It is not a fantasy of perfect virtue. It is a practical program: rules that change payoffs. Reduce rents. Increase transparency. Constrain discretion. Protect whistleblowers. Strengthen oversight. Enforce symmetrically. Restore competition. Make public service incompatible with private extraction.

If Part II taught us that corruption can become a stable attractor, Part III now insists that stable attractors can be changed, but only by redesigning the game. The anti-capture state redesigns the game so that the dominant strategy shifts away from rent extraction and toward public-serving governance.

In the next chapter, we will examine the complementary design challenge: **how to build "smart friction" that blocks destabilizing behavior—misinformation cascades, constitutional hardball, emergency-power abuse—without freezing the system into brittle paralysis.** The anti-capture state changes payoffs; smart friction changes dynamics. Together, they form the foundation of institutional resilience in nonlinear times.

Chapter 9

A Prosperity Architecture: Security, Dignity, and Meaning

Prosperity is commonly measured by numbers: GDP growth, employment rates, stock market indexes, and household income. Democracies have long assumed that if the economy "performs," legitimacy will follow. Yet in nonlinear times that assumption is increasingly fragile. A society can grow economically yet remain politically unstable. It can generate wealth and still experience widespread insecurity. It can produce abundance and still feel starved—for dignity, for belonging, for moral coherence, for meaning. When that happens, democratic stability erodes not because people reject prosperity, but because they experience prosperity as *uneven, humiliating, or hollow.*

This chapter advances a different thesis: **democratic resilience requires a prosperity architecture**—an institutional and economic design that produces not only material output but durable security, equal dignity, and meaningful social participation. These are not sentimental aspirations. They are system variables. They shape citizens' and elites' incentives, determine whether politics becomes existential, and influence whether information disorder and polarization become contagious. A democracy without a prosperity architecture can still hold elections, but it becomes easier to capture, destabilize, and be more vulnerable to bad attractors: corruption, resentment, delegitimation, and episodic violence.

Part III is about "Designing Institutions for Nonlinear Times." The anti-capture state (Chapter 8) aimed to change the payoffs that make extraction rational. This chapter complements that project by asking: **What institutional architecture makes broad-based prosperity—and the lived experience of equal citizenship—structurally likely?** The answer is not one policy but a system of interlocking stabilizers. A prosperity architecture is a *resilience architecture.*

We will build this argument in four steps:

1. Define prosperity as a three-part structure—security, dignity, meaning—rather than a single economic metric.
2. Explain why each component is a stabilizer in nonlinear democracies.
3. Describe the institutional modules that produce these components in a durable way.
4. Show how these modules interact with the book's broader system dynamics: dampeners, bad attractors, and tipping points.

1. Why Prosperity Must Be Redesigned as an Institution, Not a Slogan

In public debate, "prosperity" is often treated as something that naturally emerges from markets and can be distributed afterward by policy. But prosperity is not only an outcome; it is an *architecture*—a set of rules that determines how risk is shared, how rewards are distributed, how work is valued, how citizens are treated, and how the future feels.

When prosperity is architected poorly, societies develop chronic instability mechanisms:

- **High insecurity** lowers trust, raises anxiety, and intensifies threat-based politics.
- **Dignity deficits** (humiliation, exclusion, disrespect) push people toward identity tribes and authoritarian cravings for recognition.

- **Meaning deficits** (alienation, purposeless work, social atomization) weaken solidarity and increase susceptibility to narrative extremism.

In nonlinear times, these deficits interact. Insecurity makes dignity more fragile; dignity threats make meaning collapse; meaning collapse makes misinformation and scapegoating more attractive. The result is not just discontent but dynamical risk: the system becomes easier to push into regime shifts.

Prosperity architecture, then, is not only "economic policy." It is stability engineering: designing the conditions under which citizens can tolerate disagreement, accept electoral losses, and cooperate across differences. A society that feels secure, dignified, and meaningfully included is harder to destabilize. A society that feels precarious, humiliated, and purposeless becomes volatile and more easily captured.

2. Security: The Stabilizer That Lowers Existential Stakes

2.1 Security as "risk containment"

Security is often misconstrued as comfort. In this framework, security means *risk containment*: the ability to plan a life without constant fear of ruin. A security-centered prosperity architecture does not eliminate hardship; it prevents ordinary shocks from becoming catastrophic.

Catastrophic risk in modern economies comes from predictable sources:

- health costs,
- job loss and wage volatility,
- housing instability,
- debt traps,
- caregiving burdens,
- and geographic immobility.

When these risks are unmanaged, citizens experience the economy as a hostile environment. They become time-poor and psychologically depleted, which reduces civic participation. They become more sensitive to threat narratives, which intensifies polarization. And they become more willing to support extreme political solutions because "normal politics" feels incapable of protecting them.

Security, therefore, functions like a dampener: it reduces amplitude. It lowers the "gain" on political shocks because people are not already at the edge of ruin.

2.2 Security and democratic legitimacy

A democracy's legitimacy is not only procedural; it is experiential. If citizens encounter the state primarily through punitive bureaucracy, humiliating welfare hoops, or indifferent market outcomes, they infer that the system is not theirs. This erodes legitimacy even if elections are formally fair.

A prosperity architecture that provides security in a universal, predictable, non-stigmatizing way strengthens legitimacy. Citizens may disagree about many things, but they can feel that the republic protects them from falling through the floor. That creates a baseline of reciprocity: people are more willing to pay taxes, comply with rules, and accept temporary losses when the system has their back.

2.3 Security as an anti-capture strategy

Security also reduces capture incentives. When citizens are insecure, they become dependent on patronage—political favors, informal networks, local bosses. Patronage is a capture channel. A secure society can resist patronage because people do not have to bargain for survival through political loyalty.

Thus, security is not just a social goal. It is an anti-capture design element.

3. Dignity: The Stabilizer That Makes Citizenship Real

If security lowers existential stakes, dignity lowers existential *humiliation.* Many political pathologies in modern democracies are not driven only by material deprivation but by the perception of disrespect—being unseen, disposable, mocked, or culturally erased. Dignity is the currency of democratic life. Without it, citizens are tempted by movements that promise recognition through domination.

3.1 Dignity as equal standing

Dignity in a democracy means equal standing: the belief that one's voice matters, one is treated fairly by institutions, and one is not socially invisible. Dignity is created or destroyed in daily encounters with:

- employers,
- schools,
- police,
- hospitals,
- welfare agencies,
- courts,
- and media narratives.

A prosperity architecture must therefore address not only income but *institutional dignity*: how systems treat people.

3.2 The dignity deficit and polarization

Dignity deficits fuel polarization by turning politics into identity warfare. When people feel disrespected, they interpret policy debates as battles over worth. They become drawn to zero-sum narratives: "they hate us," "they look down on us," "they want to replace us," "they don't care if we live or die." These narratives are emotionally powerful and algorithmically amplifiable, which makes them contagious.

Dignity thus serves as a stabilizer because it reduces the emotional fuel for polarization. A society where people feel respected—even amid disagreement—has lower baseline hostility.

3.3 Dignity and the rule of law

The rule of law depends on perceived fairness. If people believe law is selective and humiliating, compliance becomes surrender. Dignity-centered institutions emphasize procedural justice: being heard, being treated consistently, and being protected from arbitrary power.

This is why dignity is not "soft." It is a resource for legal and political stability.

4. Meaning: The Stabilizer That Prevents Moral and Civic Hollowing

Security and dignity can still coexist with emptiness. A society can provide material stability and formal equality yet feel meaningless—atomized, spiritually barren, and culturally exhausted. In such societies, people search for meaning in extreme narratives, factional identity, conspiracy, or scapegoating. Meaning becomes a political resource.

4.1 Meaning as participation in something larger than the self

Meaning arises when people feel their lives contribute to something valued: family, skills, community, nation, or moral purpose. Modern economies often undermine meaning through:

- precarious work and fragmented careers,
- loss of local institutions and civic associations,
- geographic displacement,
- digital substitution for community,
- and status hierarchies that reduce many jobs to invisibility.

When meaning collapses, people become vulnerable to movements that offer moral clarity through antagonism: "we are the righteous; they are the corrupt." This is an epistemic and political vulnerability. It increases susceptibility to information disorder because conspiracy stories provide a ready-made moral universe.

4.2 Meaning and democratic resilience

Democracies require more than rules; they require civic motivation. People must care enough to participate, to compromise, to accept losses, to protect institutions they do not control. Meaning provides that motivation. Without meaning, citizens retreat into private survival or cynical spectacle. Politics becomes a distant drama rather than a shared project.

A prosperous architecture, therefore, must include *civic meaning-making institutions*: arenas where people feel connected and useful.

5. THE PROSPERITY ARCHITECTURE: INSTITUTIONAL MODULES

A "prosperity architecture" is built from modules that generate security, dignity, and meaning in structurally durable ways. It is not a single program; it is a system. Below are the core modules, organized by the three pillars and then by cross-cutting integration.

Pillar I: Security Modules

Module 1: Universal risk floors

A prosperity architecture begins with a floor beneath which citizens do not fall. This includes:

- accessible, reliable healthcare protection,
- unemployment insurance designed for modern labor markets,
- income supports that are predictable and non-stigmatizing,
- and disability and caregiving supports that prevent ruin.

The essential design principle is **automaticity**: benefits should expand in downturns and contract in upturns without requiring extraordinary legislation. Automatic stabilizers are not only economic tools; they are legitimacy tools. They prevent recessions from becoming regime crises.

Module 2: Housing stability and geographic mobility

Housing is the primary driver of insecurity for many households. A prosperity architecture includes:

- policies that expand housing supply and affordability,
- tenant protections against sudden displacement,
- zoning and land-use reforms that reduce artificial scarcity,
- and mobility supports (relocation assistance, portable benefits).

Housing stability reduces the psychological intensity of politics because displacement and rent anxiety are chronic stressors that make societies volatile.

Module 3: Debt containment and predatory market constraints

Debt can function as a privatized welfare system: people borrow to survive. A prosperity architecture reduces debt traps by:

- regulating predatory lending,
- expanding access to fair credit,
- restructuring student and medical debt burdens,
- and improving bankruptcy pathways.

Debt containment is a stabilizer because debt shame and debt fear are dignity-destroying and politically combustible.

Module 4: Wage stability and bargaining power

Security requires a predictable income. A prosperity architecture strengthens:

- wage floors indexed to productivity or cost of living,
- labor standards enforcement,
- portable benefits for gig and contract work,
- and mechanisms that increase worker bargaining power.

This is not merely distributive. It reduces insecurity, increases trust, and lowers the attraction of scapegoating politics.

Pillar II: Dignity Modules

Module 5: Procedural dignity in the welfare state

Means-tested systems can inadvertently humiliate citizens through surveillance and paperwork. A dignity-centered design emphasizes:

- simplified eligibility,
- respectful service delivery,
- minimal intrusive monitoring,
- and appeal pathways with real due process.

The point is not to remove accountability but to align assistance with democratic standing: citizens should not have to surrender dignity to receive basic support.

Module 6: Justice and policing legitimacy

Every interaction with law enforcement is a legitimacy event. A dignity-centered prosperity architecture includes:

- transparent standards for use of force,
- accountability mechanisms perceived as fair,
- community legitimacy-building practices,
- and investments in non-police crisis response where appropriate.

This is not only about crime; it is about consistency in the rules and equal citizenship.

Module 7: Education as equal-status formation

Education is not only human capital; it is also a form of dignity. A prosperity architecture includes:

- equitable funding and resources,
- civic education emphasizing systems literacy and democratic norms,
- pathways for vocational and technical dignity (not only university prestige),
- and lifelong learning mechanisms.

If education becomes a caste system, dignity collapses and polarization rises.

Module 8: Anti-discrimination and inclusion as stability policy

In pluralistic democracies, dignity requires credible protection against discrimination in employment, housing, lending, and public services. This is not only a moral imperative; it is a stability requirement. Systematic humiliation produces identity radicalization and legitimacy collapse.

Pillar III: Meaning Modules

Module 9: Civic infrastructure and associational life

This means that it is built into institutions that connect people beyond markets and screens. A prosperity architecture includes:

- revitalized local civic institutions (libraries, community centers),

- support for civic associations,
- public-interest local media ecosystems,
- and spaces where cross-cutting interaction occurs.

This is an anti-polarization investment because it builds bridging ties.

Module 10: National service and civic contribution pathways

A society can provide meaning by creating pathways for contribution:

- voluntary national service programs,
- public works and community resilience projects,
- climate adaptation and infrastructure corps,
- and recognition systems that honor civic contribution.

The goal is not militarization; it is shared purpose and cross-group cooperation.

Module 11: Work as craft and recognition

Work is where many people experience dignity and meaning—or humiliation and emptiness. A prosperity architecture promotes:

- predictable scheduling,
- worker voice in workplace decisions,
- training and apprenticeships,
- and career ladders that allow pride and development.

This is not only labor policy; it is moral ecology.

Module 12: Cultural pluralism and narrative integration

Meaning also depends on narrative: what does it mean to be a citizen? Democracies need integrative stories that allow pluralism without fragmentation. This is not propaganda; it is civic narrative capacity—rituals, public commemorations, shared civic education, and leadership language that emphasizes equal dignity.

6. Integration: Prosperity Architecture as a Stability System

The modules above matter individually. Their deeper power is systemic. A prosperity architecture stabilizes democracy through four integrative mechanisms.

6.1 Lowering baseline stress reduces contagion

Polarization and misinformation behave like contagions in high-stress environments. Security and dignity lower baseline stress, increasing skepticism toward extreme narratives and reducing the emotional appeal of scapegoating.

6.2 Broad-based prosperity reduces capture vulnerability

Capture thrives where citizens are dependent and time-poor. When people are secure, they can monitor politics, join associations, and resist patronage. Prosperity architecture is therefore complementary to the anti-capture state.

6.3 Meaning builds civic immune function

Societies with strong associational life and shared civic contributions have stronger "immune systems" against disinformation because people trust local networks and verification norms. Meaning is epistemic resilience.

6.4 Prosperity reduces tipping-point probability

Tipping points become likely when grievances stack, dampeners fail, and shocks hit a brittle system. Prosperity architecture deepens dampeners by increasing trust and legitimacy. It makes crises less likely to produce regime shifts.

7. Tradeoffs and Design Risks

A prosperity architecture must be designed carefully. Poorly designed systems can backfire.

7.1 Bureaucratic humiliation risk

Even well-funded programs can destroy dignity if delivered with suspicion and complexity. The design must prioritize respectful service and procedural justice.

7.2 Dependency narratives and legitimacy

If programs are framed as gifts rather than rights, they can become politically fragile and culturally polarizing. Universal or broadly inclusive designs tend to be more stable because they build shared ownership.

7.3 Fiscal sustainability and credibility

Security systems must be fiscally credible to maintain trust. That implies prudent financing, predictable automatic stabilizers, and transparency about costs and trade-offs. Unfunded promises become legitimacy liabilities.

7.4 Moral hazard and perverse incentives

Programs must avoid creating traps that discourage work or mobility. This can be managed through phased benefits, portability, and supportive services.

The principle is **credible universality with smart design**: broad coverage, low stigma, high respect, and incentives aligned with participation.

8. The Prosperity Architecture in a Nonlinear Environment: A "Resilience Dividend"

In nonlinear times, a prosperity architecture produces a resilience dividend:

- It reduces the amplitude of political oscillations.
- It increases tolerance for disagreement.
- It lowers the payoff to demagoguery.
- It increases trust in institutions through lived experience.
- It reduces susceptibility to information disorder.
- It makes reforms plausible without rupture.

This dividend is often invisible in calm times and decisive in crisis times—much like insurance. Democracies often underinvest in it because it doesn't look urgent until it is too late. Part III argues that designing institutions for nonlinear times requires treating prosperity architecture as essential infrastructure rather than optional generosity.

9. Conclusion: Prosperity Is the Moral Ecology of Stability

A democracy is stable when citizens can lose an election without losing their lives, their dignity, or their future. That requires more than constitutional rules. It requires a lived experience of security, respect, and meaningful inclusion. It requires a prosperity architecture.

Security ensures that ordinary shocks do not become existential disasters. Dignity ensures that institutions treat citizens as equals rather than as suspects or subjects. Meaning ensures that public life is more than consumption and conflict—that it is a shared project worthy of participation.

Together, these pillars strengthen the dampeners discussed in Part II and reduce the capture and tipping-point dynamics that threaten modern democracies. They are not merely social ideals. They are the system conditions that make self-government viable in turbulent environments.

In the next chapter, we will turn to the "operating system" that connects these architectures: **how to build smart friction and adaptive governance so reforms can be implemented, revised, and defended without triggering legitimacy crises.** The anti-capture state changes payoffs; the prosperity architecture changes lived experience; smart friction changes dynamics. Combined, they form a coherent design strategy for democratic stability at the edge of chaos.

Chapter 10

Systems Humanism: A Practical Program for Human Flourishing and Democratic Repair

A democracy is not repaired the way a machine is repaired. You cannot replace a broken part and assume the system will run smoothly again. Democracies are complex adaptive systems made of people—agents who learn, fear, imitate, coordinate, and retaliate. They are built from rules and institutions, yes, but also from norms, identities, narratives, and lived experiences. Their stability depends not only on constitutional architecture but on the moral ecology that sustains cooperation: trust, dignity, reciprocity, and the sense that shared life is worth the effort.

Part III has argued that nonlinear times require an institutional design that is resilient in the face of turbulence. Chapter 8 described the anti-capture state: rules that change payoffs so extraction becomes a losing strategy. Chapter 9 proposed a prosperity architecture that delivers security, dignity, and meaning as stabilizers of democratic life. This chapter now introduces the integrative framework that binds those designs together: **Systems Humanism**: a practical program for human flourishing and democratic repair.

Systems Humanism begins with a simple claim: **human flourishing is a systems property**, not a private luxury. It emerges from the interaction between individuals and the structures around them: markets, schools, media, law, neighborhoods, workplaces, families, and civic institutions. When those structures reward extraction, humiliation, and zero-sum competition, even decent people behave in ways that degrade the commons. When structures reward reciprocity, dignity, and contribution, even imperfect people can build stable and humane societies. The moral character of a polity is not only a matter of virtue; it is also a matter of incentives and feedback.

This framework rejects two common errors. The first is technocratic reductionism: the belief that social life can be engineered purely through metrics and policy levers, as if meaning and dignity were side effects. The second is moral romanticism: the belief that civic virtue alone can defeat structural forces like inequality, platform-driven outrage, or capture. Systems Humanism insists on both—**structure and spirit**—and it aims to design institutions that make humane behavior rational and stable in a turbulent environment.

The chapter proceeds in six parts:

1. Define Systems Humanism and the "moral ecology" of democratic stability.
2. Describe the pathologies it addresses: extraction, humiliation, and cognitive capture.
3. Articulate core principles for human flourishing under nonlinear conditions.
4. Offer a practical program: institutional modules and reforms aligned with Systems Humanism.
5. Explain how the program reduces polarization, improves legitimacy, and prevents tipping points.
6. Conclude with a pragmatic theory of hope: why repair is possible and how to stage it.

I. What is Systems Humanism?

Systems Humanism is an interdisciplinary philosophy of governance that treats human dignity, moral development, and democratic stability as emergent outcomes of complex social systems. It is "humanist" because it centers on the worth of persons and the moral meaning of equal citizenship. It is "systems" because it refuses to treat suffering and instability as merely personal failings or cultural decadence. Instead, it asks how structures—economic rules, information ecosystems, institutional design—shape the behaviors and beliefs that constitute public life.

1. The core premise: flourishing is emergent, not merely individual

In the standard liberal story, flourishing is primarily private: individuals pursue happiness, and government protects rights and provides public goods. That story remains important, but it underestimates how much flourishing depends on systemic conditions:

- the stability of livelihoods,
- the fairness of institutions,
- the integrity of information,
- the availability of community,
- the meaning of work,
- and the reality of equal standing.

In nonlinear times, these conditions are not background; they are decisive. A society can have formal rights and still produce widespread despair. It can have elections and still produce domination. It can have prosperity and still produce humiliation. The problem is not that individuals are insufficiently virtuous. The problem is that the system may be producing predictable pathologies.

2. Moral ecology: the environment that shapes civic character

Systems Humanism treats society as a moral ecosystem. In any ecosystem, organisms adapt to incentives. If the environment rewards predation, predatory behavior spreads. If it rewards cooperation, cooperative behavior becomes stable. This is not a denial of agency; it is a recognition that agency is situated at the human level.

A "moral ecology" includes:

- **incentive gradients** (what behaviors are rewarded),
- **normative signals** (what behaviors are honored),
- **institutional constraints** (what behaviors are prevented),

- **information flows** (what narratives dominate attention),
- **social networks** (who influences whom),
- and **material security** (how scarcity shapes moral choices).

When the moral ecology is healthy, civic virtues—restraint, reciprocity, truthfulness, empathy—are not constantly punished. When the moral ecology is degraded, virtues become liabilities. People do not become saints or demons; they become adaptively cynical. The result is political instability and moral exhaustion.

3. Systems Humanism as a bridge between ethics and engineering

The phrase "Physics of Democratic Stability" implies constraints and dynamics. Systems Humanism supplies the ethical content within those constraints. It says: stability is not enough. A stable tyranny is stable. What we want is **stable freedom**: a democracy that remains legitimate under stress because it protects dignity and supports flourishing.

Systems Humanism, therefore, functions as a design ethic: it guides institutional engineering toward human ends, and it disciplines moral aspiration with systems realism. Its hallmark is an insistence that reforms must be:

- **dignity-preserving**,
- **incentive-compatible**,
- **resilient to bad actors**,
- **transparent and accountable**,
- **and capable of learning over time**.

II. The Pathologies Systems Humanism Confronts

If Systems Humanism is a repair program, it must name what it repairs. In modern democracies, three pathologies dominate the moral ecology: **extraction**, **humiliation**, and **cognitive capture**. Each is a system phenomenon; each undermines democratic stability.

1. Extraction: when the system rewards taking over creation

Extraction is the conversion of public authority and market power into private rent. It is the capture problem described in Chapter 8. Extraction manifests as:

- monopoly and market concentration,
- political corruption and influence markets,
- regulatory loopholes and tax engineering,
- privatization of public goods without accountability,
- and "pay-to-play" access to opportunity.

Extraction undermines stability by producing inequality and distrust. It teaches citizens that rules are for sale. It teaches elites that politics is a profitable investment. Over time, it transforms democracy into a contest over the extractive machine. Systems Humanism treats extraction not only as unfair but as morally degrading. It makes citizens feel disposable and makes elites morally insulated. It converts civic life into a zero-sum game of domination.

2. Humiliation: when institutions make people feel inferior or unseen

Humiliation is not merely emotional injury. It is political fuel. Societies that systematically humiliate groups—through disrespect, surveillance, arbitrary bureaucracy, or cultural contempt—produce resentment and identity radicalization. Humiliation manifests as:

- punitive welfare systems that treat recipients as suspects,
- unequal treatment in policing and courts,
- status hierarchies that shame certain kinds of work,
- geographic and class contempt ("left behind" narratives),
- and media ecosystems that profit from mocking the other side.

Humiliation damages stability because it turns politics into a battle for recognition. When dignity feels scarce, people seek it through domination. This is how identity politics becomes existential. Systems Humanism insists that **dignity is a stability resource**.

3. Cognitive capture: when narratives become constraints

Cognitive capture is the degradation of shared reality through information disorder and manipulative narrative ecosystems. It includes misinformation, disinformation, and propaganda, but also the subtler phenomenon of incentive-driven attention economies that reward outrage, certainty, and tribal identity.

Cognitive capture damages stability by:

- making accountability impossible (no shared facts),
- turning institutions into contested objects,
- accelerating polarization and delegitimation,
- and making crisis response chaotic.

Systems Humanism treats cognitive capture as a systems problem: the information environment is structurally misaligned with democratic needs. The repair program must therefore include epistemic resilience—not censorship, but verification capacity and smart friction.

III. PRINCIPLES OF SYSTEMS HUMANISM

Systems Humanism becomes practical when it yields design principles. The following principles guide the program.

Principle 1: Dignity is non-negotiable infrastructure

Dignity is not a cultural preference. It is the foundation of legitimacy. Institutions must treat people as ends, not as obstacles. Policies must be delivered in ways that preserve equal standing: respectfully, accessibly, consistently, and transparently.

Principle 2: Security is a stabilizer; catastrophic risk is a democratic toxin

When citizens live near ruin, politics becomes existential. A humane society builds risk floors and automatic stabilizers so ordinary shocks do not become radicalizing catastrophes.

Principle 3: Meaning is a public good; civic participation must be rewarded

A society that provides material goods but no moral purpose will become vulnerable to extremism and nihilism. Institutions must cultivate pathways for contribution: dignified work, civic service, local association, and recognition of care and community building.

Principle 4: Design for bad faith—without becoming authoritarian

Systems must assume strategic exploitation and still preserve freedom. This requires transparent constraints, auditability, and symmetric enforcement. It rejects both naïve trust in norms and authoritarian suppression.

Principle 5: Change payoffs, don't just shame behavior

Moral appeals matter, but durable change occurs when incentives shift. The anti-capture state is Systems Humanism's economic-structural arm: reduce rents, constrain discretion, increase detection, and enforce fairly.

Principle 6: Build epistemic resilience rather than narrative control

Democracies need shared reality. The answer is not a ministry of truth; it is verifiable public data, independent auditing, provenance tools, and information "firebreaks" that reduce viral manipulation.

Principle 7: Legitimacy must be visible, not assumed

Fairness must be legible. Processes must be transparent and understandable. Institutions must demonstrate restraint and consistency to rebuild trust.

Principle 8: Create adaptive institutions that learn under stress

Nonlinear environments require iteration. Policies must have review cycles, sunset clauses where appropriate, and feedback mechanisms that translate results into revisions without crisis.

IV. A Practical Program: Systems Humanism in Institutional Modules

Systems Humanism becomes a repair program when translated into modules that can be implemented. The modules below build on the anti-capture state (Chapter 8) and prosperity architecture (Chapter 9), integrating them into a coherent democratic renewal agenda.

Module A: The Dignity State — redesigning public services for equal standing

Goal: Replace humiliating bureaucracies with dignified, rights-based service delivery.

Key elements:

1. **One-door access to services:** Simplified enrollment and integrated portals that reduce paperwork and stigma.
2. **Procedural justice standards:** Clear timelines, explanations, appeal rights, and respectful communication.
3. **Non-punitive compliance:** Replace suspicion-driven surveillance with verification proportional to risk.
4. **Frontline professionalism:** Invest in training and pay for public-facing workers; treat them as civic ambassadors.
5. **Citizen experience metrics:** Track fairness, respect, and accessibility—not only cost and fraud rates.

Why it matters: Every interaction with the state is a legitimacy event. Dignified services repair trust at the daily level, which is the foundation for national legitimacy.

Module B: The Security Floor — automatic stabilizers for nonlinear economies

Goal: Prevent ordinary shocks from becoming existential crises.

Key elements:

1. **Automatic unemployment and income supports** that expand during downturns.
2. **Healthcare cost risk containment** so illness does not bankrupt families.
3. **Housing stability mechanisms** to prevent mass displacement in shocks.
4. **Portable benefits** for contingent work (health, retirement, paid leave).

5. **Debt shock absorbers**—restructuring pathways for medical and predatory debt.

Why it matters: Security lowers the temperature of politics. People who are not constantly threatened by ruin are less vulnerable to extremist mobilization and scapegoating.

Module C: The Anti-Capture Package — rules that invert extraction incentives

Goal: Make capture unprofitable, visible, and punishable.

Key elements:

1. **Transparent influence pathways:** real-time disclosure of political spending and lobbying.
2. **Procurement firewall:** open contracting, audits, and debarment for collusion.
3. **Revolving-door constraints:** cooling-off periods and conflict-of-interest enforcement.
4. **Beneficial ownership transparency** to prevent hidden money flows.
5. **Competition policy revitalization** to reduce concentrated power.
6. **Independent oversight** with protected budgets and mandatory reporting.

Why it matters: Extraction destabilizes democracy by eroding trust and raising inequality. Anti-capture is both a form of justice and a form of stability engineering.

Module D: Epistemic Infrastructure — verification capacity for a shared reality

Goal: Rebuild the epistemic commons without censorship.

Key elements:

1. **Independent statistical agencies** protected from political interference.

2. **Open data standards** for key public metrics (budgets, enforcement, health, elections).

3. **Auditability tools**: routine election audits, procurement audits, and public dashboards.

4. **Provenance and transparency for political messaging**: disclosure of sponsors, targeting practices, and coordinated campaigns.

5. **Research access and platform accountability**: independent audits of amplification mechanisms and manipulation patterns.

6. **Local journalism support** insulated from partisan control.

Why it matters: Democracy cannot self-correct without shared facts. Epistemic resilience is a core stabilizer and an antidote to cognitive capture.

Module E: The Contribution Society — meaning through civic participation

Goal: Expand pathways for contribution that create shared purpose and bridging ties.

Key elements:

1. **Voluntary civic service corps** (infrastructure, climate resilience, elder care support, tutoring).

2. **Apprenticeships and craft pathways** with real prestige and mobility.

3. **Community-building incentives**: support for civic associations and local institutions.

4. **Recognition systems** that honor care work, community leadership, and civic contribution.

5. **Public works as dignity projects**: infrastructure and rebuilding efforts that employ and unite across groups.

Why it matters: Meaning and contribution create the social glue that reduces polarization. They build "moral capital" that can be spent during crises.

Module F: Smart Friction and Rule Consistency — preventing escalation without paralysis

Goal: Create constraints that block destabilizing tactics while preserving reform.

Key elements:

1. **Transparent emergency power rules** with time limits and oversight.
2. **Anti-hardball procedural reforms** in legislatures and elections to reduce manipulation.
3. **Consistent enforcement standards** to avoid selective punishment perceptions.
4. **Independent referees with redundancy**: inspectors general, auditors, bipartisan election bodies.
5. **Institutional stress tests** and crisis protocols that prioritize legitimacy.

Why it matters: In nonlinear times, small manipulations can trigger cascades. Smart friction reduces the system's gain without freezing it.

Module G: Civic Education for Systems Literacy and Democratic Virtue

Goal: Build citizens capable of living in a complex democracy.

Key elements:

1. **Systems literacy curriculum**: feedback loops, polarization dynamics, media incentives, civic institutions.
2. **Epistemic humility training**: how to evaluate sources, uncertainty, and propaganda.
3. **Deliberation practice**: structured dialogue across differences.
4. **Civic rights and responsibilities education**: law, institutions, and the meaning of equal citizenship.

Why it matters: Institutions alone cannot do everything. A resilient democracy needs citizens who understand the dynamics that threaten it.

V. How Systems Humanism Repairs Democracy: The Stabilizing Mechanisms

The modules above form a program. But why should they work? Systems Humanism claims democratic repair occurs when we shift the system's dynamics. Four mechanisms are especially important.

1. Lower baseline stress reduces contagion amplitude

Security floors and dignity-centered services reduce chronic stress. Lower stress reduces susceptibility to outrage contagion and scapegoating. This dampens polarization and makes tipping points less likely.

2. Changing payoffs reduces the supply of destabilizers

Anti-capture rules reduce the profitability of extraction, which reduces the incentives for corruption, media manipulation, and institutional hardball. When capture is less profitable, fewer actors invest in it.

3. Epistemic infrastructure restores self-correction

Shared reality is democracy's steering mechanism. By increasing verification capacity—audits, transparency, independent data—Systems Humanism restores negative feedback. This makes correction possible without a crisis.

4. Meaning and contribution rebuild bridging ties

Civic service and community institutions create cross-cutting relationships, which reduce affective polarization. When people have real ties across difference, they are less easily manipulated by demonization narratives.

Together these mechanisms rebuild the dampeners from Part II—trust, legitimacy, rule consistency—while reducing the attraction of bad attractors and lowering the probability of tipping points.

VI. Sequencing: How to Implement Systems Humanism Without Triggering Backlash

A repair program must be staged. In fragile environments, reforms can be interpreted as a form of capture. Systems Humanism, therefore, emphasizes sequencing:

1. **Credibility first:** transparency, audits, independent oversight, symmetric ethics enforcement.

2. **Daily dignity next:** redesign public services; improve competence and fairness.

3. **Security floors:** automatic stabilizers that reduce existential anxiety.

4. **Anti-capture structural reforms:** competition policy, procurement firewalls, influence pathway reforms.

5. **Meaning infrastructure:** civic service, local institutions, recognition systems.

6. **Long-horizon transformation:** deeper reforms become feasible once trust and legitimacy rebound.

This sequencing is not an ideological compromise. It is a systems strategy: rebuild dampeners first so reforms are seen as legitimate rather than as domination.

VII. A Practical Philosophy of Hope

Systems Humanism is, ultimately, a theory of hope anchored in mechanism rather than sentiment. It refuses two forms of despair:

- the moral despair that concludes "people are too selfish for democracy,"
- and the technocratic despair that concludes "institutions are too broken to fix."

Instead, it claims that **people behave better when systems make better behavior stable.**

Democracies have recovered before—not because citizens became saints, but because incentives and institutions were redesigned. The path is difficult, but it is not mysterious. Repair occurs when:

- extraction is made costly,
- dignity is made real in daily life,
- shared reality is rebuilt,
- security prevents existential panic,
- and contribution creates meaning beyond faction.

This is the Systems Humanist program: not utopia, but durable improvement; not perfection, but resilience; not naïve unity, but a moral ecology where pluralism can coexist with stability.

Conclusion: Systems Humanism as the Operating System of Democratic Renewal

In nonlinear times, democracy needs more than policy debates. It needs an operating system—a coherent framework that integrates incentives, dignity, meaning, and stability. Systems Humanism offers that framework. It treats flourishing as a systems property, legitimacy as moral infrastructure, and institutional design as the practical craft of making humane behavior rational.

The anti-capture state (Chapter 8) changes payoffs so extraction is less profitable. The prosperity architecture (Chapter 9) stabilizes life through security, dignity, and meaning. Systems Humanism integrates these into a single repair program: a moral ecology engineered for resilience.

A democracy repaired through Systems Humanism is not conflict-free. It is conflict-capable. It can absorb disagreement without rupture because citizens feel protected from ruin, respected as equals, and connected to a shared project. Its institutions are credible because rules are consistent and enforcement is symmetric. Its economy is productive because capture is constrained. Its information ecosystem supports self-correction by strengthening verification. And its civic life is meaningful because contributions are honored and the community is rebuilt.

This is not a romantic vision. It is a practical one. In turbulent times, the republic must be designed for turbulence. Systems Humanism is the program for doing so—one that treats human dignity not as ornament, but as the central stabilizer of democratic life.

In the next chapter, we will turn from the program to its mechanics of implementation: how to build *adaptive institutions* that can learn under stress, revise policies without legitimacy collapse, and maintain the republic's safe operating space as conditions evolve.

Part IV

Implementation and the Politics of Repair

Parts I–III built a diagnosis and a design language for democratic stability under nonlinear conditions. We treated democracy not as a settled equilibrium but as a complex adaptive system—one whose stability depends on dampeners (trust, legitimacy, rule consistency), whose failures can harden into bad attractors (corruption, capture, delegitimation), and whose proximity to critical thresholds can turn small shocks into regime shifts. We then moved from diagnosis to blueprint: the anti-capture state that changes payoffs, a prosperity architecture that anchors security, dignity, and meaning, and Systems Humanism as the integrative operating system for human flourishing and democratic repair.

Part IV begins where most reform books quietly end: **implementation**. The challenge here is not whether we can write a coherent design. The challenge is whether we can *install* it inside a real political system—one already polarized, information-disordered, unequal, and saturated with strategic actors who will exploit procedural vulnerabilities. This part of the book argues that in nonlinear times, implementation is not a mere administrative phase after ideas. Implementation is the main battlefield. It is where legitimacy is won or lost, where coalitions form or fracture, and where the system either deepens its stabilizing basin or slides back into the same extractive attractors that necessitated repair.

A central premise of this part is therefore simple: **democratic repair is an implementation problem under adversarial conditions.** The "politics of repair" is the politics of sequencing, constraint design, credibility-building, coalition maintenance, and learning under stress. It is about changing payoffs and narratives simultaneously, without tipping the system into backlash, paralysis, or a delegitimation spiral.

In linear times, implementation is often treated as a technical exercise: pass the law, write the regulations, hire the staff, roll out the program. In nonlinear times, implementation is a *dynamic intervention* in a sensitive system. Every reform attempt sends signals. Every enforcement action is interpreted through factional lenses. Every administrative error becomes fuel for narrative warfare. Every policy that touches perceived identity or status can be weaponized, amplified, and converted into regime-level conflict. The republic is not a passive object being repaired; it is a living system that responds, resists, adapts, and sometimes retaliates.

This introduction sets the frame for Part IV by answering four questions:

1. **Why implementation becomes the decisive arena in nonlinear times**
2. **Why repairs fail even when the designs are sound**
3. **What it means to "engineer legitimacy" without propaganda**
4. **How to build repair as a staged, learning process rather than a single legislative event**

It closes by previewing the five chapters of Part IV—each focused on a core implementation challenge: sequencing, coalitions, legitimacy engineering, stress testing, and measurement.

1. The Shift from Policy Arguments to System Interventions

The ordinary language of reform is policy language: healthcare policy, tax policy, election policy, education policy. That language is necessary, but it is incomplete. In a nonlinear democracy, reforms do not operate only through their substantive content. They operate through **feedback effects**: on trust, perceived fairness, threat perception, elite incentives, and narrative ecosystems.

Consider two reforms with identical policy content but different implementation dynamics. One is rolled out transparently, with clear rules, consistent enforcement, and visible auditability; the other is rolled out through opaque discretion, inconsistent enforcement, and improvisational messaging. The first tends to increase trust, even among skeptics, because it demonstrates rule consistency; the second tends to decrease trust, even among supporters, because it confirms suspicions. In other words, implementation is not downstream of legitimacy. **Implementation is a primary producer of legitimacy.**

This is why Part IV treats reforms as **system interventions** rather than isolated policies. System interventions must be evaluated not only by whether they are morally desirable or economically efficient, but by whether they strengthen or weaken the stabilizing dampeners that keep democracy in its safe operating space.

Part II emphasized that democracies fail when negative feedback mechanisms weaken, and positive feedback loops dominate. Implementation is the arena where this balance is decided. Poor implementation can turn good reforms into destabilizers. Competent implementation can turn contested reforms into stabilizers by demonstrating fairness and restraint. The politics of repair is therefore the politics of controlling gain, reducing cascade pathways, and increasing the visibility of procedural justice.

2. The Paradox of Repair: Why the Most Necessary Reforms Are the Hardest to Legitimate

Democratic repair faces a paradox that becomes sharper as systems become more fragile:

- The reforms that are most necessary are often those that threaten concentrated interests (anti-capture rules, competition policy, transparency, ethics enforcement, procurement reform).
- But those are precisely the reforms that generate intense resistance, narrative warfare, and strategic sabotage.
- In a low-trust environment, that resistance can be reframed as proof that reform itself is illegitimate, either as "tyranny," "persecution," "politicization," or "corruption by another name."

In other words, repair is undermined by the very dynamics it must reverse. Capture fights anti-capture. Information disorder fights epistemic resilience.

Patronage fights rule consistency. Humiliation politics fights dignity architecture. The system behaves like an organism defending an infection because the infection has rewired its immune response.

This is one reason corruption becomes a stable attractor (Chapter 6): it produces not just material rents but **cognitive and institutional defenses**—narratives, networks, and procedural sabotage that protect extraction. The anti-capture state (Chapter 8) is therefore not merely a moral aspiration; it is a fight against an adaptive opponent.

This is also why the prosperity architecture (Chapter 9) cannot be treated solely as "social policy." Insecure societies are easier to manipulate. When citizens live near ruin, they are more susceptible to threat narratives and more willing to accept exceptional measures. Thus, security, dignity, and meaning are not only humane; they are stabilizers that make anti-capture politics possible. An anxious, humiliated, meaning-starved society is the ideal terrain for capture: citizens are fragmented, exhausted, and more easily divided.

Systems Humanism (Chapter 10) insists that flourishing is emergent. Part IV extends that logic: **repair is emergent, too.** It requires aligning incentives, institutions, and narratives so that reform becomes self-reinforcing rather than self-defeating.

3. Legitimacy Is Not a Mood; It Is a Measurable, Engineered Condition

One of the most damaging errors in modern governance is to treat legitimacy as public relations: if people distrust institutions, institutions should "communicate better." This is a half-truth that becomes lethal in nonlinear times. Better communication cannot substitute for consistent enforcement, visible fairness, and competent delivery. When messaging tries to substitute for reality, it accelerates cynicism and deepens distrust.

Legitimacy is best understood as an engineered condition produced by three things:

1. **Procedural integrity**: rules are stable, known, and applied consistently.

2. **Visible fairness**: people can *see* that decisions are made through accountable processes.

3. **Competent performance**: institutions can deliver basic governance without improvisational chaos.

Part IV uses a phrase that may sound cold but is morally urgent: **legitimacy engineering**. This does not mean manufacturing consent. It means building systems in which consent is rational because citizens can observe fairness and reliability. It means designing institutions that generate trust as a byproduct of repeatable evidence.

In Part II, we described dampeners: trust, legitimacy, and rule consistency. These are not abstract ideals floating above society. They are the outputs of daily encounters with governance. If the state appears arbitrary, people behave defensively. If the state appears captured, people withdraw. If enforcement appears selective, people escalate. The politics of repair must therefore focus on what citizens experience:

- Do rules apply to the powerful as well as the ordinary?
- Are decisions explainable in plain language?
- Can people predict how institutions will behave?
- When mistakes occur, are they acknowledged and corrected?
- Are there credible channels to challenge decisions without humiliation?

These are legitimacy questions. They are also design questions.

A crucial implication is that in **low-trust environments, legitimacy must be front-loaded into the implementation itself.** Reforms must be structured so their fairness is legible even to skeptics. That means clear standards, constrained discretion, independent audits, public dashboards, and symmetric enforcement. Without these, even good reforms become narrative fuel for delegitimation and political fracture.

4. Implementation in Nonlinear Environments: The Five Failure Modes

Reforms fail in nonlinear times not only because they are opposed, but because they are implemented in ways that trigger predictable failure modes. Part IV will return to these repeatedly. They form the hazard map for democratic repair.

Failure Mode 1: Backlash cascades

A reform triggers identity threat, status resentment, or economic fear. These emotions are amplified by information ecosystems and then converted into political mobilization. The mobilization pressures institutions to retreat, overreact, or weaponize enforcement, each of which deepens polarization. The reform becomes a trigger event rather than a stabilizer.

Failure Mode 2: Selective enforcement and the persecution narrative

Anti-corruption or accountability measures are interpreted as factional targeting, especially when enforcement patterns are uneven or opaque. The result is delegitimation of enforcement institutions and increased hardball retaliation. This is how a necessary anti-capture agenda can accidentally generate a legitimacy crisis.

Failure Mode 3: Administrative incompetence as legitimacy sabotage

A reform is substantively sound but operationally chaotic: delays, errors, unclear rules, contradictory guidance. In a high-trust society, such errors are corrected. In a low-trust society, errors are interpreted as proof of bad faith or incompetence. Competence is not technocratic vanity; it is legitimacy infrastructure.

Failure Mode 4: Capture through complexity

A reform is implemented with enough complexity and discretion that concentrated interests can exploit loopholes, reshape rule-making, or create compliance burdens that exclude smaller competitors and citizens. The reform inadvertently deepens capture.

Failure Mode 5: Reform without learning

A reform is implemented as a one-time legislative victory rather than a learning system. When it produces problems (as all complex interventions do), the system cannot revise it without a crisis. The reform becomes brittle: an object of permanent warfare rather than adaptive governance.

Part IV is designed to address these failure modes. It treats repair as a practice: staged, monitored, audited, iterated, and shielded by legitimacy safeguards.

5. The Central Strategy: Keystone Reforms, Sequencing, and the "Minimum Viable Legitimacy" Threshold

In complex systems, not all interventions are equal. Some are **keystone** interventions—small changes that disproportionately alter the system's dynamics. In democratic repair, keystone reforms are those that quickly increase rule consistency and credibility, because credibility changes behavior. When citizens and elites believe enforcement is real and rules are stable, a cascade of adaptations follows: less cheating, less hardball, less cynicism, more compliance, and more willingness to invest in long-horizon cooperation.

But there is a sequencing problem: reforms must be staged so they do not appear as domination or capture. In fragile environments, the first goal is not maximal policy transformation. The first goal is to cross a threshold we can call **minimum viable legitimacy**: the minimum level of trust and procedural credibility necessary for major reforms to be interpreted as lawful rather than factional.

Minimum viable legitimacy is not warm feelings. It is measurable behavior:

- willingness to accept election outcomes as binding,
- willingness to comply with laws even when disliked,
- belief that courts and enforcement institutions are not purely partisan weapons,
- and belief that public procedures are not merely theater.

Part IV argues that repair should begin by building credibility: transparency, audits, constrained discretion, consistent enforcement, and competence upgrades. Only after credibility rises should the system attempt deeper redistributive or structurally disruptive reforms, because without credibility, those reforms will be interpreted through the lens of capture and will trigger backlash cascades.

This is not an argument for timid reform. It is an argument for **strategic reform under nonlinear conditions**. The order of operations matters because it determines whether reforms stabilize or polarize.

6. Repair as Coalition Engineering in a Polarized Polity

Implementation is inseparable from coalition strategy. Laws do not implement themselves; institutions do not defend themselves; reforms do not legitimate themselves. Coalitions—electoral, legislative, and civic—provide the political oxygen repair needs.

Yet nonlinear times punish coalition-building. Attention economies reward maximalism. Primary dynamics reward purity. Social media incentives reward humiliation and dunking rather than bargaining. Political entrepreneurs gain by escalating conflict. In this environment, coalition-building must be designed, not assumed.

Part IV treats coalitions as stability devices. A reform coalition is not merely a set of votes; it is a narrative structure and an alignment of incentives. The coalition must satisfy three conditions:

1. **Shared benefit**: reforms must produce visible, broadly distributed gains.
2. **Dignity framing**: reforms must avoid humiliating opponents or implying cultural contempt.
3. **Procedural fairness**: reforms must be implemented in ways that skeptics can evaluate as legitimate.

The prosperity architecture in Chapter 9 is crucial here. Broad-based security and dignity are not only moral goals; they create the social foundation for coalition politics. When citizens are less desperate and less humiliated, they are more capable of cross-cutting cooperation. When they are anxious and status-threatened, coalitions fracture into zero-sum camps.

Part IV will therefore treat coalition-building as a systems intervention: designing packages that reduce existential stakes, create multiple entry points for support, and minimize humiliation dynamics.

7. THE ETHICS OF REPAIR: RESTRAINT, SYMMETRY, AND THE DANGER OF "REPAIR AUTHORITARIANISM"

A repair agenda is vulnerable to a seductive mistake: believing that the ends justify the means. When democracies are fragile, reformers may be tempted to centralize power, bypass procedures, or weaponize institutions "for the greater good." But the book's physics framework warns against this: legitimacy is the binding constraint. A democracy cannot restore itself by destroying the procedural foundation that makes it democratic.

Thus, Part IV insists on three ethical constraints that are also stability constraints:

- **Restraint**: winners must avoid maximal entrenchment even when tempted.
- **Symmetry**: enforcement must apply across factions and status levels.
- **Procedural transparency**: rule changes must follow legitimate pathways and be auditable.

These constraints are hard to maintain in polarized environments. But abandoning them is how repair becomes its opposite: **repair authoritarianism**, where anti-corruption rhetoric becomes purge logic, where disinformation policy becomes censorship, and where crisis governance becomes permanent emergency. That is merely a different bad attractor.

Systems Humanism provides the moral discipline here: flourishing requires stable freedom, not stable domination. The politics of repair must therefore be a politics of constraint as much as a politics of change.

8. LEARNING UNDER STRESS: BUILDING REPAIR AS AN ADAPTIVE PROCESS

Nonlinear times demand institutions that can learn. Part IV treats repair as iterative. Policies should have review mechanisms, measurable indicators, and revision pathways that do not require regime-level conflict. Otherwise, reforms become brittle and politicized: any failure becomes proof that "the whole thing is illegitimate," and the system oscillates between overreach and repeal.

Adaptive repair requires:

- **clear goals** (what problem is this intervention solving?),
- **transparent metrics** (how will we know if it works?),
- **feedback loops** (how will results change practice?),
- **stress tests** (how will it behave under crisis?),
- and **revision pathways** (how can we adjust without implying failure or betrayal?).

This is not technocracy. It is democratic humility, an acknowledgment that complex systems cannot be perfectly engineered in advance. The goal is to create reforms that improve over time rather than collapse under their first confrontation with reality.

9. The Implementation Landscape: Why Today's Environment Magnifies Risk

Part IV also confronts a defining feature of the current era: **implementation occurs in a hostile media and narrative environment**. Reform is implemented in real time under surveillance by factions, platforms, and opportunists who benefit from outrage. That means even small administrative errors can turn into national scandals. It also means that reform must anticipate sabotage—not only from formal opponents but from the incentive structure of attention itself.

This has several implications:

- **Legibility is survival**: opaque processes invite conspiratorial interpretation.
- **Speed matters, but not at the cost of procedural integrity**: delays breed cynicism; reckless speed breeds chaos.
- **Frontline competence is politics**: a poorly run benefits system or election administration office can destabilize national legitimacy.
- **Narratives must be met with verifiable evidence**: the antidote to rumor is not insult; it is auditability.

Part IV will emphasize that democratic repair requires not only laws and programs but **also institutional performance capacity to deliver services and to operate** reliably in the public eye.

10. A PREVIEW OF PART IV'S FIVE CHAPTERS

With these premises in mind, Part IV is organized as a practical pathway from blueprint to construction. The chapters correspond to the core implementation tasks.

Chapter 11 — Sequencing the Repair: Keystone Reforms and the Order of Operations

This chapter develops a staged strategy: credibility first, then capability, then bigger structural change. It identifies keystone reforms that quickly raise rule consistency and public trust—transparency, auditing, procurement reform, ethics enforcement, and election administration integrity—so that later reforms can be seen as legitimate rather than as factional capture. It also introduces the idea of minimum viable legitimacy and explains why reforms attempted below that threshold often backfire.

Chapter 12 — Coalitions for Nonlinear Times: Bargaining, Bridging, and the New Majority

Repair requires durable coalitions that survive inevitable setbacks. This chapter describes coalition design in a polarized environment: how to structure reforms to create shared wins; how to avoid humiliation framing; how to build geographic and cross-class alliances; and how to make mutually reinforcing anti-capture and prosperity policies. It treats coalition-building as a stability device rather than just electoral arithmetic.

Chapter 13 — Legitimacy Engineering: Communication, Transparency, and Procedural Fairness at Scale

This chapter focuses on the operational production of legitimacy. It offers a blueprint for making fairness visible: public dashboards, routine audits, plain-language explanations, oversight independence, and consistent standards. It also addresses a central danger: the temptation to replace legitimacy with messaging. The chapter argues for legitimacy as evidence, not performance.

Chapter 14 — Stress Tests and Crisis Protocols: Governing Shocks Without Regime Shifts

Democracies must be prepared to absorb shocks without flipping regimes. This chapter proposes democratic stress testing: contested elections, disinformation waves, corruption exposure, economic shocks, and emergency power triggers. It outlines crisis protocols designed to preserve legitimacy: time-limited emergency powers, independent oversight, transparent reporting, and after-action reviews that become institutional learning rather than blame theater.

Chapter 15 — Measuring What Matters: A Democratic Stability Scorecard and the Flourishing Index

Repair needs measurement—not as a technocratic fetish, but to detect drift toward tipping points and bad attractors. This chapter operationalizes the book's variables: trust, legitimacy, rule consistency, capture risk and rent extraction, information integrity, and the prosperity architecture pillars (security, dignity, meaning). It proposes a scorecard and early warning indicators to guide policymakers and civic actors—and to make accountability possible without relying on rumors.

11. The Purpose of Part IV: Making Democratic Repair Credible

The ultimate purpose of Part IV is to answer a question that haunts every serious reform effort: **How do we make repair credible in a society that distrusts repair?** How do we reform institutions without triggering legitimacy collapse? How do we constrain capture without producing persecution narratives? How do we build prosperity without producing backlash cascades? How do we improve information integrity without becoming censorial? How do we reduce polarization without moralizing contempt?

There is no single answer. But there is a strategy: treat repair as a systems intervention, stage it through keystone reforms that rebuild credibility, design coalitions around dignity and shared benefit, engineer legitimacy through transparency and rule consistency, stress test the system for shocks, and measure what matters so drift is detected early rather than discovered in crisis.

Part IV, therefore, shifts the tone from blueprint to craft. It is the part of the book where ideals meet the realities of implementation, where Systems Humanism must prove it is not only a philosophy but also a workable program. The stakes are not abstract. In nonlinear times, democracies can drift toward critical thresholds without recognizing it, until a small shock triggers a regime shift. Implementation is how we widen the safe operating space before that happens.

If Parts I–III argued that democratic stability is the product of dampeners, incentive structures, and moral ecology, Part IV argues something equally consequential: **democratic repair is possible, but only if it is designed as a staged, legitimacy-preserving, learning process—one that assumes adversarial conditions and still refuses to abandon democratic constraint.** That is the politics of repair. That is the work ahead.

Chapter 11

Sequencing the Repair: Keystone Reforms and the Order of Operations

Democratic repair fails more often because of bad sequencing than because of bad ideas. In fragile systems, the order in which reforms are introduced can determine whether the same policy is interpreted as lawful improvement or factional domination, whether enforcement is seen as accountability or persecution, whether administrative mistakes are treated as correctable errors or proof that "the system is rigged," and whether reform momentum compounds into trust—or collapses into backlash.

In linear models of governance, sequencing is treated as a convenience: you pass the law, then you implement it, then you adjust. In nonlinear democracies, sequencing is a stability strategy. The system is sensitive. Incentives are adversarial. Information is disordered. Legitimacy is contested. Under those conditions, the reform agenda is not simply a list of "good things to do." It is a **dynamical intervention** in a complex adaptive system. The sequence you choose changes the feedback loops you activate. It changes who mobilizes, how narratives form, and whether the republic's dampeners—trust, legitimacy, and rule consistency—thicken or thin.

This chapter argues for a principle that should sit at the center of reform politics in nonlinear times:

> **Do not begin with the most morally maximal reform. Begin with reforms that quickly raise system credibility and rule consistency, because credibility changes behavior—then use that credibility to accomplish bigger structural change.**

That is not a call for timidity. It is a call for systems realism. In fragile democracies, reforms can be "correct" in substance and still fail catastrophically in dynamics. The order of operations matters because legitimacy is the binding constraint. If legitimacy collapses, even the best reforms become brittle, politicized, and reversible. If legitimacy strengthens, even contested reforms can become stable.

This chapter develops a practical sequencing framework built around three ideas:

1. **Minimum Viable Legitimacy (MVL):** the threshold of procedural credibility needed for major reforms to be interpreted as lawful rather than factional.

2. **Keystone Reforms:** high-leverage interventions that quickly increase rule consistency, auditability, and public confidence.

3. **The Repair Ladder:** a staged order of operations that moves from credibility → capacity → security and dignity → anti-capture restructuring → meaning and long-horizon transformation.

We will also address the risks—backlash cascades, persecution narratives, administrative sabotage—and the techniques that prevent sequencing from becoming mere political slogans: implementation design, transparency scaffolding, and learning loops.

1. Why Is Sequencing the Core Problem in Nonlinear Reform

Parts II and III showed how democratic systems drift into fragility: capture deepens inequality, inequality increases existential stakes, information disorder amplifies polarization, rule consistency erodes, and small shocks become regime shifts. Part IV begins with a simple extension of that logic: **repair must be staged because the system cannot absorb maximal interventions while its dampeners are degraded.**

In stable democracies, citizens tend to interpret reform efforts in good faith and tolerate imperfection. In fragile democracies, reforms are interpreted through the lens of threat and suspicion. The same proposal—say, ethics enforcement or election administration reform—can be read as a neutral integrity measure by one camp and as a plot by the other. Implementation errors become "evidence" of conspiracy. Enforcement becomes "weaponization." Reforms intended to reduce capture can be attacked as attempts to capture.

This is the nonlinearity of legitimacy: in low-trust conditions, the signal-to-noise ratio collapses. The system becomes high-gain. Small procedural deviations trigger disproportionate outrage. Narrative entrepreneurs exploit ambiguity. And because modern attention systems reward escalation, the loudest interpretation spreads fastest.

Sequencing is the way you lower the system's gain before you attempt deep structural moves. In engineering terms, you stabilize the platform before you change the payload. In political terms, you rebuild the credibility of rules and referees so that the next reforms are received as governance rather than conquest.

2. Minimum Viable Legitimacy: The Threshold Without Which Reform Backfires

The temptation in crisis is to move fast and move big. The moral pressure is intense: inequality is unjust, capture is intolerable, disinformation is corrosive, and institutions are failing. But crisis intensity is precisely what makes sequencing vital. When legitimacy is weak, maximal moves are interpreted as domination. The system responds not with cooperation but with escalation.

To navigate that reality, we introduce **Minimum Viable Legitimacy (MVL)** the threshold of procedural credibility required for a democracy to implement major reforms without triggering cascading destabilization.

MVL is not popularity. It is not whether people like the government. It is whether enough people believe the system's procedures are binding—even when they lose. MVL is observable in behaviors:

- **Outcome acceptance:** losing factions accept election outcomes as legitimate enough to comply.

- **Institutional respect:** courts, election officials, auditors, and investigators are seen as constrained by rules rather than operating as partisan weapons.
- **Compliance baseline:** citizens comply with laws and taxation at levels consistent with functional governance.
- **Correctability:** mistakes are interpreted as correctable, not as proof of bad faith.
- **Non-violence norms:** political conflict remains largely nonviolent; rhetoric may be hot, but the baseline rejects coercion.

Below MVL, reform efforts trigger failure modes:

- transparency becomes "surveillance,"
- enforcement becomes "persecution,"
- competence errors become "fraud,"
- and any redistributive or structural change becomes "confiscation" or "capture."

Above MVL, the same reforms can be contested but still processed through institutions.

Therefore, the first sequencing aim is not "pass everything we want." It is: **cross MVL by rebuilding rule consistency, auditability, and credible fairness.** Once MVL rises, the democracy's capacity for ambitious reform expands dramatically—because the system can process conflict without flipping regimes.

3. Keystone Reforms: The Interventions That Shift Dynamics Early

In ecological systems, a keystone species disproportionately shapes the environment. In institutional systems, a **keystone reform** is an intervention that produces outsized stability gains by strengthening dampeners and reducing early cascade pathways.

A keystone reform has five characteristics:

1. **High visibility of fairness:** citizens can *see* the integrity effect.
2. **Symmetry:** it applies across factions and status groups.

3. **Auditability:** it increases evidence and reduces rumor space.
4. **Low identity threat:** it does not immediately trigger existential cultural fear.
5. **Fast credibility returns:** it produces early proof that rules bind.

Keystone reforms are not necessarily small. They can be significant. But they are chosen for their stabilizing effects, not for ideological satisfaction.

Examples of keystone reforms

A. Election administration integrity (credibility keystone)

- Transparent procedures, routine audits, clear chain-of-custody rules, bipartisan oversight bodies with public reporting.

Why keystone? Because election legitimacy is the principal dampener. When elections are widely contested, everything else becomes factional warfare.

B. Procurement and contracting transparency (anti-capture keystone)

- Open contracting data, published evaluation criteria, routine audits, and debarment for fraud/collusion.

Why keystone? Because it demonstrates "the state is not for sale" in the most concrete, legible way—where money flows.

C. Independent oversight with protected capacity (enforcement keystone)

- Empowered inspectors general, independent audit agencies, and whistleblower protections.

Why keystone? Because credible oversight increases detection probability and deters corruption while appearing procedurally constrained.

D. Conflict-of-interest rules and disclosure (trust keystone)

- Clear recusal rules, financial disclosure, revolving-door constraints, gift bans.

Why keystone? Because it targets elite impunity and is relatively legible to the public.

E. Service competence upgrades (legitimacy keystone)

- Simplify benefits delivery, reduce delays, improve frontline service; publish performance metrics.

Why keystone? Because competence is experienced daily, it produces trust at the micro-level.

Notice: these keystone reforms emphasize **credibility and fairness** rather than maximal redistribution. That does not mean redistribution is unimportant; it means that without credibility, distribution fights become existential and destabilizing. Sequencing makes ambitious justice possible by building the legitimacy platform first.

4. THE REPAIR LADDER: AN ORDER OF OPERATIONS FOR NONLINEAR DEMOCRACIES

Sequencing is not a single timeline. Different societies have different constraints. But a general order of operations emerges from the dynamics described in Parts II–III. We can frame it as a **Repair Ladder** with five stages. Each stage unlocks the next by raising MVL and lowering system sensitivity.

Stage 1: Credibility first — rebuild the referees and rule consistency

Goal: Cross MVL by making fairness visible and enforcement symmetric.

Core moves:

- routine election audits and transparent administration
- empowered independent oversight (IGs, auditors)
- procurement transparency and anti-collusion enforcement
- conflict-of-interest and disclosure rules
- public dashboards for key integrity and performance metrics

Logic: This stage reduces the space for rumors and increases predictable constraints. It signals that winners will be bound by rules, too.

Stage 2: Capacity next — competence as legitimacy infrastructure

Goal: Improve the state's ability to deliver reliably.

Core moves:

- modernize benefits and service delivery
- improve administrative professionalism and frontline training
- streamline regulatory procedures for clarity and predictability
- invest in data systems that allow real-time performance monitoring

Logic: Competence reduces cynicism. In fragile environments, implementation errors are political accelerants. Fixing capacity reduces future backlash risk.

Stage 3: Security and dignity floors — reduce existential stakes and humiliation dynamics

Goal: Lower baseline stress and decrease susceptibility to threat narratives.

Core moves:

- automatic stabilizers (unemployment/income supports)
- housing stability measures
- healthcare cost containment
- procedural dignity reforms in welfare and policing interfaces
- portable benefits and wage stability mechanisms

Logic: Security and dignity are not "extras." They reduce the emotional temperature that fuels polarization and manipulation.

Stage 4: Structural anti-capture — change payoffs at scale

Goal: Reduce rent extraction and the profitability of capture.

Core moves:

- campaign finance transparency and influence pathway constraints
- revolving-door restrictions and lobbying transparency
- robust antitrust and competition policy
- procurement firewall expansion
- beneficial ownership transparency and anti-money laundering nodes

Logic: Once MVL is higher and the state is more competent, deep structural reforms are harder to dismiss as factional grabs and easier to implement effectively.

Stage 5: Meaning and long-horizon flourishing — deepen the moral ecology

Goal: Build civic "immune function" against future instability.

Core moves:

- civic infrastructure and associational life
- voluntary national service/contribution pathways
- educational reforms for systems literacy and civic competence
- local journalism and epistemic commons investments
- long-horizon climate and infrastructure projects as dignity projects

Logic: This stage strengthens bridging ties, builds shared purpose, and creates long-run resilience so the system doesn't drift back toward fragility.

The Repair Ladder is not a rigid script. Sometimes stages overlap. Sometimes crises force partial jumps. But the principle holds: **credibility and competence are preconditions for ambitious transformation.** The fastest way to fail is to invert the ladder—attempting maximal structural change before establishing legitimacy scaffolding.

5. Sequencing Is Also About Narrative Timing: Reforms Must Become Legible Wins

Reforms succeed when they create visible improvements that ordinary people can recognize as fairness. In nonlinear times, the public's interpretive environment is saturated with noise. That makes *legibility* decisive. Keystones are powerful because they are legible: audits, transparency portals, debarments, conflict-of-interest enforcement, and improved service delivery are easier for citizens to evaluate than abstract macro reforms.

This does not mean democratic repair is a marketing project. It means it must produce verifiable evidence. The sequencing strategy, therefore, includes an evidence logic:

- Start with reforms that produce **publicly observable proof** that rules bind.
- Use that proof to weaken cynicism and delegitimation narratives.

- Then introduce deeper reforms that would otherwise be interpreted as partisan conquest.

The politics of repair depends on this: when reforms do not produce early, legible benefits, the coalition fractures and opponents gain narrative dominance. Early wins are not cosmetic; they are stabilizers.

6. The "Credible Restraint" Principle: Reform Must Not Look Like Entrenchment

One of the hardest truths in polarized democracies is that even good reforms can look like entrenchment if implemented without restraint. The first stages of repair must therefore include **credible restraint** by winners:

- avoid procedural hardball that maximizes advantage
- avoid humiliating rhetoric toward opponents
- submit reforms to transparent processes
- accept independent audits and oversight—even when inconvenient
- enforce ethics rules against one's own side

Why does restraint matter so much? Because repair is always vulnerable to the suspicion that it is really capture-by-other-means. In a low-trust society, the only way to reduce that suspicion is to behave in ways that are costly for one's own faction but beneficial for the system—symmetry, transparency, and enforceable constraints. This is legitimacy engineering at its most concrete.

Credible restraint is not naïve virtue. It is strategic in nonlinear systems. It prevents backlash cascades and raises MVL by proving that procedures bind even when power is available.

7. Avoiding the Four Classic Sequencing Disasters

Sequencing errors tend to recur. Here are four classic disasters and how the Repair Ladder prevents them.

Disaster 1: Maximal redistribution before credibility

When legitimacy is low, redistribution is interpreted as confiscation or favoritism, especially if opponents believe institutions are captured. This triggers backlash and may strengthen capture by encouraging elites to invest even more in influence warfare.

Fix: Build credibility by establishing the keystones of credibility first; then implement redistribution as part of a security-and-dignity architecture with transparent standards and broad eligibility.

Disaster 2: Enforcement without symmetry

Anti-corruption campaigns perceived as selective become persecution narratives, delegitimizing oversight and increasing retaliation.

Fix: Front-load symmetric ethics rules, independent oversight, transparent enforcement criteria, and public reporting—before high-profile prosecutions.

Disaster 3: Technocratic complexity without legibility

Complex reforms create loopholes and opacity that enable capture. They also create public confusion that opponents weaponize.

Fix: Prioritize auditability, simplicity where possible, and public dashboards. Build reforms that citizens can verify.

Disaster 4: Policy without capacity

Even good reforms fail when agencies cannot implement them. Failure becomes evidence of incompetence and fuels distrust.

Fix: Stage 2 capacity upgrades are not optional. Invest in administrative competence early, especially in frontline services.

8. A Practical Sequencing Method: The Keystone Matrix

To operationalize sequencing, reformers can use a simple tool: a Keystone Matrix that scores candidate reforms along four dimensions:

1. **Legitimacy gain:** Does it increase trust, fairness visibility, and rule consistency quickly?
2. **Implementation risk:** Can it be executed competently with existing capacity?

3. **Backlash potential:** Does it trigger identity threat or existential framing?

4. **Capture resistance:** Is it robust to strategic exploitation and loophole gaming?

High-priority early reforms score high on legitimacy gain and capture resistance, and moderate-to-low on backlash and implementation risk.

Here is the sequencing logic:

- **Early stage:** high legitimacy gain + low backlash + high auditability
- **Mid stage:** capacity-building + security/dignity floors with broad, non-stigmatizing design
- **Later stage:** high-conflict structural reforms once MVL is higher and coalitions are sturdier

This matrix does not choose values for a society. It determines the order in which values can be stabilized.

9. THE "REPAIR STACK": DEPENDENCIES THAT MUST BE BUILT IN ORDER

Many reforms fail because they ignore hidden dependencies. The Repair Ladder can be viewed as a stack with prerequisites:

Layer 1: Referees

- election integrity mechanisms
- independent audit bodies
- clear procedural standards

Without referees, every conflict becomes legitimacy warfare.

Layer 2: Auditability

- open contracting
- public data
- conflict-of-interest disclosure

Without auditability, rumor dominates, and enforcement becomes politicized.

Layer 3: Capacity

- professionalized administration
- digital infrastructure and service delivery competence

Without capacity, reforms become chaotic and delegitimizing.

Layer 4: Security and dignity

- automatic stabilizers
- respectful public service design

Without security and dignity, politics remains existential and easily manipulated.

Layer 5: Structural change

- anti-capture payoffs, antitrust, influence market reforms

Without earlier layers, structural change looks like domination and provokes backlash.

Layer 6: Meaning and civic immune function

- civic institutions, contribution pathways, systems literacy

Without meaning, long-run repair decays into cynicism and fragmentation.

A society can attempt Layer 5 without Layers 1–3, but it tends to yield brittle, reversible outcomes. The order of operations is not a moral hierarchy; it is a system dependency.

10. Windows of Opportunity: Shocks as Moments of Redesign (and the Ethics of Restraint)

Nonlinear systems often undergo abrupt changes at critical moments. Crises can open "windows" for reform that would otherwise be impossible. But crises are also moments when legitimacy is fragile, and fear is high—precisely when repair can slip into emergency authoritarianism.

Sequencing in crisis requires two disciplines:

1. **Use the window to install keystones and guardrails**, not to entrench factions.

2. **Prioritize reforms that increase auditability and constrain discretion**, so crisis governance does not become the new normal.

Crisis windows are best used to implement reforms that improve **future crisis handling**: transparent emergency power constraints, independent oversight, routine audits, and competence upgrades. These are stability-enhancing even when politics is heated.

The ethical risk is the "shock doctrine" temptation: using a crisis to push through maximal agendas without deliberation. In nonlinear times, that can trigger backlash cascades and delegitimation spirals—making the crisis worse and deepening polarization. A Systems Humanist approach insists: crisis is for stabilizing the platform, not for converting temporary power into permanent dominance.

11. Composite Vignettes: How Sequencing Succeeds or Fails

To make sequencing concrete, consider two composite scenarios—stylized, but realistic.

Vignette A: The "Integrity First" pathway

A newly elected government inherits a low-trust environment with contested election narratives. Instead of immediately launching aggressive prosecutions and maximal reforms, it begins with:

- bipartisan election administration audits and transparent reporting
- procurement transparency portals with routine audits
- conflict of interest rules applied to its own officials first
- strengthened inspectors general with protected budgets
- public service delivery upgrades (benefits, licensing, permits) with visible metrics

Opposition leaders still criticize, but the reforms are hard to dismiss as partisan because they constrain everyone and produce public evidence. Within a year, a modest rise in MVL occurs: fewer citizens believe the system is purely rigged; compliance improves; some opponents cooperate because refusing looks unreasonable.

Only then does the government move to deeper reforms: influence market constraints, antitrust actions, and broader security floors. The coalition holds because early wins created credibility and reduced fear.

The lesson: **repair began with legitimacy-producing constraints and competence, not with punishment and maximalism.**

Vignette B: The "Maximal First" failure

A different government enters office in a similarly low-trust environment, but chooses immediate maximal confrontation. It launches aggressive investigations perceived as targeting opponents, proposes sweeping structural reforms with complex rules, and pushes them through quickly. Implementation is chaotic; agencies lack capacity; early errors occur; opponents amplify them as proof of conspiracy. Supporters cheer, opponents radicalize, and moderates recoil. The reforms become the new axis of polarization. Courts are attacked. Agencies are delegitimized. The system experiences protests, counter-protests, and legislative paralysis.

Even where reforms were substantively justified, the sequence produced a backlash cascade. The government may still win short-term battles, but MVL declines, and the system becomes more brittle. A later shock—such as an economic downturn or a foreign crisis—pushes the system toward a regime shift.

The lesson: **reform can be correct in content but catastrophic in dynamics if sequencing ignores the prerequisites of legitimacy.**

12. Sequencing and Coalition Durability: How to Keep Repair from Collapsing Midstream

Sequencing is also coalition management. A repair agenda is long. Coalitions weaken over time, especially when attention systems reward conflict and when opponents frame reforms as domination. The sequencing strategy must therefore include coalition durability mechanisms:

12.1 Early shared wins

Keystone reforms should deliver early, broadly visible benefits: less corruption in procurement, simpler services, clear election procedures, faster response times, and fairer enforcement. These benefits keep moderates invested and make it harder for opponents to claim reform is purely partisan.

12.2 Non-humiliation framing

The coalition must avoid rhetoric that treats opponents as irredeemable. Humiliation escalates identity threat, lowering MVL. Systems Humanism insists on dignity even in conflict: criticize behavior, not personhood; condemn corruption, not entire populations.

12.3 Cross-class and cross-geography packaging

Reforms should be packaged so that multiple constituencies benefit. Anti-capture reforms appeal to taxpayers and small businesses; security floors appeal to workers and families; procurement transparency appeals to everyone. Packaging reduces "tribal ownership" of reform and makes it harder to repeal later.

12.4 Symmetric constraint as coalition glue

Nothing stabilizes coalitions like symmetry. When people see rules applied to allies and opponents alike, they infer institutional seriousness. Symmetry is the antidote to "weaponization" narratives.

13. The Implementation Discipline: How to Design Reforms so They Don't Collapse Under Execution

Sequencing is not only the order of laws; it is the order of implementation capacity.

13.1 Build implementation scaffolding into the reform itself

Every keystone reform should include:

- clear standards and minimal discretion
- audit requirements and public reporting
- timelines and responsible agencies
- funding for implementation capacity
- complaint and appeal pathways
- and "red alert" assessments for loopholes and capture risk

13.2 Treat frontline performance as political stability

A benefits portal that fails, a licensing office that delays for months, a confusing enforcement policy—these are not minor. In nonlinear environments, they become national legitimacy issues. Capacity-building is therefore a stability investment.

13.3 Use iterative rollout with feedback loops

Implement reforms in stages with pilots, public metrics, and revision pathways. This reduces brittleness and prevents a single failure from delegitimizing the entire agenda.

14. The Long Game: Why Later-Stage Reforms Become Easier after MVL Rises

Once credibility and competence are established, a remarkable dynamic often appears: reforms become easier because behavior changes. Elite actors invest less in hardball if enforcement is credible. Citizens are less vulnerable to rumors if audits and transparency exist. Opponents can criticize reforms without rejecting procedures. The system's gain lowers.

This is the nonlinear reward of sequencing: **small legitimacy improvements can produce cascading improvements in governability**, which then allow deeper reforms—antitrust actions, influence market restructuring, large-scale investments—to be implemented without triggering regime-level conflict.

This is also why sequencing is morally important. A society that tries to force justice without legitimacy can end with less justice and less democracy. A society that builds legitimacy as infrastructure can implement justice more durably.

15. A Staged Blueprint: A Concrete 24–48 Month Sequencing Outline

While each country differs, a plausible sequencing outline for a fragile democracy might look like this:

Months 0–6: Credibility keystones and "visible fairness."

- routine election administration audits and transparent reporting

- procurement transparency portal + independent audits
- conflict-of-interest rules and public disclosures
- strengthen inspectors general and whistleblower channels
- launch a public "rule consistency dashboard" (enforcement statistics, audit results)

Months 6–18: Capacity and service legitimacy

- modernize benefits delivery and frontline service standards
- reduce bureaucratic humiliation (simplify eligibility, clear appeal rights)
- professionalize key agencies; invest in data and performance monitoring
- implement procurement enforcement and debarment processes

Months 12–24: Security and dignity floors (broad and non-stigmatizing)

- automatic stabilizers for downturns
- housing stability measures
- healthcare cost containment pathways
- portable benefits frameworks
- procedural justice upgrades in policing and courts

Months 18–36: Structural anti-capture

- lobbying and revolving-door restrictions
- campaign finance transparency and dark-money constraints
- antitrust and market structure enforcement agenda
- beneficial ownership transparency; AML enforcement in key nodes

Months 30–48: Meaning infrastructure and civic immune function

- civic service pathways and contribution programs
- local civic institution investments
- systems literacy and civic education reforms
- local journalism and epistemic commons support
- institutional stress tests and crisis protocols as routine practice

This outline is not a promise that politics will be calm. It is a design for keeping politics governable.

Conclusion: Sequencing Is the Ethics of Realism

In nonlinear democracies, sequencing is not a technocratic detail. It is the ethics of realism: the recognition that good ends require durable legitimacy, and durable legitimacy requires the right order of operations.

The central claim of this chapter can be stated plainly:

> **Repair must begin with keystone reforms that make fairness visible, enforcement symmetric, and institutions competent—because without those, ambitious reforms will be interpreted as capture, will trigger backlash cascades, and may push the system toward tipping points.**

Sequencing is how a democracy climbs out of a bad attractor without falling into another. It is how it rebuilds the dampeners—trust, legitimacy, rule consistency—before it attempts the heavier work of restructuring payoffs and building prosperity and meaning at scale. It is how Systems Humanism becomes more than an ideal: a practical program that respects the dynamics of fragile systems while refusing to abandon democratic constraint.

In the next chapter, we turn from sequencing to coalition formation: **how to build durable coalitions for repair in a polarized, attention-driven environment—coalitions that can withstand sabotage, sustain legitimacy, and keep the ladder intact long enough to reach structural transformation.**

CHAPTER 12

COALITIONS FOR NONLINEAR TIMES: BARGAINING, BRIDGING, AND THE NEW DEMOCRATIC MAJORITY

DEMOCRATIC REPAIR IS not primarily a policy problem. It is a coalition problem. Policies are ideas; coalitions are power. And in nonlinear times—when polarization is identity-saturated, information is disordered, and incentives reward maximalism—coalition-building is not the natural byproduct of shared interest. It is an engineered practice. It is the art of assembling durable, cross-cutting alliances that can survive sabotage, withstand inevitable implementation errors, and maintain legitimacy as the rules of the game change.

Parts I–III described the dynamics that make repair urgent: the erosion of trust, legitimacy, and rule consistency; the stabilization of corruption as a bad attractor; and the proximity to tipping points where small shocks produce regime shifts. Chapter 11 argued that repair must be sequenced: begin with keystone reforms that raise minimum viable legitimacy, then move toward bigger structural change. This chapter addresses the complementary question: **Who carries the repair agenda across time?** Not just into law, but through the long, contested period of implementation.

In stable democracies, coalitions can be relatively straightforward. Parties compete within shared procedural norms. Majorities alternate, and losing factions accept outcomes. In such environments, coalition-building is often a matter of policy alignment and electoral arithmetic. In nonlinear democracies, those assumptions fail. Coalitions must contend with:

- **Affective polarization:** opponents are not merely wrong; they are perceived as dangerous or illegitimate.
- **Information disorder:** shared facts are scarce; rumors are fast; narratives precede evidence.
- **Attention incentives:** outrage outcompetes compromise; humiliation is rewarded; nuance is punished.
- **High stakes:** inequality and insecurity make losing feel existential.
- **Adversarial strategy:** capture networks and political entrepreneurs exploit fractures and weaponize procedural ambiguity.

Under these conditions, coalition-building is no longer primarily about persuading citizens that your policies are better. It is about **reducing existential threat, creating shared ownership of procedures, and designing reform packages that generate visible, broadly distributed gains while avoiding humiliation dynamics**. It is also about cultivating civic and institutional allies—auditors, local leaders, professional communities, journalists, civic associations—who function as legitimacy scaffolding during turbulent implementation.

This chapter advances a central thesis:

> **The new democratic majority in nonlinear times is not a simple ideological bloc. It is a "repair coalition": a cross-cutting alliance built around rule consistency, anti-capture fairness, broad security and dignity, and the restoration of a shared epistemic commons.**

Such a coalition does not require cultural uniformity. It requires agreement on constraints: that democracy must remain governable, that capture must be constrained, that citizens deserve basic security and dignity, and that public procedures must be credible. It is less a "party" coalition than a **system-preservation coalition**—a coalition capable of reforming institutions without triggering regime shifts.

We will build this argument in seven parts:

1. Why coalitions collapse in nonlinear times
2. The coalition paradox: repair requires unity, but polarization punishes it
3. The architecture of a repair coalition: pillars, constituencies, and shared interests
4. Bargaining under identity threat: the new rules of compromise
5. Bridging strategies: cross-cutting ties, dignity framing, and civic infrastructure
6. Coalition defense: resisting sabotage, narrative warfare, and "defection cascades"
7. A practical blueprint: how to assemble and sustain a new democratic majority

1. Why Coalitions Collapse in Nonlinear Times

Coalitions collapse not only because people disagree, but because modern systems amplify the forces that turn disagreement into fragmentation. In nonlinear times, the coalition problem has three layers.

1.1 The psychological layer: threat and humiliation

When politics becomes identity-saturated, compromise feels like betrayal. Citizens do not simply evaluate proposals, they evaluate whether the proposal threatens their status, their community, or their moral universe. Threat transforms policy into an existential contest. Humiliation transforms disagreement into rage.

Coalitions fail when they inadvertently trigger humiliation dynamics:

- treating a group as "backward" or "deplorable"
- implying cultural superiority
- dismissing grievances as ignorance rather than experience
- reducing communities to stereotypes
- or communicating reform as punishment rather than renewal

Humiliation is a contagion accelerant. It drives people toward maximalist leaders who promise recognition through domination.

1.2 The informational layer: narrative competition and epistemic fracture

Coalitions require coordination, and coordination requires shared understanding. When the epistemic commons is fragmented, coalition members cannot even agree on what happened, let alone on what to do. In such conditions, rumors and propaganda can break coalitions cheaply.

Information disorder produces two coalition pathologies:

- **factional epistemologies:** each subgroup consumes different realities, creating internal distrust
- **accusation spirals:** coalition members suspect each other of bad faith because narratives outpace verification

1.3 The incentive layer: attention markets and political entrepreneurship

Modern attention systems reward outrage, certainty, and antagonism. They punish nuance and cross-partisan bargaining. This creates a supply of political entrepreneurs who gain by breaking coalitions: they monetize conflict. Even within a governing coalition, the incentive is to defect publicly to gain purity status and attention.

This is one reason why repair coalitions must include internal norms and structures that reduce the payoff to defection and increase the payoff to disciplined cooperation.

2. The Coalition Paradox: Repair Requires Unity, but Polarization Punishes It

A repair agenda must do difficult things: constrain capture, enforce ethics, reform information systems, expand security floors, and redesign institutions for stability. Each of these threatens some interest group or identity narrative. As a result, repair requires broad support. But broad support requires bargaining, and bargaining triggers suspicion in polarized environments.

This is the coalition paradox: **to repair democracy, you must bargain across divides, but the environment punishes bargaining by framing it as corruption, betrayal, or weakness.** Coalitions, therefore, face attacks from both sides:

- Opponents attack them as illegitimate.
- Purists within attack them as compromised.

In nonlinear times, coalition-building requires three strategic moves that are often missing from reform politics:

1. **Design reforms that generate shared wins early** (legibility and distribution matter).
2. **Adopt dignity-centered framing that avoids humiliation** (recognize grievances without validating scapegoating).
3. **Build institutional and civic scaffolding** so that coalition cohesion does not rely only on leadership charisma.

Part III's Systems Humanism is crucial here: it insists on dignity as a stability resource, security as a dampener, and meaning as a civic immune function. These are not only policy goals; they are coalition glue.

3. The Architecture of a Repair Coalition: Pillars and Constituencies

A durable coalition is built around shared interests, constraints, and identity. In a diverse society, you cannot demand uniform values. You can, however, build a coalition around a shared commitment to the conditions that make pluralism viable.

A repair coalition rests on four pillars:

1. **Rule consistency and procedural fairness**
2. **Anti-capture and competition—fairness against extraction**
3. **Security and dignity floors—risk containment and equal standing**
4. **Epistemic resilience—shared reality, verifiable accountability**

These pillars correspond to the book's dampeners and to the key structural threats. They also provide a language that can unify constituencies that otherwise disagree.

3.1 Pillar 1: Rule consistency and procedural fairness

This pillar appeals to citizens who care about stability, due process, and equal treatment—often moderates, institutionalists, professionals, many religious communities, many immigrants seeking predictability, and many working-class citizens who feel rules are selectively applied.

Coalition message: "A democracy worth living in is one where rules bind everyone—especially the powerful."

3.2 Pillar 2: Anti-capture and competition

This pillar appeals to both left and right constituencies when framed properly:

- On the left: anti-corruption, anti-oligarchy, fairness, labor, and community protection.
- On the right: anti-cronyism, free enterprise, small business freedom, anti-bureaucratic favoritism.
- For independents: basic taxpayer fairness.

Coalition message: "The economy should reward work and innovation, not political favoritism."

3.3 Pillar 3: Security and dignity floors

This pillar appeals broadly when designed as risk containment rather than moral charity:

- healthcare cost risk containment
- housing stability
- portable benefits
- automatic stabilizers
- dignified service delivery

It can unify working families, rural and urban communities, younger cohorts priced out of housing, and older cohorts fearful of medical ruin.

Coalition message: "No one should be one illness or one layoff away from collapse. Security is freedom."

3.4 Pillar 4: Epistemic resilience

This pillar appeals to people exhausted by misinformation and distrust—parents, educators, professionals, institutional leaders, many faith communities, and many local leaders.

It must be carefully framed to avoid censorship concerns. It should emphasize transparency, audits, provenance, and independent verification.

Coalition message: "We don't need enforced agreement. We need verifiable facts and accountable procedures."

4. CONSTITUENCY MAPPING: WHO CAN BELONG TO THE NEW DEMOCRATIC MAJORITY?

The term "new majority" does not mean a single demographic. It means a *functional alliance* capable of sustaining repair. The constituencies below often share overlapping grievances, even though they differ culturally.

4.1 The "competence constituency"

Citizens who are not ideologically extreme but want government that works: reliable services, predictable rules, competent crisis management. They are often swing voters and stabilizers of coalitions.

What they need: evidence of competence and restraint; visible fairness; reduced chaos.

4.2 The "anti-extraction constituency"

Small businesses squeezed by concentrated power, workers facing wage stagnation, entrepreneurs blocked by licensing and gatekeeping, taxpayers angry at cronyism, and progressive anti-oligarchy voters.

What they need: competition policy, procurement fairness, and anti-crony enforcement that is symmetric, not partisan.

4.3 The "security constituency"

Households facing healthcare, housing, and debt insecurity. This includes many who do not identify as ideological left but experience the economy as precarious.

What they need: risk containment framed as freedom; universal or broad eligibility; low stigma.

4.4 The "dignity constituency"

Communities that feel culturally mocked or administratively humiliated; racial and ethnic groups facing discriminatory treatment; rural communities feeling ignored; urban communities experiencing policing injustice.

What they need: recognition without condescension; procedural dignity; equal protection; respect for place and identity.

4.5 The "epistemic constituency"

Educators, health professionals, scientists, journalists, parents, and local leaders—those alarmed by truth collapse and online manipulation.

What they need: transparency tools, audits, provenance systems, civic education, and support for local journalism.

4.6 The "institutional guardians"

Civil servants, judges, election officials, auditors, inspectors general, military professionals—those who maintain the procedural spine of the republic.

What they need: protection from politicization, clear standards, and leadership that defends institutional constraint.

A repair coalition is built by linking these constituencies under shared pillars. The key is not to demand identical cultural commitments, but to create a shared narrative of equal citizenship and fair rules.

5. Bargaining Under Identity Threat: The New Rules of Compromise

In nonlinear times, compromise triggers an identity threat. Coalition bargaining must therefore follow different rules than in a high-trust era.

5.1 The "dignity-first" bargaining rule

Before negotiating policy, signal respect. Not performatively, but substantively:

- acknowledge legitimate grievances even when rejecting scapegoating
- separate cultural worth from policy disagreement
- avoid contempt cues in language and media
- prioritize listening forums that are visible and sincere

Coalition bargaining collapses when one side feels it is being asked to surrender dignity as the price of inclusion.

5.2 The "constraint-based" compromise rule

In polarized conditions, agreeing on substantive outcomes is harder than agreeing on constraints. So begin with constraints:

- rules apply symmetrically
- audits are routine
- discretion is limited
- enforcement is transparent
- emergency powers are constrained

Once constraints are accepted, policy bargaining becomes less existential because the losing side believes it can recover later without being crushed.

5.3 The "shared-win packaging" rule

Repair coalitions survive when reforms deliver shared wins across groups, not only targeted wins. Examples:

- procurement transparency benefits taxpayers and small businesses
- antitrust benefits consumers and entrepreneurs
- healthcare cost containment benefits employers and families
- housing supply reforms benefit young and old
- service competence reforms benefit everyone

Packaging reforms as shared wins reduces identity sorting and makes it harder to demonize the coalition.

5.4 The "anti-defection" rule: reduce incentives for purity spirals

Coalitions fail when members gain more by defecting than by cooperating. To reduce defection incentives:

- allocate visible credit across coalition factions
- create joint oversight committees and shared ownership
- build internal dispute resolution mechanisms
- avoid humiliating internal criticism in public

In a media environment that rewards betrayal, coalitions must intentionally reward discipline.

6. BRIDGING: BUILDING CROSS-CUTTING TIES IN A FRAGMENTED SOCIETY

Coalitions are not only legislative alliances. They are social structures. A majority of repairs must be supported by bridging institutions that create cross-cutting ties—relationships that reduce demonization and increase trust.

6.1 Bridging institutions as "civic shock absorbers"

Local associations, unions, faith communities, civic clubs, service programs, and local media create bridging ties. These ties function like dampeners: they reduce the amplitude of outrage contagion because people are less willing to believe the worst about those they know personally.

Part III's "meaning" pillar becomes coalition infrastructure here. Civic contribution programs and local institutions are not only moral goods; they are coalition stabilizers.

6.2 Civic service as coalition technology

A voluntary civic service corps—focused on infrastructure, climate resilience, elder care, tutoring—creates shared purpose and cross-group collaboration. It builds narrative integration: "We built something together."

6.3 Place-based dignity: repair must honor local identity

Coalitions fracture when reforms are perceived as contempt for place. Place-based programs—rural broadband, local manufacturing revitalization, local health systems, community college funding—should be framed not as charity but as investment in national cohesion.

6.4 Bridging through procedural fairness

Even without cultural agreement, procedural fairness can bridge. When people see consistent enforcement and transparent rule-making, they may still disagree on values but can accept outcomes as legitimate enough to coexist.

7. Coalition Defense: Resisting Sabotage and Narrative Warfare

In nonlinear times, any coalition that threatens capture will be attacked. Coalition defense is therefore part of coalition design.

7.1 Anticipate "delegitimation attacks" and inoculate with auditability

Opponents will claim reforms are corrupt, partisan, or tyrannical. The antidote is not counter-insult; it is evidence:

- routine audits
- public dashboards
- independent oversight
- transparent procurement data
- clear enforcement criteria

Auditability is coalition armor. It reduces rumor space.

7.2 Prevent "persecution narratives" through symmetry

Anti-capture enforcement must apply equally to coalition allies and opponents. Nothing destroys coalition legitimacy faster than selective enforcement. Symmetry is not only ethics; it is strategy.

7.3 Protect institutional guardians

Auditors, inspectors general, election officials, judges, and civil servants must be protected from intimidation and politicization. If they collapse, the coalition loses the procedural spine that makes reform credible.

7.4 Build redundancy: coalition support beyond a single leader

Charismatic leadership can ignite reform, but it cannot be the only support. Coalitions must embed reforms in:

- local governments and civic networks
- professional associations
- community institutions
- nonpartisan oversight structures
- and policy designs that create beneficiaries across factions

Redundancy prevents reform from collapsing when leadership changes.

7.5 Avoid internal humiliation

Coalitions often destroy themselves by publicly shaming internal dissenters. In nonlinear times, humiliation triggers defection cascades. Internal disagreement must be managed through private negotiation and shared narrative discipline.

8. The "Repair Coalition Narrative": A Language That Unifies Without Homogenizing

Coalitions require a story. Not propaganda, but a shared interpretive frame that makes cooperation meaningful.

A Systems Humanist repair narrative has four elements:

1. **Equal citizenship:** everyone deserves dignity and fair treatment.
2. **Rules that bind:** no one is above the law; capture is constrained.
3. **Security as freedom:** risk floors enable autonomy and reduce fear politics.
4. **Shared reality:** verifiable facts and audits protect self-government.

This narrative avoids both moralistic contempt and technocratic coldness. It frames repair as a renewal of equal citizenship rather than a conquest of opponents. It makes coalition membership morally honorable: not "we defeated them," but "we rebuilt the rules that allow us to live together."

9. A Practical Blueprint: Assembling the New Democratic Majority

How do you actually build this coalition? Below is a staged blueprint consistent with the sequencing in Chapter 11.

Stage 1: Build a "credibility coalition" around keystone reforms

Start with reforms that almost everyone can endorse in principle:

- election administration transparency and audits
- procurement transparency and anti-collusion enforcement
- conflict-of-interest rules
- empowered inspectors general and whistleblower protections
- service competence upgrades

These reforms create early wins and reduce existential fear. They also make later reforms more legitimate.

Coalition targets: moderates, institutional guardians, small businesses, civic groups, local leaders.

Stage 2: Expand into a "security-and-dignity coalition"

Once credibility begins to rise, introduce broadly designed security floors and dignity reforms:

- healthcare cost risk containment
- housing stability
- portable benefits
- dignified service delivery
- procedural justice improvements in policing and courts

Frame these as stability and freedom, not paternalism.

Coalition targets: working families, younger cohorts, seniors, rural and urban communities, and faith organizations.

Stage 3: Consolidate into an "anti-capture and competition coalition"

Now push deeper structural reforms:

- influence pathway transparency
- revolving-door constraints
- competition policy
- beneficial ownership transparency
- procurement firewall expansion

At this stage, the coalition can sustain conflict because MVL is higher, and early wins have built trust.

Coalition targets: anti-extraction voters across the left/right, entrepreneurs, labor, and consumer advocates.

Stage 4: Deepen with "meaning and contribution" infrastructure

Finally, invest in civic immune function:

- civic service programs
- local civic institutions
- systems literacy education
- local journalism support
- community-building investments

These deepen bridging ties and make the coalition resilient across election cycles.

10. The New Majority as a Stability Regime, Not an Election Win

The goal of the repair coalition is not merely to win once. It is to establish a new stability regime—an institutional configuration where:

- capture is harder and less profitable,
- security reduces existential fear,
- dignity is institutionalized,

- shared reality is supported by audits and transparency,
- and civic meaning reduces susceptibility to polarization contagion.

Once those conditions exist, coalition politics becomes easier because the system's gain is lower. The republic becomes less sensitive. Disagreement becomes processable again.

This is the deeper idea: **the coalition builds the reforms, and the reforms rebuild the conditions for normal coalition politics.** Repair is a virtuous loop if sequenced and defended properly.

11. Conclusion: Coalition-Building as Democratic Resilience Engineering

In nonlinear times, coalition-building is not a rhetorical skill; it is resilience engineering. The new democratic majority is the coalition capable of implementing and defending repair without triggering regime shifts. It is not a monolith. It is a cross-cutting alliance organized around constraints and stabilizers: rule consistency, anti-capture fairness, security and dignity floors, and epistemic resilience.

Such a coalition will always be contested. It will be attacked by capture networks and by maximalist entrepreneurs. It will suffer from internal tension. But it can endure if it follows the Systems Humanist logic: treat dignity as infrastructure, treat security as freedom, treat truth as verification rather than coercion, and treat rules as constraints that bind everyone.

The politics of repair is not politics as usual. It is politics under sensitivity. It requires bargaining that avoids humiliation, bridging that rebuilds civic ties, and disciplined cooperation that resists the incentives of attention markets.

In the next chapter, we turn to the operational heart of coalition stability: **Legitimacy Engineering—how to make fairness visible, how to communicate in an information-disordered environment without propaganda, and how to build procedural credibility at scale so the repair coalition can survive its inevitable storms.**

Chapter 13

Legitimacy Engineering: Communication, Transparency, and Procedural Fairness at Scale

Legitimacy is the load-bearing beam of democratic stability. When it holds, democratic societies can tolerate disagreement, absorb shocks, and revise policy without breaking the constitutional frame. When it fails, politics becomes existential: opponents are not merely wrong but illegitimate; institutions are not merely imperfect, but enemy infrastructure; and every controversy becomes a struggle over the right to rule rather than a contest over how to govern.

Parts I and II argued that democracies drift toward fragility as dampeners weaken—trust, legitimacy, and rule consistency—and as positive feedback loops dominate—polarization, capture, and information disorder. Part III proposed designs: the anti-capture state that changes payoffs; a prosperity architecture that delivers security, dignity, and meaning; and Systems Humanism as a practical program for flourishing and democratic repair. Part IV turns to implementation—the politics of installing these designs under adversarial conditions. Chapter 11 presented sequencing: credibility first, then capacity, then deeper structural transformation. Chapter 12 addressed coalitions: a repair majority built around fair rules, anti-capture constraints, security and dignity floors, and a rebuilt epistemic commons.

This chapter focuses on a central question that determines whether sequencing and coalitions succeed: **How do you build legitimacy at scale in a low-trust, high-velocity environment without sliding into propaganda, censorship, or performative "messaging" that accelerates cynicism?**

The answer is what we will call **legitimacy engineering**—the deliberate design of institutions, procedures, transparency systems, and communication practices so that fairness becomes *visible*, accountability becomes *verifiable*, and governance becomes *predictable enough* that pluralistic conflict remains processable rather than regime-threatening.

Legitimacy engineering is not public relations. It is not spin. It is not the manipulation of belief. It is the construction of repeatable evidence that institutions are constrained, symmetric, and competent. It is the creation of an environment where citizens and factions can disagree without concluding that the system is fundamentally fake.

In nonlinear times, this is not optional. The acceleration of information flows, the fragmentation of epistemic authority, and the strategic weaponization of narratives mean that legitimacy cannot be assumed. It must be produced—continuously—through institutional design and disciplined practice. And because legitimacy itself is a complex systems variable—highly sensitive to shocks, narratives, and cumulative lived experiences—legitimacy engineering must be approached as a resilience discipline: building dampeners, lowering system gain, and creating firebreaks against cascades of distrust.

This chapter develops legitimacy engineering in five parts:

1. **What legitimacy is** (and what it is not) in a nonlinear democracy
2. **The legitimacy stack**: where legitimacy is produced (daily, procedural, and constitutional layers)
3. **Transparency as infrastructure**: auditability, legibility, and the design of public evidence
4. **Communication under information disorder**: truth-telling, uncertainty, and narrative inoculation without propaganda
5. **Procedural fairness at scale**: rules that bind, due process that is visible, and service delivery as a legitimacy practice

We close with a concrete implementation blueprint: the legitimacy engineering toolkit, a staged rollout plan, and a set of metrics—because in nonlinear times, you cannot defend legitimacy with rhetoric. You defend it with evidence.

1. LEGITIMACY AS A SYSTEMS VARIABLE

1.1 The three faces of legitimacy

Legitimacy is often spoken of as a mood—trust is high, trust is low. That is too thin. Legitimacy is better understood as a three-part structure:

1. **Procedural legitimacy:** the belief that decisions are made through fair, known rules applied consistently.
2. **Performance legitimacy:** the belief that institutions can deliver basic governance competently and reliably.
3. **Moral legitimacy:** the belief that the system treats people with equal dignity and does not function as a machine of domination.

These forms are distinct but coupled. A state can be competent and still morally illegitimate (competent repression). It can be procedurally elaborate but incompetent (lawful chaos). It can be morally aspirational but procedurally arbitrary (benevolent whim). Democratic stability requires all three—especially in nonlinear times, when errors and scandals can cascade across domains.

A useful diagnostic question is: **When citizens reject legitimacy, what exactly are they rejecting?** Often, it is not "democracy" in the abstract. It is the experience of procedural arbitrariness (selective enforcement), performance failure (bureaucratic humiliation, chaotic service), or moral insult (feeling disposable, mocked, excluded). Legitimacy engineering aims to repair these experiences, not merely persuade citizens to feel differently.

1.2 What legitimacy is not: popularity, unity, or narrative control

Legitimacy is not the same as popularity. A government can be unpopular and legitimate if procedures are fair, enforcement is consistent, and rights are protected. Conversely, a government can be popular and illegitimate if it rules through arbitrary power or selective punishment.

Legitimacy is not unity. Democracies contain conflict. The goal is not to eliminate disagreement, but to keep it within a shared procedural framework.

Legitimacy is not narrative control. Attempts to "manage perception" without improving fairness and competence produce what we might call **legitimacy inflation**: a temporary boost in proclaimed trust that collapses into deeper cynicism when reality contradicts messaging. In nonlinear environments, this collapse is fast and contagious. People do not merely disagree; they learn that the institution is lying—and then they generalize that inference to all institutions. The system's gain increases: rumor becomes default; conspiratorial thinking becomes adaptive.

The rule is harsh but clarifying **in low-trust societies; messaging that substitutes for evidence reduces legitimacy.** Legitimacy engineering, therefore, begins with humility: stop treating distrust as a communications deficit. Treat it as a systems output.

1.3 Nonlinearity: why legitimacy collapses suddenly and recovers slowly

Legitimacy behaves like a threshold variable. It can degrade gradually and then collapse quickly. A scandal, a contested election, a perceived double standard—these can serve as triggers when the reservoir of underlying legitimacy is already depleted.

Recovery is slower because legitimacy is a cumulative inference. Citizens require repeated experiences of fairness, competence, and constraint before they revise beliefs. This is why early keystone reforms (Chapter 11) must be **legible and repeatable**: audits that happen routinely, dashboards that update regularly, and enforcement that applies consistently. One symbolic act is not enough; legitimacy is rebuilt through a cadence of evidence.

2. The Legitimacy Stack: Where Legitimacy Is Produced

To engineer legitimacy, you need to know where it is made. In a complex system, outcomes emerge from many interactions. Legitimacy is produced at multiple layers—some visible, some hidden.

2.1 Layer 1: Daily legitimacy (the "street-level state")

Most citizens experience the state through everyday encounters:

- applying for benefits or permits

- dealing with schools, hospitals, and police
- paying taxes and receiving services
- navigating courts, administrative hearings, or local agencies
- interacting with infrastructure: transit, utilities, housing codes

These experiences generate **micro-legitimacy**—small inferences about whether the system is fair, competent, and respectful. Micro-legitimacy is the substrate upon which macro-legitimacy rests. If daily interactions are humiliating, confusing, or arbitrary, citizens will not believe in lofty constitutional rhetoric.

This is why service delivery is not technocratic detail; it is legitimacy infrastructure. A benefits portal that crashes is a legitimacy event. A permitting process that takes months is a legitimacy event. A police interaction that feels arbitrary is a legitimacy event. In nonlinear times, these events are amplified by social media and narrative entrepreneurs, turning local failures into national delegitimation.

2.2 Layer 2: Procedural legitimacy (the rule system)

Procedural legitimacy is produced by institutions that define "how decisions are made":

- elections and election administration
- legislative procedures (how laws are passed)
- regulatory processes (how rules are written)
- courts and enforcement agencies
- audits, oversight, and ethics systems

Here, the key variable is **rule consistency**. People can tolerate losing if they believe rules are stable and apply to all. They become radicalized when rules appear selective, improvised, or manipulated.

Procedural legitimacy is particularly fragile in polarized environments because each side suspects the other of gaming procedures. Therefore, legitimacy engineering must prioritize **constraint visibility**: making procedural constraints observable rather than merely asserted.

2.3 Layer 3: Constitutional legitimacy (the moral frame)

At the deepest layer is the belief that the system expresses equal citizenship rights, dignity, and protection from domination. This includes:

- equal protection under law
- protection of speech and pluralism
- constraints on coercion and emergency powers
- fairness across groups and classes
- a credible pathway for reform without rupture

Constitutional legitimacy is threatened not only by formal violations but by the lived perception that the system is captured or indifferent. When citizens believe the state exists for elites, constitutional legitimacy decays even if legal forms remain intact.

2.4 The coupling: why the layers must be repaired together

The legitimacy stack is coupled. You cannot repair constitutional legitimacy while daily legitimacy is humiliating. You cannot repair procedural legitimacy while enforcement is selective. You cannot repair performance legitimacy while the state cannot deliver.

This coupling yields a key principle for Part IV: **legitimacy engineering must be multi-layered.** It cannot be reduced to a single transparency law or a single communications strategy. It requires a coherent architecture: daily competence, procedural constraint, and moral dignity.

3. Transparency as Infrastructure: Auditability, Legibility, and Evidence

Transparency is often treated as a moral good: sunlight is the best disinfectant. In nonlinear democracies, transparency is also a stability technology—if designed well. If designed poorly, it can backfire, overwhelming citizens with data, fueling rumors, and creating surveillance fears.

Legitimacy engineering uses transparency in a disciplined way: **not as data dumping, but as auditability and legibility.**

3.1 Auditability vs. transparency theater

Transparency theater is when institutions publish information that does not enable accountability. It is performative disclosure: PDFs no one can analyze, delayed releases, selective summaries, or data presented without context. Transparency theater can worsen cynicism: it signals that the institution wants credit without constraint.

Auditability, by contrast, means information is:

- timely
- machine-readable
- complete enough to evaluate decisions
- tied to clear standards
- and accompanied by independent verification pathways

Auditability turns rumor into a falsifiable claim. It changes the epistemic environment. It lowers the payoff to disinformation because citizens and journalists can check.

3.2 Legibility: making fairness visible to non-experts

Even auditable data can fail if it is not legible. Legibility means ordinary people can understand:

- what decision was made
- what rule governed it
- what evidence was used
- how to challenge it
- and how outcomes are monitored

Legibility is legitimacy. If citizens cannot interpret processes, they fill the gap with narratives.

Therefore, transparency systems must include:

- **plain-language explanations**
- **standardized templates** for decisions and enforcement actions
- **public dashboards** showing trends (not just raw documents)
- **independent summaries** from auditors or oversight bodies
- and **clear pathways** for inquiry and appeal

The aim is not to make everyone an analyst. It is to make key fairness indicators visible.

3.3 The legitimacy dashboard: a public evidence layer

A core tool of legitimacy engineering is a **legitimacy dashboard**—a publicly accessible set of metrics updated regularly that demonstrates rule consistency, competence, and fairness.

A legitimacy dashboard might include:

- election audit results and chain-of-custody compliance rates
- procurement data: bids, awards, evaluation criteria, debarments
- enforcement statistics: complaints received, investigations opened, outcomes, timelines, demographic and geographic distributions (with privacy safeguards)
- administrative performance: benefit application processing times, error rates, appeal outcomes
- ethics compliance: disclosures filed, recusals, violations found, sanctions applied
- service accessibility: wait times, user satisfaction, complaint resolution

The dashboard is not a propaganda tool; it is an accountability tool. Its power lies in routine updating. It creates a cadence of evidence that crowds out rumors.

3.4 Independent verification: transparency without referees is fragile

Transparency alone is insufficient because citizens distrust the source. The system needs referees: independent auditors, inspectors general, ombuds offices, bipartisan election boards, or nonpartisan statistical agencies. These institutions provide a **credible interpretation** of data.

Legitimacy engineering, therefore, includes:

- protected independence of oversight bodies
- guaranteed access to records
- mandatory reporting timelines
- public disclosure of methods
- and structured oversight redundancy (multiple watchdogs)

Redundancy matters because single referees can be attacked or captured. Multiple verification channels make delegitimation harder.

3.5 Open contracting and procurement as the most legible anti-capture transparency

Procurement is a keystone domain because it is where public money becomes private contracts. Citizens intuitively understand corruption here. Therefore, open contracting is one of the highest-leverage transparency infrastructures:

- publish solicitations, bids (with justified redactions), scoring criteria
- disclose beneficial ownership of contractors
- publish contract modifications and change orders
- require conflict-of-interest declarations for evaluators
- conduct randomized audits and publish findings
- debar corrupt contractors and publish debarment reasons

This produces visible proof that the state is not for sale. It builds legitimacy at the daily level—taxpayer fairness—and at the procedural level—rule consistency.

3.6 Transparency and privacy: avoiding surveillance backlash

Transparency can trigger fear if it feels like surveillance. Legitimacy engineering must respect privacy and avoid humiliating disclosure. The principle is:

- **Make institutions transparent, not citizens.**
- **Make decisions auditable, not lives exposed.**

Publish process data, aggregate statistics, enforcement outcomes, and decision rationales—while protecting personal privacy. Where personal data is necessary (e.g., financial disclosures for officials), scope it carefully and enforce consistently.

3.7 Transparency as a firebreak against information cascades

In nonlinear information environments, rumors spread because verification is slow. Transparency infrastructure speeds verification, thereby reducing cascade risk.

Think of transparency as an epistemic firebreak:

- If election audits are routine and published, fraud rumors have less fuel.
- If procurement data is open, cronyism claims can be tested quickly.
- If enforcement statistics are public, "weaponization" claims can be evaluated.
- If service performance metrics are public, competence claims become falsifiable.

Firebreaks do not eliminate misinformation; they reduce their ability to trigger mass coordination around false narratives.

4. Communication Under Information Disorder: Truth-Telling Without Propaganda

Legitimacy engineering includes communication—not as spin, but as an extension of procedural fairness. Communication is how institutions explain constraints, acknowledge uncertainty, and make processes legible. In information-disordered environments, communication is also how institutions prevent rumors from becoming default.

The challenge is that communication itself is distrusted. Therefore, legitimacy engineering adopts a disciplined, constrained, and evidence-based communication posture.

4.1 The communication triangle: truth, restraint, and verification

Effective legitimacy communication rests on three commitments:

1. **Truthfulness:** do not lie, do not exaggerate, do not claim certainty where none exists.
2. **Restraint:** avoid humiliating opponents, avoid triumphalism, avoid moral contempt.
3. **Verification:** link claims to public evidence—audits, data, procedures, and independent reports.

This posture is slower than propaganda but stronger. Propaganda can win attention; it cannot build durable legitimacy.

4.2 Uncertainty as credibility: communicating what you don't know

In low-trust environments, institutions often fear acknowledging uncertainty, as they assume it will be exploited. But pretending certainty when uncertainty exists is more damaging. When reality contradicts claims, trust collapses. Therefore, legitimacy engineering treats uncertainty as credibility:

- specify what is known, what is unknown, and when updates will occur
- explain why uncertainty exists (data lag, investigation process)
- commit to public release of findings under clear timelines
- avoid premature conclusions

This is procedural fairness in speech. It signals constraint. It also reduces rumor space by providing a stable update cadence.

4.3 The "explain the rule" discipline: process-first communication

In polarized conditions, content arguments often trigger identity threat. Process explanations can reduce threat by emphasizing constraint. Therefore, legitimacy engineering prioritizes:

- what rule governed the decision
- what evidence was considered
- what oversight exists
- how appeals work
- what protections prevent abuse

This is especially important in contentious areas: enforcement actions, election administration decisions, emergency powers, and disinformation responses. When institutions lead with process, they demonstrate that they are bound by rules rather than ruling by whim.

4.4 Pre-bunking and inoculation: slowing rumor without censorship

Information disorder is not only "false stories." It is a system of incentives that rewards viral claims. Institutions can reduce susceptibility through **inoculation**—pre-bunking likely manipulations by explaining the techniques and providing verification pathways.

Examples:

- Before elections: explain how ballots are handled, how audits work, what anomalies mean, and what does *not* indicate fraud.
- Before policy rollouts: explain what early errors might look like, how to report them, and how corrections will occur.
- Before crisis measures: explain emergency power limits, oversight, and sunset provisions.

The goal is not to preempt criticism. It is to reduce the shock value of predictable events and to provide citizens with cognitive tools to interpret them.

4.5 The humility protocol: admitting mistakes without collapsing authority

Mistakes are inevitable. In nonlinear environments, how institutions handle mistakes determines whether they experience legitimacy collapse or legitimacy gain.

A humility protocol includes:

- rapid acknowledgment of errors
- clear explanation of cause
- concrete correction steps
- independent review if appropriate
- public reporting on prevention measures

This is difficult because it invites attack. But concealment invites a worse attack when discovered. Humility, properly executed, demonstrates constraint and seriousness. It is often legitimacy-enhancing, especially when contrasted with defensive denial.

4.6 The dignity rule: never communicate contempt

In Chapter 12, we emphasized dignity as the glue of the coalition. Communication that signals contempt is a legitimacy toxin. It activates humiliation dynamics and drives polarization contagion.

Legitimacy engineering, therefore, insists on:

- respect for persons even when condemning behaviors
- avoidance of caricature and moral mockery
- rejection of "owning" rhetoric and humiliating triumphalism
- commitment to equal citizenship language

This is not etiquette. It is systems management. Humiliation raises the gain on conflict and increases the probability of defection cascades.

4.7 Decentralized trust: communicating through local intermediaries

In fragmented societies, national institutions may be distrusted even when truthful. Legitimacy communication must therefore be **distributed** through credible local intermediaries:

- local election officials
- community organizations
- faith leaders

- professional associations
- local journalists and civic groups

These intermediaries can translate procedures into the local language and provide trusted verification. This creates redundancy in the legitimacy system: if one channel is attacked, others still function.

4.8 Crisis communication: the "cadence, constraint, and calm" doctrine

In crises, information velocity increases. Rumors spread faster. The public is emotionally primed. Crisis communication should therefore follow a doctrine:

- **Cadence:** regular updates on a predictable schedule
- **Constraint:** emphasize rule limits and oversight
- **Calm:** avoid panic language, avoid demonization, avoid blame theater

Crisis communication that is erratic or triumphalist accelerates distrust. Steady, controlled crisis communication can dampen contagion.

5. Procedural Fairness at Scale: Rules That Bind and Due Process That Is Visible

Procedural fairness is the heart of legitimacy engineering. It is how institutions show citizens that they are not subjects of arbitrary power. But procedural fairness must be visible and scalable—not only in courts, but across the administrative state and public services.

5.1 The symmetry principle: enforcement that binds allies and opponents

In Chapter 8, we argued that the anti-capture state must change payoffs, and in Chapter 11, we argued that legitimacy must be built early. The critical bridge is symmetry:

- ethics rules apply to all parties
- audits apply regardless of who wins
- enforcement targets behaviors, not identities
- penalties are consistent across status and faction

Symmetry is the most powerful antidote to "weaponization" narratives. Without symmetry, enforcement becomes perceived as factional dominance and triggers retaliation spirals.

Symmetry does not require identical outcomes. Cases differ. It requires consistent standards and transparent reasoning.

5.2 Due process as a legitimacy technology

Due process is often treated as a legal formality. In legitimacy engineering, it is a technology that prevents coercive drift and makes citizens feel safe during contestation.

Due process at scale includes:

- clear notice of rules and consequences
- the right to be heard
- access to evidence used against one
- appeal pathways
- timely decisions
- and independent review

These elements matter not only in criminal justice but in administrative enforcement: licensing, benefits, inspections, school discipline, and tax disputes. People form legitimacy judgments when they encounter power.

5.3 The "plain-language due process" standard

One reason due process fails in practice is that it is unintelligible. People feel powerless when procedures are opaque.

Therefore, legitimacy engineering insists that every major enforcement or administrative decision include:

- a plain-language explanation of the rule
- what evidence was used
- what factors mattered
- how to appeal
- and where to get assistance

This is not only compassionate; it reduces rumor space and increases compliance.

5.4 Procedural justice in policing and public safety

Public safety institutions are legitimacy amplifiers: they can build trust quickly or destroy it quickly. Procedural justice principles—being heard, being treated respectfully, being treated consistently—are essential.

Legitimacy engineering in public safety includes:

- clear use-of-force policies and public reporting
- independent review of serious incidents
- complaint systems with visible outcomes
- training and accountability aligned with respect
- non-police crisis response where appropriate
- and community engagement that is not performative but continuous

Again, the aim is not to eliminate conflict; it is to make enforcement credible and constrained.

5.5 Service delivery as procedural fairness: the "dignity state"

Chapter 9 described security and dignity as pillars of prosperity architecture. Here, we translate dignity into administrative design.

A dignity-centered service system has:

- minimal unnecessary paperwork
- predictable timelines
- respectful communication
- non-stigmatizing access
- and correction pathways that do not require humiliation

This reduces the feeling that citizens must beg to receive what they are entitled to. It strengthens constitutional legitimacy: the state treats people as equals.

5.6 The legitimacy incident model: treating failures like safety events

Complex systems manage safety through incident reporting and learning. Legitimacy engineering borrows this discipline: treat major legitimacy failures as incidents requiring a structured response.

A **legitimacy incident** could be:

- a major administrative failure (system outage during benefit enrollment)
- a scandal with corruption implications
- an enforcement action perceived as selective
- a contested election procedure
- a crisis policy that triggers rights concerns

The incident model includes:

- rapid stabilization (stop the bleeding)
- transparent facts gathering
- independent review
- public reporting of findings
- corrective actions
- and follow-up monitoring

This turns crises into learning rather than blame theater. It demonstrates seriousness and increases trust over time.

6. Legitimacy Engineering in Practice: The Toolkit

We now consolidate the chapter into a toolkit—concrete design objects that can be installed.

6.1 The Legitimacy Charter: constraints in writing

A legitimacy charter is a publicly stated set of procedural commitments:

- symmetry in enforcement
- transparency standards and timelines
- audit routines and publication schedules
- conflict-of-interest rules
- emergency power constraints
- and service dignity standards

The charter is not a manifesto; it is a contract. Its value lies in making commitments checkable.

6.2 Routine audits as democratic ritual

Audits should not be exceptional. They should be routine and boring—like safety checks in aviation. Boring audits are stabilizing because they normalize verification and reduce scandalization.

Examples:

- routine post-election audits
- periodic procurement audits
- random inspections and compliance checks with published outcomes
- annual ethics audits and disclosure compliance reports

Ritualized audits reduce the novelty that rumor feeds on.

6.3 Open data with independent interpretive institutions

Publish machine-readable data, but also fund independent institutions that interpret it:

- nonpartisan audit agencies
- university consortia
- civic data labs
- local journalism collaborations
- public interest technologists

Interpretation is where legitimacy is won, because citizens cannot process raw data alone.

6.4 The Public Reason Template: standardized explanations for major decisions

Create a standardized template for public explanations of major decisions:

- purpose and authority
- rule basis
- evidence summary
- tradeoffs acknowledged
- oversight and review
- appeal pathways
- timelines for updates

Standardization is legitimacy engineering because it reduces discretion and increases predictability.

6.5 Ombuds and complaint systems that actually resolve

Many institutions have complaint systems that function as vents, not remedies. Legitimacy engineering requires complaint systems with:

- tracking numbers and timelines
- public reporting of resolution rates
- escalation pathways
- independent ombuds authority
- and user-centered design

When citizens can resolve issues without humiliation, trust grows.

6.6 Procurement firewall package

As in Chapter 8, procurement reform is both anti-capture and legitimacy-building:

- open contracting
- beneficial ownership disclosures
- audit and debarment mechanisms
- conflict-of-interest protections
- and public performance reporting

This is one of the most visible ways to prove the state is not a private spoils machine.

6.7 Crisis legitimacy safeguards

In crises, legitimacy can be lost quickly. Safeguards include:

- clear emergency power triggers
- time limits and sunset clauses
- oversight committees with public reporting
- judicial review pathways
- and after-action reviews

The message is: we can act fast without abandoning constraint.

7. The Staged Rollout: Legitimacy Engineering Over 18 Months

To make the chapter operational, here is a sequencing-consistent rollout plan.

Months 0–3: Establish the legitimacy frame

- publish a legitimacy charter with clear standards
- set audit schedules (election, procurement, ethics, service performance)
- create public dashboards and update cadence
- appoint or empower independent oversight with protected access and reporting timelines
- implement a humility protocol and crisis communication cadence

Months 3–9: Build auditability and daily competence

- launch open contracting platform and procurement reporting
- implement conflict-of-interest disclosure improvements and recusal reporting
- modernize key service systems (benefits, permits) with published performance metrics
- create ombuds systems with resolution tracking
- begin routine public briefings tied to dashboard updates

Months 9–18: Scale procedural fairness and expand the legitimacy reserve

- implement due-process templates across agencies
- publish enforcement statistics and standards to counter weaponization narratives
- expand civic intermediaries: partnerships with local institutions for procedure explanation and verification
- institutionalize after-action reviews for major incidents
- integrate legitimacy metrics into agency performance goals

This rollout is designed to raise Minimum Viable Legitimacy so deeper reforms—security floors and anti-capture restructuring—can be implemented without triggering backlash cascades.

8. MEASURING LEGITIMACY: INDICATORS THAT MATTER

If legitimacy is engineered, it must be measurable—not perfectly, but usefully. A legitimacy scorecard should track:

Procedural legitimacy indicators

- audit completion rates and publication timeliness
- consistency of enforcement outcomes across comparable cases
- appeal outcomes and reversal rates
- compliance with disclosure and recusal requirements
- election administration error rates and audit findings

Performance legitimacy indicators

- service delivery wait times and error rates
- complaint resolution rates
- administrative capacity metrics (staffing, training completion)
- consistency of rule implementation across jurisdictions

Moral legitimacy indicators

- perceived fairness surveys (procedural justice measures)
- disparities in enforcement and service outcomes (with careful interpretation)
- trust in institutions at local and national levels
- measures of dignity experience in service interactions

The goal is not a single "trust number." The goal is to detect drift and to provide early warning when legitimacy reservoirs are thinning.

9. The Deeper Point: Legitimacy Is Democracy's Operating Capital

Why devote an entire chapter to legitimacy engineering? Because legitimacy is the operating capital that makes all other reforms feasible. Without it, anti-capture measures are read as purges; security floors are read as patronage; epistemic resilience measures are read as censorship; crisis governance becomes permanent emergencies.

Legitimacy engineering is therefore not a cosmetic layer. It is the enabling condition for the repair agenda itself. It is how the system changes its own dynamics, how negative feedback is restored, how rumors lose their monopoly, how citizens can accept losses without rejecting the system.

In Systems Humanist terms, legitimacy is also a moral condition: it is the felt reality of equal citizenship. A person who experiences the state as respectful and consistent is less likely to seek dignity through domination. A person who experiences the state as humiliating and arbitrary is more likely to radicalize. Legitimacy is the moral ecology that shapes political character at scale.

CONCLUSION: BUILD EVIDENCE, NOT ILLUSIONS

Legitimacy engineering can be summarized in one sentence:

> **Do not ask citizens to trust; give them repeated, visible reasons to trust.**

That requires transparency designed as auditability and legibility, not theater. It requires communication disciplined by truthfulness, restraint, and verification. It requires procedural fairness that is visible and scalable rules that bind, due process that is understandable, and service delivery that treats people as equals. It requires independent oversight and routine audits that turn rumors into falsifiable claims.

In nonlinear times, legitimacy cannot be restored by speeches, slogans, or nostalgia. It can be restored only by redesigning the institutions that generate daily experience and by building a public evidence layer robust enough to withstand narrative warfare.

In the next chapter, we turn to the stress environment in which legitimacy is most at risk: crises. Chapter 14—"Stress Tests and Crisis Protocols: Governing Shocks Without Regime Shifts"—will propose a practical resilience playbook: democratic stress testing, crisis procedures that preserve constraint, and learning systems that convert shocks into institutional strengthening rather than cascading collapse.

Chapter 14

Stress Tests and Crisis Protocols: Governing Shocks Without Regime Shifts

Democracies rarely die from a single decisive blow. More often, they drift into fragility and then experience a shock that turns drift into rupture. The shock can be economic—an inflation spike, a banking failure, a sudden unemployment surge. It can be political—a contested election, a corruption scandal, a constitutional hardball escalation. It can be informational—an engineered disinformation wave, a viral lie that triggers mass outrage. It can be physical—pandemic, climate disaster, infrastructure collapse, terrorism, war. In a stable democracy, shocks are absorbed, institutions flex, legitimacy holds, and the system returns toward equilibrium. In a fragile democracy near critical thresholds, the same shocks can trigger cascades: legitimacy collapses, norms snap, and the polity shifts into a new regime, often a bad attractor of emergency rule, factional retaliation, and durable distrust.

Parts I and II framed democratic stability as a dynamical property: dampeners (trust, legitimacy, rule consistency) keep the system within a safe operating space; positive feedback loops (polarization, capture, information disorder) push it toward tipping points; and corruption can become a stable attractor. Part III proposed a design program: the anti-capture state, a prosperity architecture, and Systems Humanism as the integrative ethic of flourishing and repair. Part IV has turned to implementation: sequencing repair (Chapter 11), building coalitions (Chapter 12), and engineering legitimacy through transparency and procedural fairness (Chapter 13). This chapter now confronts the environment that tests all those designs: **crisis.**

The claim of this chapter is blunt: **In nonlinear times, crisis governance is the central determinant of regime continuity.** Democracies can have good policies, but if they cannot govern shocks without losing legitimacy, they will eventually break. Conversely, democracies can survive hard periods if they have protocols that preserve procedural constraint, maintain a credible evidence layer, and prevent emergency measures from becoming permanent domination.

What follows is a practical resilience playbook: **stress tests** and **crisis protocols** designed for democracies operating under adversarial narrative conditions. The goal is not to eliminate crises. The goal is to prevent crises from becoming regime shifts.

We will proceed in six parts:

1. Why shocks become regime shifts: the dynamics of crisis cascades
2. The democratic stress test framework: how to simulate failure before it happens
3. Crisis protocols: the "constraint-first" doctrine for emergency governance
4. The shock portfolio: election crises, corruption crises, economic crises, information crises, and physical crises
5. Learning systems: after-action reviews, institutional memory, and adaptive repair
6. A blueprint for installation: building crisis resilience without normalizing emergency rule

1. WHY SHOCKS BECOME REGIME SHIFTS: CRISIS CASCADES IN FRAGILE DEMOCRACIES

1.1 The difference between a shock and a regime shift

A shock is an event. A regime shift is a systemic transition: the rules of interaction change, expectations change, and behavior reorganizes around new incentives. A contested election is a shock; the normalization of election denial and retaliatory institutional hardball is a regime shift. A corruption scandal is a shock; the acceptance of selective enforcement and impunity as normal is a regime shift. An economic downturn is a shock; the emergence of permanent emergency economic governance is a regime shift.

The book's physics metaphor is useful here: regimes are basins of attraction. A democracy with strong dampeners returns toward stable procedures after shocks. A democracy with weakened dampeners can be pushed into a different basin—authoritarian emergency rule, captured institutions, chronic street violence, or extreme polarization.

1.2 Crisis cascades: how failure spreads across domains

Crisis cascades occur when a shock in one domain triggers reinforcing failures in others:

- **Economic shock → insecurity → polarization → delegitimation**
- **Election shock → distrust → information disorder → violence risk**
- **Corruption shock → cynicism → compliance collapse → weaker state → more capture**
- **Disinformation shock → panic → emergency powers → rights backlash → legitimacy collapse**
- **Climate disaster → service failure → humiliation → anti-state radicalization**

These cascades are not hypothetical. They are the predictable consequence of tight coupling in modern societies, where information spreads instantly, institutions are interdependent, and polarization turns every event into a factional weapon.

1.3 The three crisis multipliers

Three factors multiply crisis risk in nonlinear democracies:

1. **Low legitimacy reserve:** when trust is already depleted, any shock is interpreted as proof of bad faith.
2. **High narrative velocity:** attention markets amplify fear, anger, and certainty, outpacing verification.
3. **Procedural ambiguity:** unclear rules, discretionary emergency powers, and inconsistent enforcement invite conspiracy and retaliation.

Therefore, crisis resilience is largely about building:

- legitimacy reserves (Chapter 13),
- verification capacity (audits and public evidence layers),
- and procedural constraints that bind crisis response.

1.4 The paradox of speed: why fast action can destroy legitimacy

Crises demand speed. But speed often requires discretion, and discretion can destroy legitimacy if it appears arbitrary. In fragile democracies, a swift but opaque response can trigger backlash, worsening the crisis. The solution is not paralysis. The solution is **pre-designed protocols** prepared in advance that allow speed with constraints.

The rule is: **pre-commitment enables legitimate speed.** If emergency powers are defined and bounded before the crisis, their use is less likely to be interpreted as a coup.

2. The Democratic Stress Test Framework: Simulating Failure Before It Happens

Complex systems that cannot tolerate failure must be stress tested. Aviation, nuclear power, and financial systems evolved stress testing because the costs of real-world failure are catastrophic. Democracies now face comparable systemic stakes. A modern democracy should therefore adopt **democratic stress testing**—structured simulations and audits designed to reveal vulnerabilities before they become crises.

2.1 What to stress test

Democratic stress tests should target the high-risk nodes where failures cascade:

- elections and vote counting
- emergency powers and crisis declarations
- communications and verification systems
- enforcement institutions (justice, inspectors general, ethics bodies)
- critical service delivery (healthcare, unemployment systems, disaster response)
- procurement and contracting under crisis (where corruption spikes)
- platform and information ecosystem vulnerabilities
- intergovernmental coordination failures

2.2 The stress test method: tabletop exercises + red teams + audits

A practical stress test program has three components:

1. **Tabletop exercises:** structured simulations involving agencies, local officials, and oversight bodies.
2. **Red teams:** adversarial groups tasked with finding ways to exploit systems (disinformation, hacking, legal loopholes, corruption opportunities).
3. **Audits:** formal evaluations of preparedness, including data integrity, chain-of-custody, procurement safeguards, and contingency capacity.

These components should be routine, widely publicized, and partially transparent in their findings (with security-sensitive details protected). Routine testing builds legitimacy by demonstrating seriousness.

2.3 The "stress test outputs": what must be produced

A stress test should output:

- a vulnerability map (where cascades can occur)
- a set of protocol revisions (rules and procedures updated)
- training requirements and capacity investments

- and a public summary (plain-language explanation of preparedness steps)

Without outputs, stress testing becomes theater. The goal is institutional learning.

2.4 Legitimacy benefits of stress testing

Stress testing is not only preparation; it is legitimacy engineering. It signals:

- humility (we anticipate errors and plan for them)
- constraint (we commit to rules before crises)
- competence (we train and practice)
- and transparency (we report what we can)

These signals build a legitimacy reserve, which is crucial when real crises occur.

3. Crisis Protocols: The Constraint-First Doctrine

Crisis protocols are pre-designed rules that govern how the state responds in times of shock. The aim is to prevent crisis response from becoming arbitrary or permanent. A Systems Humanist approach insists that crisis governance must preserve dignity and equal citizenship even when fear is high.

We propose a **constraint-first doctrine** built around seven principles.

Principle 1: Pre-defined triggers and definitions

Emergency powers should have clear triggers: measurable conditions, defined thresholds, and explicit scope. "Emergency" cannot be whatever the executive says it is. Ambiguity invites abuse and delegitimation.

Principle 2: Time limits and sunset provisions

Emergency measures must expire automatically unless renewed through ordinary procedures. Automatic sunset clauses prevent normalization of emergency rule.

Principle 3: Independent oversight and routine reporting

Oversight bodies must monitor emergency actions in real time:

- inspectors general
- auditors
- legislative oversight committees
- and where appropriate, judicial review

Reporting should be routine and public where possible because cadence builds trust.

Principle 4: Minimal necessary infringement
Crisis measures should follow the principle of proportionality: do the minimum necessary to meet the crisis goal, and lift constraints as soon as conditions permit. Overreach becomes a legitimacy crisis.

Principle 5: Transparent criteria for enforcement
Emergency rules are only as legitimate as their enforcement. Enforcement criteria must be public, consistent, and appealable. Selective enforcement during crises accelerates polarization.

Principle 6: Procurement firewalls
Crises create massive spending flows. Without procurement safeguards, corruption spikes. Open contracting, beneficial ownership checks, and auditability must be built into crisis procurement.

Principle 7: A communication cadence anchored in evidence
Crisis communication must be regular, calm, and evidence-linked. Uncertainty should be acknowledged. Updates should follow a predictable schedule. This reduces rumor cascades.

These principles transform crisis response from improvisation into constrained action. They are how democracies govern quickly without abandoning legitimacy.

4. The Shock Portfolio: Protocols For Major Crisis Types

Democratic resilience requires protocols for the crises most likely to trigger regime shifts. Below, we outline five crisis categories and the protocols that prevent cascades.

4.1 Election crises: contested outcomes, procedural failures, and violence risk

Elections are legitimacy fulcrums. If election legitimacy collapses, the system loses its steering mechanism. Election crises require pre-commitment to verification.

Protocol A: Routine audits as default

Post-election audits should be automatic and standardized, not discretionary responses to allegations. Routine audits normalize verification and reduce suspicion.

Protocol B: Transparent chain-of-custody and process visibility

Publicize how ballots are handled, where they are stored, and how recounts work. Provide clear timelines and live reporting of procedural milestones.

Protocol C: Independent election administration bodies

Where possible, insulate election administration from direct partisan control through bipartisan boards, professional standards, and protected staffing.

Protocol D: Contested-election adjudication rules

Define how disputes are resolved: which courts, what evidence standards, what timelines. Ambiguity invites legal hardball and rumor.

Protocol E: Violence prevention coordination

Coordinate with local law enforcement under clear constraints to protect polling places and counting centers without intimidation. Ensure visible neutrality.

Protocol F: Communication cadence

During counting and disputes, provide scheduled updates that explain processes rather than just outcomes. Emphasize that delays often reflect verification, not fraud.

The aim is to make elections boring again—procedurally intense but socially non-existential.

4.2 Corruption crises: scandals, elite impunity, and weaponization narratives

Corruption crises are explosive because they combine moral outrage with factional suspicion. If handled poorly, they can produce a persecution narrative that delegitimizes accountability.

Protocol A: Independent investigative pathways

Use inspectors general, independent prosecutors, or special oversight mechanisms with transparent legal authority.

Protocol B: Symmetric enforcement commitments

Enforce ethics and corruption rules across factions; publish enforcement criteria and statistics. This is critical to avoid perceptions of selective targeting.

Protocol C: Evidence-first public reporting

Avoid inflammatory rhetoric. Release facts in structured reports with clear sourcing. Use plain-language summaries and publish update timelines.

Protocol D: Procurement lockdown during scandal

Corruption scandals often reveal procurement vulnerabilities. Immediately implement open contracting transparency, audit triggers, and debarment processes.

Protocol E: Institutional humility and reform linkage

Tie accountability to structural reforms: "We are not just punishing; we are fixing the system that allowed this." This shifts the narrative from factional battle to repair.

The goal is to turn scandal into legitimacy gain: proof that rules bind, not proof of factional war.

4.3 Economic crises: inflation spikes, unemployment, financial shocks

Economic crises can trigger regime shifts by raising existential stakes and fueling scapegoating. The stabilizer is automaticity: pre-designed responses that kick in without political improvisation.

Protocol A: Automatic stabilizers

Unemployment support expansions, income supplements, and targeted relief should activate automatically based on indicators (jobless claims, GDP contraction). This reduces delay and politicization.

Protocol B: Transparent distribution rules

Relief must be rule-based and legible. Discretionary relief invites capture and corruption narratives.

Protocol C: Anti-price gouging enforcement with due process

Enforce against clear abuses while avoiding overreach. Publish enforcement criteria and allow appeals.

Protocol D: Financial system stress testing and resolution plans

Where relevant, ensure banks and critical financial institutions have resolution plans to prevent panic cascades.

Protocol E: Communication discipline on tradeoffs

Inflation and crisis measures involve tradeoffs. Acknowledge them. Explain goals and timelines. Avoid false promises that later collapse trust.

Economic crisis governance is legitimacy governance because insecurity fuels polarization contagion.

4.4 Information crises: disinformation waves, deepfakes, viral lies

Information crises can trigger regime shifts by collapsing shared reality and provoking panic. The danger is overreaction: censorship efforts can become delegitimizing and authoritarian.

The solution is epistemic resilience: verification and transparency rather than narrative control.

Protocol A: Rapid verification unit

A cross-institutional verification team that quickly assesses viral claims and publishes evidence-linked clarifications. This is not "truth ministry" but a public fact-checking function tied to auditable sources.

Protocol B: Provenance and disclosure requirements

Require transparency for political ads, coordinated campaigns, and synthetic media disclosures where feasible. Focus on disclosure rather than content suppression.

Protocol C: Platform coordination with safeguards

Coordinate with platforms on detection of coordinated inauthentic behavior, foreign interference, and fraudulent amplification—under transparent standards and oversight.

Protocol D: Public education and inoculation

Before elections and major events, educate citizens on likely manipulations. Provide verification pathways.

Protocol E: Lawful response boundaries

Define what the state will not do: no criminalizing ordinary speech, no broad censorship. Clear boundaries protect legitimacy.

The aim is to reduce viral manipulation without becoming the manipulator.

4.5 Physical crises: pandemics, climate disasters, infrastructure collapse, security shocks

Physical crises test state capacity and dignity. Poor response becomes humiliation, which becomes anti-state radicalization.

Protocol A: Disaster response competence and dignity standards

Ensure aid delivery is efficient, respectful, and accessible. Bureaucratic humiliation during disaster is politically explosive.

Protocol B: Crisis procurement firewall

Disasters trigger massive emergency contracting. Open contracting and audits are essential.

Protocol C: Mutual aid and civic coordination

Work with local civic organizations, faith groups, and community networks to deliver services—distributed trust increases compliance.

Protocol D: Emergency powers constraints

Time limits, oversight, and public reporting must be explicit. A crisis does not justify indefinite rule.

Protocol E: After-action reviews

Publish lessons learned and implement reforms. Visible learning turns failure into credibility.

Physical crisis governance is where citizens experience the state most directly. It can generate legitimacy or destroy it.

5. Learning Systems: Converting Shocks into Institutional Strengthening

Crises are inevitable. The difference between resilient and fragile democracies is whether crises lead to learning or to denial. Learning is not automatic; it must be institutionalized.

5.1 After-action reviews as democratic practice

An after-action review (AAR) should be routine after major events:

- election cycles
- major corruption investigations
- economic crisis interventions
- disaster responses
- major disinformation incidents

AARs should include:

- what happened (facts)
- what worked
- what failed
- what should change (procedures, staffing, laws)
- who is responsible and by when
- and a public summary

The point is not to blame the theater. It is adaptive governance.

5.2 Institutional memory: avoiding "amnesia cycles"

Democracies often forget lessons because leadership changes. Institutional memory requires:

- permanent crisis response offices with professional staff
- documented protocols and training programs
- routine drills and exercises
- and public reporting that creates continuity

Without memory, each crisis is handled as improvisation, increasing legitimacy risk.

5.3 Metrics and early warning indicators

Part IV's final chapter will propose a scorecard. Here, we emphasize that crisis resilience requires early warning signals:

- rising distrust in election administration
- growing enforcement disparity perceptions
- increased rumor virality metrics
- procurement irregularities
- service delivery failure rates
- spikes in political violence indicators
- and elevated economic insecurity measures

Early warning enables preventive action—reducing the likelihood that a small shock triggers a cascade.

5.4 The "repair loop": crisis → evidence → reform → legitimacy gain

The Systems Humanist approach treats crises as opportunities for learning that strengthen dignity and legitimacy. The repair loop looks like:

1. crisis occurs
2. facts are gathered and published under constraints
3. independent oversight verifies
4. reforms address structural vulnerabilities
5. new protocols reduce future risk
6. legitimacy increases because citizens observe learning and constraint

This loop converts shocks into stabilizers rather than regime threats.

6. Installing Crisis Resilience Without Normalizing Emergency Rule

The final design challenge is paradoxical: to prepare for emergency governance without making emergency governance the norm. Stress tests and protocols can themselves be used to justify permanent surveillance or executive dominance. Therefore, crisis resilience must include constraints that prevent the "emergency creep" attractor.

6.1 The anti-creep architecture

To prevent emergency creep:

- define emergency powers narrowly
- require renewals through normal procedures
- publish oversight reports regularly
- enforce transparency on crisis procurement
- and maintain judicial review and appeal rights

Emergency powers should be treated like hazardous materials: used when necessary, stored securely, monitored constantly, and disposed of promptly.

6.2 Distributed resilience: local capacity and civic networks

Centralization can increase efficiency, but it also increases the stakes of central failure. Distributed resilience—local capacity, civic networks, mutual aid partnerships—reduces cascading collapse. It also enhances legitimacy by fostering citizens' trust in local intermediaries.

6.3 Professionalization and depoliticization of crisis functions

Crisis response units should be staffed by professionals under clear standards, not partisan loyalists. Depoliticization reduces suspicion and improves performance legitimacy.

6.4 Public rituals of verification

Democracies need rituals—shared practices that reinforce norms. Routine audits, stress tests, and after-action reviews become legitimacy rituals: they normalize verification and learning, reducing the novelty that rumor exploits.

6.5 The dignity constraint: crisis response must preserve equal standing

Systems Humanism insists on dignity. Crisis response must avoid imposing burdensome requirements, discriminatory enforcement, and stigmatizing aid delivery. Dignity is not secondary in crisis—it is the foundation of compliance and legitimacy.

Conclusion: Govern Shocks with Constraint, Evidence, and Learning

Nonlinear times guarantee shocks. The question is whether shocks become regime shifts. This chapter argued that democratic resilience requires a disciplined crisis architecture:

- **Stress tests** to reveal vulnerabilities before failure
- **Protocols** that enable speed with constraint
- **Verification systems** that reduce rumor cascades
- **Procurement firewalls** that prevent crisis capture
- **Communication cadence** anchored in evidence and humility

- **Learning systems** that convert crises into institutional strengthening
- and **anti-creep safeguards** that prevent emergency rule from becoming permanent

In the language of this book's physics, these measures widen the safe operating space. They thicken dampeners. They lower the gain on political and informational contagion. They prevent bad attractors—authoritarian emergency rule, retaliatory hardball, corruption spirals—from becoming stable.

Democracy's deepest test is not whether it can govern when the weather is calm. It is whether it can govern when the storms arrive—without abandoning the constraints that make it democratic. A polity that can do that is not merely stable. It is mature. It can endure.

In the next and final chapter of Part IV, we turn to measurement: **Chapter 15—"Measuring What Matters: A Democratic Stability Scorecard and the Flourishing Index."** There we will operationalize the book's core variables—trust, legitimacy, rule consistency, capture risk, information integrity, and the pillars of security, dignity, and meaning—so democratic repair can be guided by early warning indicators rather than discovered only after the system has crossed a tipping point.

Chapter 15

Measuring What Matters: A Democratic Stability Scorecard and Flourishing Index

Democratic repair is impossible without measurement. Not because numbers magically solve politics, but because complex systems drift silently until they cross a threshold. In nonlinear environments, where feedback loops amplify fear, rumor, and factional suspicion, drift can accelerate without obvious warning. By the time the crisis becomes visible, it is often too late to correct it with ordinary politics. The system has already moved closer to a tipping point, or into a bad attractor where capture, polarization, and delegitimation reinforce one another.

Parts I and II argued that democratic stability is not a given; it is an emergent property of dampeners (trust, legitimacy, rule consistency), a vulnerability to positive feedback loops (capture, inequality, information disorder), and a susceptibility to regime shifts when shocks hit a fragile state. Part III proposed the architecture of repair: anti-capture rules that change payoffs; a prosperity architecture that delivers security, dignity, and meaning; and Systems Humanism as a practical program for flourishing and democratic repair. Part IV addressed implementation: sequencing reforms (Chapter 11), building coalitions (Chapter

12), engineering legitimacy (Chapter 13), and governing crises without regime shifts through stress tests and protocols (Chapter 14).

This final chapter of Part IV operationalizes the entire framework. It offers two linked tools:

1. **A Democratic Stability Scorecard (DSS):** a measurement system designed to track whether the republic remains inside its safe operating space, where conflict remains processable, rules remain credible, and capture does not dominate governance.
2. **A Flourishing Index (FI):** a measurement system designed to track whether citizens experience the prosperity architecture described in Chapter 9, security, dignity, and meaning—understood as stabilizers rather than sentimental add-ons.

The goal is not to reduce democracy to a number. The goal is to build an **early warning system** and a **public evidence layer** that makes drift visible, enables accountability without rumor, and guides adaptive repair. In the language of complex dynamic systems, measurement is a way to strengthen negative feedback: detect deviations early and correct them before they become a cascade.

To do this responsibly, we must address a danger: measurement itself can become a tool of propaganda, control, or technocratic overreach. Therefore, the scorecard and index must be designed with Systems Humanist ethics in mind: transparency, dignity, pluralism, and restraint. Measurements must be auditable, interpretable, and used to support self-government rather than replace it.

This chapter proceeds in six parts:

1. Why measurement fails in democracies and how to avoid those failures
2. The principles of a Systems Humanist measurement framework
3. The Democratic Stability Scorecard: domains, indicators, and thresholds
4. The Flourishing Index: security, dignity, meaning—indicators and design choices
5. Implementation: governance of the scorecard, auditability, and public dashboards
6. Using the tools: early warning, reform sequencing, and crisis prevention

1. WHY MEASUREMENT FAILS—AND WHY WE NEED IT ANYWAY

1.1 The "GDP mistake" and the measurement trap

Modern states are accustomed to measuring what is easy: GDP, unemployment, inflation, fiscal deficits, and test scores. These metrics matter, but they can obscure what determines democratic stability. A country can grow economically while its legitimacy decays. It can meet fiscal targets while corruption deepens. It can increase aggregate wealth while insecurity, humiliation, and meaninglessness spread.

This is the "GDP mistake": treating output as a proxy for social health. The result is a governance style that optimizes for growth while ignoring the moral ecology—dignity, trust, shared reality—that makes democracy viable and worth maintaining.

The measurement trap is the opposite: believing that if we can measure something, we can control it. That can lead to technocratic hubris, surveillance, or narrow optimization that damages dignity and pluralism. The scorecard proposed here avoids both extremes by treating measurement as **diagnostic** rather than **deterministic**.

1.2 Why democracies resist measurement of stability

Democracies often resist measuring stability for three reasons:

1. **Political risk:** measurement can reveal uncomfortable facts—capture, inequity, enforcement disparities—that threaten incumbents.
2. **Narrative conflict:** in polarized environments, each side distrusts the other's metrics, fearing manipulation.
3. **Complexity:** stability is multi-dimensional; simple indices can mislead.

Yet these are precisely the reasons measurement is necessary. Without a credible public evidence layer, rumor fills the gap. Without early warning, crises become surprises. Without shared metrics, accountability collapses into narrative warfare.

Therefore, the scorecard must be designed as a **legitimacy tool**—auditable, independently governed, and transparent—so it becomes a shared reference point even amid disagreement.

1.3 The purpose: early warning and adaptive repair

The Democratic Stability Scorecard and Flourishing Index serve three purposes:

- **Early warning:** detect drift toward tipping points and bad attractors.
- **Policy guidance:** help prioritize sequencing—what to fix first, where dampeners are thin.
- **Public legitimacy:** provides verifiable evidence that reduces rumors and supports democratic self-correction.

They do not replace politics. They inform them.

2. Principles for Measuring Democratic Stability and Flourishing

A Systems Humanist measurement framework must obey principles that protect dignity and legitimacy.

Principle 1: Measure systems, not moral worth

Metrics should evaluate institutions and conditions, not declare certain citizens "better." Avoid stigmatizing categories. Measure environments and outcomes.

Principle 2: Auditability over authority

Every metric should be reproducible and open to independent verification. This prevents measurement from becoming propaganda.

Principle 3: Multiple indicators, not one magic number

Composite indices can be useful for communication but dangerous for governance if treated as definitive. Use dashboards with domain scores and underlying indicators.

Principle 4: Symmetry and fairness

Metrics should be applied consistently across jurisdictions and groups. Enforcement metrics must include context and explain limitations to avoid misinterpretation.

Principle 5: Lag awareness and uncertainty

Some variables change slowly; some rapidly. Use confidence intervals where appropriate. Communicate uncertainty explicitly (Chapter 13's truthfulness constraint).

Principle 6: Protect privacy—make institutions transparent, not citizens

Use aggregate data and anonymization. Avoid personal-level disclosure that fuels surveillance or humiliation.

Principle 7: Tie measurement to action pathways

Metrics must link to concrete responses, such as stress tests, audits, policy adjustments, and capacity investments. Otherwise, measurement becomes theater.

3. The Democratic Stability Scorecard (DSS)

The DSS tracks whether democracy remains inside its safe operating space. It focuses on the variables most central to this book's framework: trust, legitimacy, rule consistency, capture risk, polarization dynamics, and information integrity.

3.1 The DSS domains

We propose seven domains. Each domain is scored on a standardized scale (e.g., 0–100), with sub-indicators.

1. **Institutional Legitimacy and Rule Consistency**
2. **Capture and Corruption Risk**
3. **Democratic Process Integrity (Elections and Representation)**
4. **Information Integrity and Epistemic Resilience**
5. **Polarization and Social Cohesion**
6. **State Capacity and Service Competence**
7. **Crisis Resilience and Stress-Test Readiness**

These domains reflect the book's physics: dampeners, attractors, and proximity to the tipping point.

3.2 Domain 1: Institutional Legitimacy and Rule Consistency

What it measures: whether citizens experience the state as procedurally fair, predictable, and constrained.

Candidate indicators:

- **Procedural justice surveys:** perceived fairness of courts, police, agencies.
- **Consistency metrics:** variance in enforcement outcomes for similar cases (adjusted for context).
- **Appeal and reversal rates:** high reversal rates may signal initial arbitrariness or poor guidance.
- **Transparency compliance:** timely publication of audits, decisions, and disclosures.
- **Time-to-decision predictability:** standard deviation of agency processing times.

Interpretation:

- Rising variance and opaque processes indicate weakening rule consistency—a thinning dampener.

3.3 Domain 2: Capture and Corruption Risk

What it measures: whether extraction is becoming stable, whether the state is drifting into a bad attractor of rent-seeking.

Candidate indicators:

- **Procurement risk flags:** concentration of awards, frequent sole-source contracts, repeated change orders.
- **Beneficial ownership transparency compliance:** percentage of contracts with verified ownership disclosure.
- **Lobbying and revolving-door metrics:** disclosures, post-employment restrictions compliance.
- **Regulatory outcome concentration:** share of regulatory benefits accruing to top firms/actors.
- **Enforcement independence:** budget stability and staffing of inspectors general and auditors.

Interpretation:

- Rising sole-source contracting and award concentration can be early signs of crisis capture.

3.4 Domain 3: Democratic Process Integrity

What it measures: whether elections and representation remain credible enough to be binding.

Candidate indicators:

- **Audit completion rates and findings:** routine post-election audits and error rates.
- **Election administration performance:** wait times, ballot rejection rates (with context), chain-of-custody compliance.
- **Dispute resolution integrity:** timelines and transparency of adjudication processes.
- **Gerrymandering and representational distortion metrics:** measures of responsiveness and competitiveness (used carefully).
- **Voter access indicators:** registration accessibility, polling availability, barrier reports.

Interpretation:

- A key early warning sign is not only irregularities but rising *contestation* and declining acceptance of outcomes.

3.5 Domain 4: Information Integrity and Epistemic Resilience

What it measures: the health of the shared reality ecosystem.

Candidate indicators:

- **Local journalism viability:** number of local news outlets, staffing levels, circulation/engagement (quality-adjusted where possible).
- **Transparency of political messaging:** disclosure rates for sponsors and targeting.
- **Platform manipulation exposure:** prevalence of coordinated inauthentic behavior detections (from independent audits).

- **Civic information literacy:** survey-based measures of source evaluation skills.
- **Verification speed:** time between viral claims and credible public verification responses.

Interpretation:

- Rapid degradation in local news and verification capacity increases vulnerability to disinformation cascades.

3.6 Domain 5: Polarization and Social Cohesion

What it measures: the system's sensitivity to conflict: how easily disagreement becomes existential.

Candidate indicators:

- **Affective polarization surveys:** warmth/coldness toward out-groups.
- **Cross-cutting social ties:** membership in bridging civic associations, mixed networks (measured indirectly).
- **Political violence indicators:** threats, incidents, militia activity proxies (careful interpretation).
- **Segregation by ideology:** residential sorting and media consumption divergence.
- **Compromise legitimacy:** surveys on willingness to accept compromise and electoral losses.

Interpretation:

- Rising affective polarization is not just cultural; it raises the gain on shocks.

3.7 Domain 6: State Capacity and Service Competence

What it measures: the competence layer of legitimacy.

Candidate indicators:

- **Service delivery performance:** processing times, error rates, and uptime of digital services.
- **Staffing and training:** vacancy rates, training completion in key agencies.

- **Complaint resolution:** percentage resolved, time to resolution.
- **Disaster response readiness:** resource availability, response times.
- **Regulatory clarity:** rates of guidance updates, variance in interpretation across regions.

Interpretation:

- Capacity failures are legitimacy accelerants; they often precede cynicism cascades.

3.8 Domain 7: Crisis Resilience and Stress-Test Readiness

What it measures: whether the system can handle shocks without regime shifts.

Candidate indicators:

- **Stress test frequency and quality:** tabletop exercises completed, vulnerabilities addressed.
- **Emergency power constraints:** existence and enforcement of time limits and reporting.
- **Procurement firewall activation:** crisis contracting transparency compliance.
- **After-action review completion:** percentage of major incidents with published AARs.
- **Crisis communication cadence:** adherence to scheduled updates and evidence-linked briefings.

Interpretation:

- Weak stress test readiness increases the probability that a shock triggers a cascade.

4. The Flourishing Index (FI)

The Flourishing Index operationalizes the prosperity architecture from Chapter 9: **security, dignity, meaning**. It treats these as stabilizers that reduce existential politics and strengthen civic cooperation.

4.1 Pillar 1: Security (risk containment)

Core idea: people can tolerate democratic conflict when they are not one shock away from ruin.

Candidate indicators:

- **Income volatility:** frequency and magnitude of income shocks.
- **Catastrophic expense exposure:** medical and housing cost burdens; bankruptcy rates.
- **Housing stability:** eviction and displacement rates; rent burden distribution.
- **Employment stability:** underemployment, precarious scheduling prevalence.
- **Access to insurance floors:** coverage rates for healthcare, unemployment, disability, and paid leave.

Interpretation:

- Rising volatility and catastrophic risk increase susceptibility to demagoguery and scapegoating.

4.2 Pillar 2: Dignity (equal standing)

Core idea: humiliation and disrespect are political accelerants; dignity is a legitimacy infrastructure.

Candidate indicators:

- **Procedural dignity surveys:** how people feel treated by agencies, police, and schools.
- **Disparities in institutional treatment:** measured carefully with context, focusing on process fairness.
- **Workplace dignity metrics:** predictability, harassment prevalence, voice at work.
- **Civic equality perceptions:** belief that "people like me" are treated fairly by the system.
- **Administrative burden index:** time and complexity required to access basic services.

Interpretation:

- Rising administrative burdens and perceived disrespect can destabilize, even if incomes rise.

4.3 Pillar 3: Meaning (belonging and contribution)

Core idea: meaning is a public good; without it, societies become vulnerable to nihilism and extremist narratives.

Candidate indicators:

- **Civic participation:** volunteering rates, association membership, voter participation beyond presidential cycles.
- **Social connection:** loneliness measures, trust in neighbors.
- **Work meaning and development:** job satisfaction, training, and mobility access.
- **Community institution strength:** libraries, community centers, local media, and civic groups per capita.
- **Youth outlook and future confidence:** surveys on optimism, perceived opportunity, and belonging.

Interpretation:

- Meaning deficits increase the demand for identity warfare and conspiracy narratives that supply moral clarity.

5. Building the Public Dashboard: Governance, Auditability, and Legitimacy

A scorecard is only as credible as its governance. In polarized environments, measurement must be insulated from manipulation and designed to be contestable.

5.1 Governance structure: independent, plural, and redundant

A credible system would include:

- an independent statistical/audit body with protected funding
- advisory panels spanning ideological and disciplinary diversity
- published methodology with change logs

- independent replication teams (universities, civic labs)
- public comment periods for major methodological changes

Redundancy is key: multiple institutions must be able to produce or audit the measures.

5.2 Data sources: combine administrative data, surveys, and independent audits

Use a layered approach:

- administrative performance data (services, enforcement)
- routine audits (elections, procurement, ethics)
- public surveys (procedural justice, polarization, dignity)
- independent research inputs (local media health, platform audits where possible)

Each metric should include metadata: source, update frequency, confidence, and limitations.

5.3 Publishing: a "legibility first" dashboard

A dashboard should include:

- domain scores and trend lines
- underlying indicators with drill-down
- plain-language explanations of what changes mean
- a "what we're doing about it" section linking metrics to actions
- scheduled update cadence

Legitimacy engineering (Chapter 13) stressed cadence and evidence. The dashboard becomes part of that mechanism.

5.4 Privacy safeguards

Use aggregation, anonymization, and differential privacy techniques where needed. Avoid publishing data that could stigmatize individuals or small communities. The guiding principle remains: transparency of institutions, not surveillance of citizens.

6. USING THE DSS AND FI: EARLY WARNING, SEQUENCING, AND CRISIS PREVENTION

The scorecard and index matter only if they guide action. Here is how they integrate with Part IV's implementation logic.

6.1 Early warning thresholds: "drift alarms"

Set threshold bands for each domain:

- **Green:** stable range; routine monitoring
- **Yellow:** drift detected; targeted audits and policy adjustments
- **Orange:** high risk; activate stress tests and crisis protocols; accelerate keystone reforms
- **Red:** imminent regime shift risk; emergency legitimacy safeguards and stabilization measures

Thresholds should be used cautiously, more as alerts than deterministic triggers.

6.2 Sequencing decisions (Chapter 11)

If the DSS shows low procedural legitimacy and high contestation, prioritize:

- election integrity audits, transparency, and procedural fairness
- procurement transparency and oversight
- service competence upgrades

If the FI shows high insecurity, prioritize:

- automatic stabilizers and housing/healthcare risk containment
- dignified service delivery improvements

Thus, measurement becomes a guide to the Repair Ladder: fix the thinnest dampeners first.

6.3 Coalition maintenance (Chapter 12)

Metrics can strengthen coalitions if framed as a shared reality. For example:

- open contracting data can unite left-right anti-crony constituencies
- service performance improvements can win moderates

- dignity metrics can unite civil rights and working-class fairness demands

A public dashboard provides common reference points that reduce narrative warfare.

6.4 Legitimacy engineering (Chapter 13)

The dashboard is itself part of legitimacy engineering:

- routine publication reduces rumors
- independent auditing increases credibility
- plain-language explanations increase legibility
- public action plans link measurement to accountability

6.5 Crisis resilience (Chapter 14)

Use the DSS Domain 7 to ensure stress tests and crisis protocols are practiced. Use the scorecard to identify vulnerabilities before shocks:

- if information integrity metrics degrade rapidly, invest in verification infrastructure and pre-bunking
- if election contestation rises, intensify routine audits and procedural communication
- if procurement risk flags spike, activate procurement firewall protocols

Measurement thus becomes a pre-crisis intervention.

Conclusion: Measurement as Democratic Self-Correction

A democracy is stable when it can correct itself without rupture. Measurement is not the only mechanism of correction; courts, elections, civic norms, and moral leadership matter. But in nonlinear times, measurement becomes essential because drift is otherwise invisible, rumors fill the evidentiary vacuum, and crises arrive faster than institutional learning.

The **Democratic Stability Scorecard** makes the republic's dampeners and vulnerabilities visible: legitimacy, rule consistency, capture risk, process integrity, information resilience, cohesion, capacity, and crisis readiness. The **Flour-**

ishing Index makes visible the lived stabilizers that enable pluralism: security, dignity, and meaning.

Together, these tools form a Systems Humanist evidence layer: a public commons of verifiable indicators that can support adaptive repair. They do not replace politics. They make politics more governable. They reduce the likelihood that the system will cross a tipping point without warning.

In the end, measuring what matters is not a technocratic exercise. It is a democratic act. It is a way of saying: we will not govern by rumor, contempt, or improvisation. We will govern by evidence, constraint, dignity, and learning. That is the promise of democratic repair—and the practical discipline required to keep the republic inside its safe operating space at the edge of chaos.

Part V

Pulling Back from the Edge

Part V, **Pulling Back from the Edge**, turns from diagnosis to institutional necessity. The earlier sections of this book argued that democracy in nonlinear times is not a static achievement but a dynamic equilibrium: fragile, adaptive, and always vulnerable to drift. Political systems do not collapse only because of dramatic shocks. More often, they erode through cumulative feedback loops: polarization deepens, trust falls, elites become insulated, institutions lose legitimacy, and the system begins to settle into patterns that are increasingly difficult to reverse. The edge of chaos is therefore not merely a metaphor. It is the zone in which democratic societies can no longer rely on historical stability, yet have not fully surrendered to breakdown.

To pull back from that edge requires more than moral appeals or nostalgic invocations of civic virtue. It requires understanding democracy as an operating system for modern complexity. Democracy is not just a method of choosing leaders. It is the institutional architecture through which large-scale capitalist societies manage conflict, distribute legitimacy, renew consent, and correct error without destroying themselves. When that architecture weakens, the consequences are not confined to politics. Markets distort. Social trust decays. Capital allocation becomes less efficient. Long-term investment declines. Citizens cease to see the economy as a system of fair opportunity and come to see it as a system of extraction. At that point, democratic instability and economic instability become mutually reinforcing.

The chapters in this section examine three of the most powerful forces pushing democratic systems toward breakdown. First is the relationship between democracy and capitalism itself: whether a complex market order can endure without the legitimacy, accountability, and rule-governed constraints that democratic institutions provide. Second is the behavior of politicians and party systems, especially when political incentives reward spectacle, division, and self-preservation rather than stewardship. Third is the corrosive effect of income and wealth inequality, which gradually transforms democracy from a regime of equal citizenship into a regime of unequal influence.

Taken together, these chapters argue that democratic survival depends on institutional redesign, not passive hope. A democracy cannot remain stable when its political class profits from dysfunction, when its economic structure concentrates power too disproportionally, and when its citizens come to believe that neither elections nor markets are delivering justice. Pulling back from the edge, therefore, means restoring the conditions under which democracy can again function as a self-correcting system: credible representation, broad-based economic inclusion, accountable parties, and institutions capable of converting conflict into legitimate order.

This section is ultimately about recovery, but one grounded in realism. The task is not to return to an imagined past equilibrium. It is to build institutions that can withstand volatility, absorb shocks, and preserve legitimacy amid accelerating complexity. If democracy is to survive nonlinear times, it must be re-engineered not as a fragile inheritance, but as a resilient, adaptive framework for political and economic life.

Chapter 16 - Why Democracy is a Necessary and Sufficient Condition for A Capitalistic Economic System

This chapter argues that democracy is not simply compatible with capitalism; it is the political condition that makes a complex capitalist order legitimate, sustainable, and self-correcting. While markets can exist under authoritarian systems in a narrow sense, the chapter contends that a truly dynamic capitalist economy—one capable of long-term innovation, broad-based trust, contract enforcement, predictable property rights, and peaceful adaptation—depends on democratic institutions.

The chapter distinguishes between **capital accumulation** and the **capitalist order**. Authoritarian systems may generate growth, but growth alone is not equivalent to a stable capitalist system. Capitalism, properly understood, requires dispersed confidence: investors must trust that rules will not arbitrarily change, workers must believe mobility is possible, and citizens must accept that outcomes, even unequal ones, emerge within a framework they regard as procedurally legitimate. Democracy supplies that legitimacy through representation, transparency, lawful contestation, and the peaceful rotation of power.

The deeper argument is that democracy acts as capitalism's **error-correction mechanism**. Markets produce wealth, but also volatility, concentration, and periodic crises. Democratic institutions absorb these disruptions by providing channels for reform before discontent becomes systemic rupture. Elections, an independent judiciary, free media, and legislative negotiation are not external moral ornaments; they are the mechanisms by which capitalist societies recalibrate. Without them, market systems drift toward oligarchy, capture, and coercion—conditions that eventually undermine both efficiency and consent.

The chapter's central claim is therefore bold: democracy is **necessary** because capitalism without legitimacy decays into extraction, and democracy is **sufficient** because it provides the institutional framework within which conflict, innovation, and inequality can be managed without systemic collapse. The chapter concludes that when democracy weakens, capitalism ceases to be broadly productive and becomes increasingly predatory, losing the very conditions that once made it resilient.

Chapter 17 - Politicians Are Destroying Democracy: Party Systems, Incentives, and the Edge of Democratic Breakdown

This chapter examines how democratic decline is often driven not only by external enemies but also by the internal behavior of political actors operating within poorly structured incentive systems. Its central thesis is that many politicians do not merely fail to protect democracy; under certain institutional conditions, they actively destabilize it because the system rewards short-term partisan gain over long-term constitutional stewardship.

The chapter focuses on party systems as the key mechanism of transmission. Parties are supposed to aggregate interests, discipline extremism, and convert social conflict into governable coalitions. But when party structures become polarized, donor-driven, media-amplified, and identity-sorted, they can instead become engines of democratic entropy. Politicians then face perverse incentives: provoke outrage rather than build consensus, perform loyalty rather than deliberate, obstruct rather than govern, and treat institutional norms as expendable weapons in a permanent campaign.

Rather than framing the issue as individual corruption or moral weakness alone, the chapter presents a systems argument. Politicians respond to incentive fields created by primaries, campaign finance structures, media ecosystems, district design, and party competition rules. In such conditions, even rational actors can collectively produce irrational outcomes. The result is a dangerous feedback loop: polarization rewards performative extremism; extremism weakens trust; declining trust increases voter fear; fear empowers more extreme actors. Democracy is moving toward a breakdown threshold not because everyone intends collapse, but because institutional design converts ambition into destabilization.

A major theme of the chapter is the question of the **optimal number of political parties**. Two-party systems may produce clarity and alternation, but under conditions of intense polarization, they can harden conflict into binary warfare. Highly fragmented multiparty systems may broaden representation, but they can also produce paralysis and unstable coalition bargaining. The chapter argues that the healthiest democratic systems are those whose party structures preserve both competition and coalition capacity—enough pluralism to avoid tribal lock-in, but enough coherence to govern.

The chapter concludes that democratic decline is often the predictable outcome of incentive misalignment. To preserve democracy, reform must target the machinery that shapes political behavior: electoral rules, party structures, campaign incentives, and institutional guardrails. Without that redesign, politicians will continue to act less like custodians of the republic and more like accelerants at the edge of democratic breakdown.

Chapter 18 - How Income and Wealth Inequality Will Bring Down Democracy

This chapter argues that severe inequality is not merely a social problem or an economic imbalance; it is a direct structural threat to democracy's survival. Its central claim is that when income and wealth become too concentrated, democracy ceases to function as a regime of equal citizenship and becomes a hierarchy of unequal power.

The chapter traces the mechanisms by which inequality destabilizes democratic systems. At first, high inequality appears as an economic distributional issue: wages stagnate, asset ownership concentrates, and social mobility slows. But over time, those economic imbalances translate into political asymmetries. Wealth purchases access, access shapes policy, and policy protects wealth. As this cycle deepens, ordinary citizens increasingly perceive that formal political equality—one person, one vote—no longer corresponds to real influence. The result is a collapse in democratic legitimacy.

The chapter emphasizes the psychological and institutional consequences of inequality. Material insecurity breeds resentment, status anxiety, and distrust. Citizens who feel excluded from the economy's gains become more susceptible to demagoguery, scapegoating, and anti-system politics. Meanwhile, affluent actors become better able to insulate themselves from public consequences, weakening the reciprocal obligations that hold a democratic society together. The moral ecology of democracy begins to fracture: solidarity declines, common purpose erodes, and politics becomes a contest over extraction rather than a process of shared governance.

A key argument in the chapter is that inequality functions as a **slow-moving destabilizer**. Unlike coups or financial crashes, it does not always announce itself in a dramatic way. Instead, it gradually hollows out the middle class that sustains democratic moderation and institutional trust. As broad-based prosperity disappears, so too does the social ballast that allows democracies to absorb conflict without radicalization. In this sense, inequality is not peripheral to democratic breakdown; it is one of its deepest causal drivers.

The chapter concludes that if left unchecked, extreme income and wealth inequality will eventually pull democracy past a critical threshold. At that point, elections remain, but equal citizenship does not. Institutions persist, but legitimacy drains away. The democratic form survives while the democratic substance decays. The only durable response is to rebuild a political economy in which prosperity is sufficiently broad, mobility is credible, and power cannot so easily be converted from wealth into unelected rule.

Chapter 16

Why Democracy Is A Necessary and Sufficient Condition for a Capitalist Economic System

If by "capitalism" we mean not merely markets that exist, but a durable, innovative, legitimacy-preserving system of decentralized exchange and investment—one that can survive shocks, correct its own errors, and retain public consent across generations—then constitutional democracy is both necessary and (with minimal institutional complements) sufficient to sustain it. Markets can appear under autocracy, and democracies can adopt heavy state planning; those are real counterexamples to a naïve claim. But in complexity terms—the language of Democracy on the Edge of Chaos—they are typically fragile attractors: they may function for a while, yet they lack the feedback architecture that keeps capitalism from degenerating into predation, monopoly, and legitimacy collapse. Democracy is capitalism's error-correction system, anti-predation constraint, and adaptive learning loop. Without it, capitalism tends toward oligarchy; with it (and basic rule-of-law scaffolding), capitalism tends toward renewal.

What follows is an argument about institutions as nonlinear dynamics: capitalism as a complex adaptive system; democracy as the governance regime most compatible with complexity; and the joint system as a stability basin that can persist at the "edge of chaos"—innovative enough to evolve, constrained enough to avoid runaway collapse.

I. The Problem: Capitalism's Power Requires a Legitimation Machine

Capitalism is a marvel of coordination. It links strangers through prices, contracts, and expectations; it converts dispersed information into investable signals; it enables specialization at scale. But capitalism also concentrates power. It generates surplus and, without countervailing forces, channels it into rent-seeking, monopoly, political capture, and status insulation. In other words, capitalism is an engine that can either produce broad prosperity or become a self-reinforcing extraction machine.

This is the core instability: capitalism's efficiency depends on competition, but its profits tempt actors to kill competition. Successful firms lobby for privileges; wealthy actors seek favorable law; market winners try to convert economic power into political power, and political power back into economic advantage—closing the loop. In your book's vocabulary, this is a classic feedback loop that can push a society out of the stable region and into a turbulent regime: rising concentration → rising capture → declining legitimacy → declining compliance → crisis politics → even more capture.

If capitalism were only about production, it could, in principle, run under any regime that protects property and contract. But capitalism is also about consent—the public's willingness to accept inequality, creative destruction, and periodic downturns as the price of long-run growth. That consent is not automatic. It must be continuously earned and renewed. And that is where democracy enters—not as ornament, but as capitalism's legitimacy generator and self-repair mechanism.

II. Capitalism as a Complex Adaptive System (Not a Machine)

In a complex adaptive system:

1. Agents learn and change strategies.

2. Feedback loops amplify or dampen behaviors.

3. Nonlinearities produce phase transitions: small changes can trigger large shifts.

4. Information is local and partial, yet system-wide patterns emerge.

5. Stability is dynamic, not static—closer to "balancing on a bicycle" than "sitting on a chair."

Capitalism fits this perfectly. Market participants act on expectations; expectations affect prices; prices reshape investment; investment alters technology and employment; these changes alter politics and culture; politics rewrite the rules; rules reshape markets. The system is reflexive.

A crucial implication: capitalism needs governance that is itself adaptive. When technology changes, when industries consolidate, when financial innovations create hidden fragilities, when externalities (climate, public health, systemic risk) accumulate—rules must update. If the rules fail to update, capitalism enters a danger zone: the gap between system complexity and institutional capacity widens until it snaps via crisis.

Democracy—when functioning—is the political form best suited to continuous institutional learning in the face of complexity. Not because voters are omniscient (they aren't), but because democracy creates multiple channels of feedback and peaceful correction.

III. Democracy as the Meta-Institution for Error Correction

Democracy's deepest economic role is not "choosing leaders." It is enabling correction without catastrophe.

Think of democracy as a set of mechanisms:

- Voice: grievances can be expressed publicly.
- Contestability: power can be challenged without civil war.
- Alternation: leaders can be replaced without coups.
- Accountability: officials face scrutiny, hearings, courts, and elections.
- Transparency norms: a public sphere exists where claims can be tested.
- Pluralism: multiple centers of power compete and check one another.

These are not merely political virtues. They are economic stabilizers. They reduce the likelihood that capitalism will become a closed cartel. They make policy errors more reversible. They turn social conflict into institutional negotiation rather than systemic rupture.

In complexity terms: democracy supplies negative feedback (checks and constraints) to counteract capitalism's natural positive feedback loops (wealth → power → more wealth). Where democracy fails, capitalism's feedback often runs hot and self-amplifying until it flips the system into a different regime: crony capitalism, oligarchy, or populist-authoritarian reaction.

IV. Why Democracy Is Necessary for Capitalism (Properly Defined)

A critic will object: "But capitalism exists in non-democracies." True markets exist. Investment exists. Firms exist. Sometimes growth is rapid. But the necessity claim here is subtler:

Democracy is necessary for capitalism that is (a) broadly legitimate, (b) competition-preserving, (c) innovation-maximizing, and (d) stable across shocks and generations.

Call this durable liberal capitalism—not in the partisan sense, but in the institutional sense: rule of law, rights, contestability, and open entry. Democracy is necessary for at least six reasons:

1) Credible Commitment Against Predation

Capitalism requires that owners believe future governments won't arbitrarily seize assets, rewrite contracts, or selectively punish firms. Autocracy can protect property—until it doesn't. Because power is concentrated, policy can change suddenly; enforcement can be selective; elites can be purged; fortunes can be "reassigned." Even if an autocrat is benevolent, successors may not be.

Democracy disperses power and embeds constraints. It strengthens the credibility of commitments through courts, legislatures, independent institutions, and electoral punishment. Investors can price risk more accurately, and entrepreneurs can plan for the long term.

2) Competition Requires Political Anti-Monopoly Forces

Capitalism's health depends on entry and competition. But dominant firms often seek political barriers: licensing games, subsidies, procurement capture, regulatory capture, zoning barriers, or favorable tax treatment. Under non-democratic regimes, the capture channel is often simpler: influence a small circle, get a moat.

Democracy doesn't eliminate capture, but it creates countervailing coalitions: consumers, small businesses, labor, journalists, civil society, opposition parties. Antitrust is fundamentally political. So is open procurement. So are anti-corruption systems. Capitalism needs politics that can resist private empires.

3) Information Quality: Markets Need Truthful Signals

Prices are information. But information quality depends on a culture and infrastructure of truth: reliable statistics, free inquiry, whistleblowers, investigative journalism, academic independence, and the ability to criticize policy without fear.

Authoritarian systems often suppress bad news—about inflation, bank fragility, environmental damage, public health, or corruption. Suppressed information creates mispricing; mispricing creates bubbles and brittle supply chains; brittleness creates crises.

Democracy's open contest of ideas is messy, but it is a distributed error-detection network—exactly what complex economies need.

4) Legitimacy for Creative Destruction

Capitalism disrupts. It destroys firms, careers, regions, and identities. The public tolerates this only if they believe the system is fair, open, and responsive enough. Democracy supplies a narrative of agency: "We can change course. We can vote. We can reform."

Without that, disruption becomes humiliation; humiliation becomes rage; rage becomes political rupture. Many authoritarian capitalisms face a hidden timer: growth must remain high to substitute for consent. When growth slows, legitimacy evaporates quickly.

5) Public Goods and Externalities Require Collective Choice

Capitalism underproduces public goods (infrastructure, basic research, public health, resilient grids) and overproduces externalities (pollution, systemic risk). Correcting these is not optional; it is survival. The required corrections are inherently political. Democracy is the regime most capable—when healthy—of building durable social compacts around taxation, regulation, and investment.

6) Inequality Must Be Managed, or It Eats the System

Capitalism tends to generate inequality; unequal societies tend to produce political capture; capture undermines competition; undermined competition reduces growth; reduced growth intensifies conflict. That loop can drive the system to a phase transition—either into authoritarianism or into collapse.

Democracy is not automatically egalitarian, but it provides the institutional means to negotiate redistributive settlements (taxes, education, labor rules, antitrust, social insurance) that keep inequality within politically tolerable bounds. In this sense, democracy is capitalism's pressure-release valve.

Bottom line on necessity: You can have markets without democracy, but those markets tend to be conditional, personalized, and politically fragile—more "permissioned commerce" than capitalism as an open order. Durable capitalism needs democracy's constraints, legitimacy production, and learning loops.

V. Why Democracy Is Sufficient for Capitalism

The sufficiency claim is trickier because democracies can choose extensive state control. So, we must specify what "sufficient" means in institutional terms.

Here is a defensible sufficiency statement:

> **Given constitutional democracy plus baseline rule-of-law institutions (property rights, contract enforcement, an impartial judiciary, open entry norms), capitalism will emerge and persist because citizens and firms will choose decentralized exchange as the most adaptive prosperity engine available.**

In other words, democracy contains a selection mechanism. It does not guarantee laissez-faire, but it tends to generate a market economy for three structural reasons.

1) Democracy Aggregates Interests; Markets Serve Most Interests

Most voters want rising living standards, employment, innovation, and consumer choice. Fully centralized planning routinely struggles with information complexity and incentives; it becomes bureaucratic and brittle. Over time, democratic publics tend to support market mechanisms because market economies—especially mixed economies—deliver adaptability and pluralism.

2) Pluralism Creates Economic Pluralism

Democracy implies plural centers of power. Plural power tends to resist total economic centralization because it empowers whichever faction controls the state. Opposition groups, regions, and civil society often demand autonomous economic spaces—private enterprise, cooperatives, independent unions, and nonprofit sectors. That pluralism is market-compatible and usually market-generative.

3) Innovation Requires Freedom to Experiment

Capitalism's deepest advantage is decentralized experimentation: thousands of entrepreneurial trials, most failing, a few transforming society. Democracy—again, when healthy—protects the freedoms that experimentation requires: speech, association, and property security. Those freedoms naturally fertilize markets.

So, democracy is "sufficient" not because it forces capitalism, but because it creates the political ecology in which decentralized exchange is the dominant, repeatedly selected strategy for achieving prosperity under complexity.

VI. The Edge-of-Chaos Bargain: Democracy + Capitalism as a Coupled System

The book's central metaphor—the edge of chaos—captures a real governance dilemma:

- Too much rigidity and control → stagnation, corruption, and brittle failure.
- Too much volatility and fragmentation → disorder, paralysis, collapse.

Capitalism supplies creative volatility; democracy supplies stabilizing legitimacy and correction. Together they form a coupled system that can remain in a productive band: dynamic, innovative, but governable.

We can describe the coupled system as two interlocking loops:

The Market Loop (Exploration)
Innovation → productivity → growth → new industries → new risks → new inequalities → new social demands.

The Democratic Loop (Correction)
Public voice → political contestation → policy adjustment → constraint on capture → renewed legitimacy → continued compliance.

When both loops function, society stays near a stable attractor: competition stays open enough, inequality stays politically manageable, and shocks are absorbed without regime breakdown.

When either loop breaks, the system drifts:

- Market loop without democratic correction → oligarchy, cronyism, brittle growth, explosive legitimacy crises.
- Democratic loop without market dynamism → distributive conflict over a stagnant pie, populism, fiscal stress, rising polarization, institutional exhaustion.

In phase-space terms, the system's trajectory depends on whether democratic feedback can quickly dampen capitalism's runaway tendencies to prevent a regime shift.

VII. The Failure Mode: Capitalism Without Democracy Becomes "Permissioned Capitalism"

When democracy is absent or hollowed out, capitalism often mutates:

1. Political access becomes the main factor of production.
2. Law becomes selective.
3. Competition becomes managed.
4. Innovation becomes subordinated to regime security.
5. Wealth becomes a function of loyalty, not value creation.

This is not capitalism's stable form; it is a transition state that can deliver growth early (especially by mobilizing labor and investment) but tends to become brittle as complexity rises. Eventually, three problems intensify:

- Misallocation (projects chosen for politics, not productivity),
- Information suppression (bad news punished),
- Succession uncertainty (policy volatility around leadership change).

The result is often a boom-and-fracture pattern—growth punctuated by sudden crises—rather than the self-renewing adaptive capitalism that democracies can sustain.

VIII. The Other Failure Mode: Democracy Without Capitalism Risks Cognitive and Fiscal Overload

Democracy also has a fragility: it is demanding. It requires citizens to tolerate losing elections, accept pluralism, and sustain trust in institutions. When growth is weak, and opportunity closes, democratic politics can degrade into:

- constant redistribution fights,
- scapegoating,
- conspiracy-driven "epistemic civil war,"
- and incentives for politicians to promise impossible outcomes.

Markets are not morally sufficient, but they are often economically necessary for democracies to fund public goods, social insurance, and opportunity creation. That is why the democracy-capitalism pairing has historically been such a powerful stability strategy: it aligns material improvement with political consent.

IX. The Present Danger: Cognitive Capture and the Collapse of Corrective Feedback

The book's central themes—misinformation, cognitive capture, polarization—map exactly onto the coupled-system view.

Democracy's economic function depends on signal quality: voters must be able to detect failure, attribute responsibility, and coordinate around reforms. When information ecosystems fracture, democracy loses its capacity for correction. Then capitalism's pathologies intensify unchecked: capture, monopoly, inequality, and corruption. In turn, economic pain fuels more misinformation and polarization.

This is a nonlinear spiral: at first, it looks like ordinary dysfunction; then suddenly, the system tips into delegitimation, constitutional crisis, or normalized authoritarian tactics.

Therefore, the defense of capitalism today is inseparable from the defense of democratic epistemics:

- credible institutions,
- anti-corruption enforcement,
- competition policy,
- transparency,
- and a public sphere that can converge on reality often enough to govern.

X. Institutional Design: Making Democracy Capitalism's Guardian Again

If democracy is capitalism's necessary and sufficient condition in the durable sense, then the practical question becomes: what keeps democracy healthy enough to perform that role?

Several design principles follow naturally from the argument:

1) Keep Entry Open in Both Markets and Politics

- Strong antitrust and anti-monopoly tools
- Anti-gerrymandering and anti-entrenchment reforms
- Competitive procurement and anti-corruption enforcement

2) Reduce the ROI of Capture

- Transparency for lobbying and political spending
- Revolving-door limits

- Clear conflict-of-interest rules
- Independent enforcement capacity

3) Rebuild Shared-Reality Infrastructure

- Statistical integrity
- Public-interest journalism
- Civic education that emphasizes institutional literacy
- Platform accountability where necessary (without politicized censorship)

4) Make the Growth Bargain Broad-Based

- Opportunity policies (education, mobility, entrepreneurship access)
- Labor bargaining power consistent with productivity growth
- Regional investment so capitalism is not experienced as geographic humiliation

5) Create Shock Absorbers

- Automatic stabilizers in recessions
- Financial regulation that limits systemic risk
- Resilience investments (grids, climate adaptation, supply chains)

These are not "left" or "right" in the complexity frame. They are stability conditions—the guardrails that keep a democracy-capitalism system in its productive attractor basin.

XI. Conclusion: Democracy Is Capitalism's Legitimacy, Learning, and Limits

The deepest reason democracy matters for capitalism is that capitalism is not only an economic system. It is a social bargain under uncertainty. It asks citizens to accept inequality, disruption, and risk in exchange for opportunity, dynamism, and rising prosperity. That bargain holds only when people believe the system is contestable, correctable, and fundamentally theirs.

Democracy supplies what capitalism alone cannot:

- Legitimacy (consent that survives downturns),
- Learning (policy correction under complexity),
- Limits (constraints that prevent predation and monopoly),
- Voice (channels for grievance that avert rupture),
- Peaceful adaptation (change without violence).

And capitalism supplies what democracy alone struggles to generate:

- decentralized experimentation,
- innovation at scale,
- the material basis for pluralism,
- and the fiscal capacity for public goods.

So, yes—within the conceptual frame that Democracy on the Edge of Chaos implies: democracy is capitalism's necessary and sufficient condition when capitalism is defined as a durable, competition-preserving, legitimacy-maintaining open order. Without democracy, capitalism tends to mutate into extraction and brittle privilege. With democracy—and the rule-of-law minimum—capitalism tends to emerge because it is the most adaptive wealth engine available to free citizens navigating complexity. In nonlinear times, the choice is not "democracy or prosperity." The choice is whether we preserve the only political architecture that can keep prosperity from eating itself.

When Democracy Stops Being Sufficient

The Conditions Under Which Democratic Capitalism Fails to Self-Stabilize

In the main argument, democracy is "sufficient" for a durable capitalist order, provided it is paired with baseline complements: rule of law, credible property/contract enforcement, open entry, and a public sphere capable of converging on reality often enough to govern. The sufficiency claim is therefore not mystical. It is conditional—and that conditionality matters in nonlinear times.

This companion section specifies when democracy stops being sufficient—when the democratic feedback loop that normally corrects capitalism's excesses breaks down, and the coupled system (democracy + capitalism) exits its stable basin and drifts toward one of three failure attractors:

1. Oligarchic capture (capitalism without meaningful democracy)
2. Populist-authoritarian closure (democracy hollowed into plebiscitary rule)
3. Governing paralysis and fragmentation (democracy intact on paper, incapable in practice)

The point is not that democracy "fails because voters are irrational." The deeper claim—consistent with Democracy on the Edge of Chaos—is that complex systems fail when feedback becomes corrupted: signals degrade, delays lengthen, incentives distort, and small disturbances are amplified rather than dampened. Democracy becomes insufficient when it can no longer perform its economic role: error correction, legitimacy renewal, and anti-predation constraint.

1) The Sufficiency Threshold: Democracy Must Keep Three Loops Healthy

A democracy remains sufficient to sustain a stable capitalist order only if three loops remain functional:

A. The Legitimacy Loop

Performance + fairness + voice → consent → compliance → governability → performance.

When citizens believe the system is broadly fair and responsive, they accept losses, tolerate disruption, and comply with rules—even when outcomes sting.

B. The Competition Loop

Open entry + anti-monopoly enforcement → innovation → productivity → broad opportunity → support for open entry.

Capitalism needs political conditions that protect competition against the natural drift toward concentration and rent extraction.

C. The Epistemic Loop

Shared reality + trusted measurement → accountable policy → correction → trust.

Democracy requires a minimum viable shared reality: not total agreement, but enough common ground to identify failure and assign responsibility.

When any of these loops breaks, "democracy" may still exist formally (elections, parties, legislatures), yet it ceases to be sufficient to stabilize capitalism. At that point, capitalism's positive feedback loops dominate, and the system begins to slide.

2) Failure Condition One: Epistemic Collapse (Democracy Without Truth)

A democracy is not only a voting mechanism; it is a knowledge system. It depends on the public's ability to detect errors and coordinate around corrections. Sufficiency fails when truth becomes factional, and the system cannot agree on basic inputs: inflation, crime trends, election legitimacy, epidemic risk, fiscal constraints, or even who is responsible for policy outcomes.

Mechanisms of epistemic collapse

- Information fragmentation: parallel realities form; facts become identity markers.
- Misinformation as strategy: political actors gain by inflaming distrust rather than solving problems.
- Institutional delegitimation: courts, statisticians, auditors, universities, and journalists become seen as partisan weapons.
- Attention capture: outrage outcompetes nuance; democratic deliberation loses to virality.

Why this breaks capitalist stability

Capitalism requires credible signals—prices, statistics, risk assessments, and trustworthy regulation. If the epistemic loop collapses:

- markets misprice risk (bubbles, bank fragility, supply-chain brittleness),
- corruption becomes harder to detect,
- policy becomes theater rather than correction,
- and legitimacy erodes because citizens cannot tell whether failures are real, fabricated, or unavoidable.

In phase-space terms: epistemic collapse increases noise and reduces signal until the governance system oscillates—overreacting to phantoms and underreacting to real threats. That is how a democracy drifts into an authoritarian "decisiveness" attractor: people trade pluralism for the promise of certainty.

3) Failure Condition Two: Capture Saturation (When Money Eats Politics)

Democracy is sufficient only if it can restrain capitalism's conversion of wealth into power. Sufficiency fails when capture becomes so pervasive that elections no longer change policy in meaningful ways—especially on core distributional and competition questions.

Capture saturation looks like:

- regulatory agencies structurally dependent on the industries they regulate,
- procurement and subsidies concentrated among politically connected firms,
- revolving-door norms that make enforcement performative,
- policy complexity weaponized to hide rents,
- and campaign finance ecosystems that turn legislators into permanent fundraisers.

Why this breaks capitalism rather than "helping business"

At high levels of capture:

- competition dies (moats widen; entry costs rise),
- innovation slows (rent-seeking outperforms invention),
- inequality hardens into caste-like immobility, and
- public consent collapses (the system appears rigged).

This is capitalism's classic nonlinear trap: the more power concentrates, the easier it is to concentrate further. Democracy becomes insufficient when it cannot supply the negative feedback needed to break that loop.

4) Failure Condition Three: Inequality Beyond the Consent Band

In this Systems Humanism framework, the key is not inequality as a moral complaint; it is inequality as a system parameter that changes behavior, incentives, and legitimacy. Democracy remains sufficient only while inequality stays within a politically tolerable band—a zone where the majority still believes upward mobility is real, rules are roughly fair, and winners do not fully own the state.

When inequality exceeds that band, three destabilizers appear:

1. Status humiliation and resentment replace policy disagreement.
2. Polarization becomes moralized ("they're not just wrong; they're evil").
3. Politics becomes existential because the stakes are no longer marginal—they're survival.

At that point, democratic capitalism tends to bifurcate into one of two unstable strategies:

- Redistributive maximalism that triggers capital flight, investment strikes, and fiscal stress, or
- Repressive stabilization that protects property and elites by reducing democratic constraints.

Either path can end in authoritarian closure or chronic crisis.

5) Failure Condition Four: Governance Overload and State Capacity Erosion

Democracy can choose good policies only if the state can implement them. Sufficiency fails when democratic demands exceed administrative capacity—when the system becomes a permanent "promise machine" with diminishing delivery.

Drivers of overload

- escalating complexity (AI, cyber risk, financial innovation, climate shocks),
- hollowed agencies and declining professional norms,
- procurement dysfunction and contractor dependence,
- fiscal constraints that turn every reform into a zero-sum fight,
- and legal/political veto points that multiply delays.

The nonlinear effect

As delivery fails, citizens stop believing the system can act. That belief shift is itself a phase transition: it transforms politics from problem-solving into blame allocation and identity warfare. Markets then face heightened uncertainty, and investment horizons shorten. This accelerates the drift toward oligarchy (private governance) or authoritarianism (force-based coordination).

6) Failure Condition Five: Polarization That Converts Competition Into Tribal War

Democracy presumes losing is tolerable. Sufficiency fails when losing becomes intolerable—when parties and factions believe the other side's victory threatens their basic status, rights, or survival.

At high polarization:

- compromise becomes betrayal,
- procedural fairness becomes suspect,
- and institutions become battlefields rather than referees.

This fractures the legitimacy loop: if half the country believes the other half is illegitimate, democratic outcomes no longer renew consent; they intensify conflict. Capitalism then inherits a permanent instability premium: regulatory lurches, investment uncertainty, and rising security costs.

In edge-of-chaos terms: polarization pushes the system from "productive contestation" into "runaway oscillation and turbulence."

7) Failure Condition Six: The "Emergency Powers" Ratchet

Crises happen—pandemics, terror attacks, financial meltdowns, and natural disasters. Democracy remains sufficient only if it can use emergency powers temporarily and then unwind them. Sufficiency fails when emergencies become a pretext for permanent exception—when crisis governance becomes the new normal.

The ratchet effect looks like:

- expanded surveillance without robust sunset clauses,
- executive dominance over legislatures,
- politicized law enforcement,
- and the normalization of "ends justify means" thinking.

Once an exception becomes permanent, capitalism becomes permissioned: investment depends on political alignment, and property rights become contingent. The system may still produce wealth, but it loses open-entry dynamism and long-run trust.

8) Failure Condition Seven: Intergenerational and Geographic Fracture

Democracy is sufficient when citizens maintain a shared sense of mutual obligation across regions and age cohorts. Sufficiency fails when prosperity becomes geographically and generationally segregated.

Symptoms:

- superstar cities vs. hollowed regions,
- asset owners vs. wage earners,
- credentialed networks vs. precarity,
- young cohorts see homeownership, social mobility, and financial security as unattainable.

This produces a dangerous political geometry: coalitions stop forming around policy and start forming around grievance identity. That shift makes capture easier and reform harder—again weakening the correction loop.

9) The Collapse Pathways: How the System Actually Tips

In complex systems, breakdown is rarely linear. Democracies typically tip via one of these pathways:

Pathway A:
Slow corruption → sudden legitimacy break

A long period of rising capture and inequality, followed by a catalytic scandal or crisis that reveals how hollow the system is.

Pathway B:
Epistemic fracture → authoritarian "clarity" demand

When reality is contested, citizens seek a single authoritative narrator. The promise is stability; the result is closure.

Pathway C:
Capacity failure → privatization of governance

When the state can't deliver, private actors fill the vacuum: gated services, private security, private arbitration, corporate welfare systems. Democracy remains—but capitalism becomes feudalized.

Pathway D:
Polarization + emergency → rules rewritten

An emergency enables one side to entrench itself; the opposition rejects legitimacy; institutions become partisan weapons. Market dynamism survives temporarily, but long-run stability collapses.

Diagnostics: Early Warning Indicators of "Insufficiency Drift"

You can operationalize "democracy stops being sufficient" with observable indicators:

- Rising policy–opinion disconnect (public preference shifts without policy response)
- Declining trust in referees (courts, auditors, election administrators, statistics agencies)
- Concentration metrics rising while antitrust/enforcement falls
- Mobility declines (especially for the bottom 80%)
- Violence or intimidation enters normal politics
- Emergency powers persist without sunset and oversight
- Budget dysfunction becomes chronic (shutdown cycles, debt brinkmanship, fiscal paralysis)
- Media ecosystem becomes segregated by identity (minimal cross-exposure)

These indicators map neatly onto a phase-space intuition: the system is leaving the stable basin.

10) Regaining Sufficiency: The Minimal Repair Kit

If democracy has drifted toward insufficiency, the repair strategy is not utopian. It is targeted: rebuilding the loops is existential.

Rebuild the epistemic loop

- protect measurement integrity (statistics, auditing, oversight),

- reduce incentive gradients for disinformation,
- create credible cross-partisan "referee" institutions.

Reduce capture saturation

- transparency and enforceable conflict-of-interest rules,
- procurement firewalls,
- real consequences for corruption,
- competition policy with teeth.

Restore the consent band

- mobility and opportunity reforms (education, housing supply, entrepreneurship access),
- labor-market bargaining structures compatible with productivity,
- anti-monopoly to reduce rent extraction.

Strengthen state capacity

- professionalize agencies,
- simplify delivery mechanisms,
- reduce veto-point sabotage,
- insulate core functions from partisan purges.

The goal is not perfection. It is to restore sufficient negative feedback so the system can self-correct again and return to a stable basin.

Closing: Sufficiency Is a Dynamic Property, Not a Label

Democracy does not become insufficient because people suddenly become worse. It becomes insufficient when the feedback architecture degrades—when truth cannot be shared, when capture overwhelms constraint, when inequality exceeds consent, when capacity collapses, when polarization turns elections into existential war, and when emergencies become a permanent exception.

In terms of Democracy on the Edge of Chaos, democracy is sufficient for capitalism only within a bounded region of the institutional parameter space. Outside that region, the coupled system undergoes a phase transition, and capitalism mutates—either into oligarchy, authoritarian permissioning, or fragmented privatized governance.

The central warning is therefore also a prescription: protect the loops. Because when democracy loses its corrective function, capitalism does not remain "capitalism." It becomes something older and darker: extraction with a price system—an economy that still moves, but no longer learns, no longer renews legitimacy, and no longer belongs to its citizens.

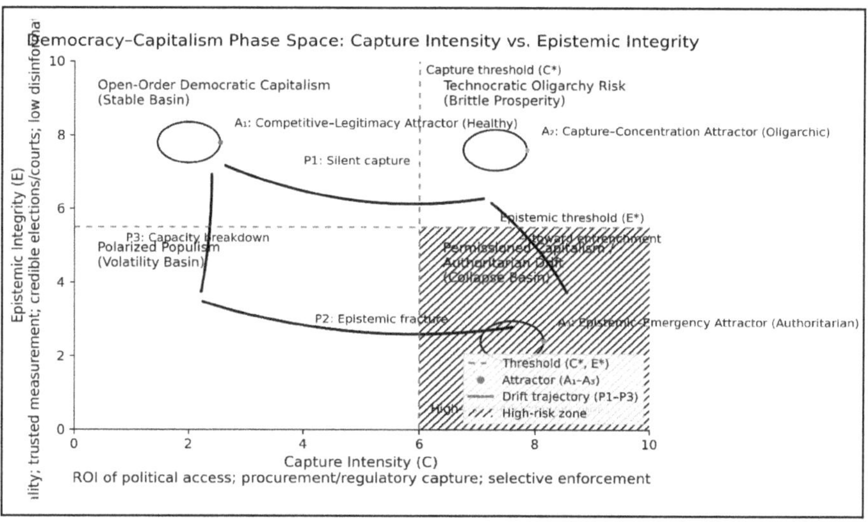

Figure 9.0: *Democracy-Capitalism Phase Space Diagram*

This phase-space diagram maps the stability of democratic capitalism using two system parameters: Capture Intensity (C) on the horizontal axis and Epistemic Integrity (E) on the vertical axis. When capture is constrained, and shared-reality institutions remain credible (upper-left), the system resides in a stable basin—an open-order regime where competition is defended politically, policy errors can be detected, and legitimacy is renewed through accountable correction. Two dotted thresholds mark tipping conditions: crossing the capture threshold (C*) means elections may still rotate leaders, but policy becomes structurally unresponsive as rents persist; crossing the epistemic threshold (E*) means democratic error-correction fails because reality becomes factional and referees (courts, elections, statistics, and congressional oversight). lose legitimacy. The three attractors summarize long-run tendencies: a healthy competitive–legitimacy loop (A_1), a capture–concentration loop that converts markets into permissioned privilege (A_2), and an epistemic–emergency loop where crisis politics ratchets permanent exception (A_3). Trajectories illustrate common drift paths—silent capture, epistemic fracture, and capacity breakdown—showing how systems can slide from stability into the high-risk lower-right zone, where rapid phase transitions toward entrenchment and authoritarian drift become more likely.

Chapter 17

Politicians Are Destroying Democracy: Party Systems, Incentives, and the Edge of Democratic Breakdown

Democracy Is Usually Destroyed in installments.

Democracy is rarely destroyed in one dramatic gesture. More often, it is consumed by accumulation: a tolerated falsehood here, a procedural abuse there, a captured appointment, a vindictive prosecution, a sham investigation, a deliberately inflammatory speech, a cynical campaign tactic, a frightened electorate, and an institution that is asked to bend just a little farther than it should. Citizens usually imagine democratic collapse as an event, but in practice, it is more often a process. The rules remain visible as their substance thins. Elections continue while legitimacy drains away. Parliaments meet, courts issue opinions, bureaucracies function, and constitutions are quoted, yet the habits that make self-government possible begin to erode. That is why the claim that politicians are destroying democracy should not be dismissed as merely rhetorical. It names a structural reality: many of the actors charged with maintaining democratic order now profit from destabilizing it. They benefit from outrage more than from restraint, from mobilization more than from settlement, and from symbolic warfare more than from competent governance.

A healthy democratic order depends on a dense network of expectations that are rarely written down but are indispensable in practice. Losers must believe they can lose an election and remain fully part of the political community. Winners must exercise restraint when they are tempted to treat temporary control as moral ownership of the state. Opponents must be regarded as legitimate adversaries rather than enemies to be extinguished. Courts, agencies, civil servants, and electoral administrators must be trusted at least enough to perform their tasks without being reduced to factional instruments the moment they do so. Citizens must believe that law can outlast personality. When those expectations weaken, democracy becomes vulnerable to nonlinear breakdown. A single scandal may not matter in a healthy polity, but in a system already overloaded with distrust, each new abuse interacts with every previous one. The result is not linear decay but compounding fragility.

In that sense, democracy should be understood as a complex adaptive system rather than a simple constitutional machine. It contains feedback loops, threshold effects, delayed consequences, and tipping points. Political behavior changes the environment in which future political behavior occurs. Leaders who discover that extreme rhetoric attracts donations, media attention, and primary support will use it more. Citizens repeatedly exposed to apocalyptic narratives become more willing to accept extraordinary measures. Opponents respond to perceived danger with their own escalation. What begins as tactical maneuvering becomes a new equilibrium of permanent conflict. Politicians do not need to abolish democracy outright to damage it. They can hollow it out from within by altering incentives, degrading norms, and converting the energy of disagreement into a business model of civic exhaustion.

I. The Incentive Structure of Democratic Arson

The first reason politicians increasingly damage democracy is that the contemporary political incentive structure rewards destructive conduct. In theory, elected officials should be rewarded for governing competently, building durable coalitions, solving public problems, and preserving trust in constitutional procedure. In practice, the rewards of political life have shifted. Fundraising, visibility, narrative control, ideological signaling, and conflict performance often matter more than legislative craftsmanship or administrative competence. The politician who can dominate the news cycle, activate donor networks, and keep supporters emotionally mobilized may survive repeated failures of governance. The politician who labors quietly to produce incremental gains may be respected in private and defeated in public.

This transformation is partly the result of the permanent campaign. Elections once punctuated governance; now, campaigning and governing are fused. Every committee hearing can be clipped into a fundraising video. Every oversight dispute can be framed as persecution or patriotic defense. Every compromise can be denounced as betrayal. The temporal logic of politics changes under these conditions. Leaders stop asking whether an action strengthens the republic over ten years and start asking whether it strengthens the coalition over ten days. Institutions built to mediate conflict are repurposed as branding stages. The legislature becomes content. The executive becomes the theater. Public administration becomes a symbolic battleground rather than a field of professional stewardship.

Systems shape character. Even good people adapt to the rewards and punishments embedded in institutions. If the ambitious politician learns that outrage is a cheaper route to recognition than expertise, he or she will tend to prefer outrage. If primary elections are dominated by a smaller, angrier, more ideologically intense subset of voters, candidates will move toward rhetorical extremes rather than toward broad civic legitimacy. If donors reward ideological combat and punish compromise, parties will select for conflict performers. Under these conditions, democratic life becomes structurally biased toward escalation. It is not merely that bad individuals enter politics; it is that politics increasingly makes bad conduct rational. That is why moral condemnation alone is insufficient. Democracies that wish to preserve themselves must re-engineer the incentive environment so that constitutional stewardship once again produces more political advantage than democratic arson.

II. The Epistemic Sabotage of Self-Government

Democracy requires more than ballots. It requires a minimally shared reality. Citizens do not need to agree on values, but they must agree enough about facts to deliberate, judge performance, and accept outcomes. When politicians strategically undermine that shared reality, they attack the cognitive foundation of self-government. This is one of the most destructive features of contemporary democratic decay. The point is not simply that politicians lie; politicians have always lied. The greater danger is that many now seek to convince citizens that truth itself is merely a factional weapon. They train supporters to interpret every inconvenient fact as propaganda, every neutral institution as captured, and every correction as an act of hostility.

The result is not ordinary misinformation but organized epistemic sabotage. Instead of persuading the public through coherent arguments, leaders flood the public sphere with contradictions, insinuations, conspiratorial narratives, selective information releases, and strategic ambiguity. These techniques are powerful because they shift the burden of proof. Citizens become exhausted. Rather than evaluating competing claims on the basis of evidence, they retreat into identity-based trust. They believe what their side says because it is their side. Once that happens, accountability collapses. A politician can fail repeatedly, contradict prior statements, or make demonstrably false claims and still retain support if followers are convinced that all external verification is corrupt.

A democratic society deprived of error-correction becomes increasingly unstable. Policy failure cannot be recognized openly, so it cannot be learned from. Institutional criticism cannot be received in good faith, so reform becomes nearly impossible. Voters no longer compare reality to rhetoric; they compare rival stories of belonging. The most dangerous political figure in such an environment is not simply the liar but the leader who teaches citizens to stop caring about whether truth exists outside partisan need. That leader immunizes the coalition against correction and converts civic judgment into tribal loyalty. Once that occurs, election disputes become easier to inflame, courts become easier to discredit, and administrative expertise becomes easier to discard. Politicians who degrade shared reality are not just distorting debate; they are attacking the operating system of democratic reason.

III.A. The Algorithmic Market for Outrage

The contemporary politician also operates inside an information environment that rewards emotional extremity. Digital platforms are not neutral carriers of speech. They are sorting and amplification systems that privilege speed, novelty, moral accusation, conflict, and emotionally activating content. A remark crafted to enrage, shame, or terrify will often travel farther than a careful explanation of institutional constraints. These change political incentives at the most practical level. The politician who wants to reach learns that procedural nuance is expensive, and outrage is cheap.

The democratic damage is intensified because the economics of attention and the economics of politics now reinforce one another. A polarizing statement can generate media coverage, social-media circulation, small-dollar donations, activist enthusiasm, and partisan solidarity at once. The politician does not merely gain publicity; they also accrue a measurable political return from escalating public tension. Conversely, the politician who speaks with moderation may receive less engagement, less coverage, and less fundraising energy. Over time, this creates a selective environment that favors figures willing to live at the edge of rhetorical irresponsibility.

Algorithmic amplification also shortens political time. Leaders are pressured to respond immediately to every controversy, often before facts are clear and before institutions have had time to act. Deliberation looks slow, while instant condemnation looks decisive. Complex policy problems are compressed into viral fragments. The result is a permanently overclocked public sphere. Citizens are exposed not to an orderly sequence of debate and decision but to a continuous stream of emotionally charged prompts. In that state, suspicion rises faster than understanding. Political identity becomes more reactive. Institutional trust erodes because every event is instantly framed in maximalist terms.

This environment does not mechanically produce a democratic breakdown, but it greatly increases the advantages enjoyed by political actors who can weaponize outrage. It also makes it harder for institutions to repair trust after it has been damaged, because every attempt at clarification competes with faster, more vivid, and more tribal forms of communication. Democracy can survive disagreement. It struggles when the dominant channels of public attention systematically reward those who intensify disagreement into hatred. Politicians who master this environment gain influence, but the republic inherits a more combustible civic culture.

III. From Opposition to Enmity

A functioning democracy depends on opposition. It cannot survive without organized disagreement, competitive parties, and the regular alternation of power. Yet democracy becomes fragile when opposition is transformed into enmity. This is the political move by which ordinary rivals are recast as traitors, usurpers, invaders, civilizational contaminants, or enemies of the people. That shift is emotionally powerful because it compresses complexity into moral combat. It relieves politicians of the obligation to persuade by allowing them to frighten. It also turns every election into a referendum on collective survival.

Once citizens are taught that the opposing party is fundamentally illegitimate, compromise begins to resemble surrender. Procedural restraint looks like weakness. Even ordinary bargaining can be reinterpreted as collaboration with evil. Politicians benefit from this atmosphere because fear is a remarkable organizing tool. It increases turnout, hardens donor loyalty, and makes ideological discipline easier to enforce. But what strengthens the campaign can weaken the republic. If every contest is existential, then every extraordinary measure to stop the other side appears justified. Rules that once seemed sacred become negotiable. Constitutional norms become tactical options. The public begins to accept the logic that defeating the enemy matters more than preserving the framework for peacefully opposing enemies.

This is how democracies drift toward reciprocal radicalization. One faction escalates because it believes the other is a mortal threat. The other faction, perceiving existential intent, responds with its own escalation. Both then claim they are merely reacting to the other's danger. Each side can point to real abuse by the other. Each side develops a moral narrative in which constitutional hardball becomes a form of patriotic necessity. In this spiral, responsibility is diffused even as the system becomes more brittle. The constitution survives on paper, but the republic's moral ecology deteriorates. What was once a bounded conflict becomes an unending contest for domination. A democracy at that point still possesses formal institutions, but it increasingly lacks the civic imagination required to use them for coexistence.

IV. The Legalism of Decay: Constitutional Hardball

One of the most misunderstood aspects of democratic erosion is that it is often carried out through legal or quasi-legal means. Citizens tend to imagine democratic collapse as an explicit suspension of the constitution. Much damage is done by actors who work aggressively within the letter of the law while ignoring its spirit. They stretch procedural advantages, weaponize timing, exploit ambiguities, delay appointments, flood courts, manipulate oversight, invoke emergency powers, redraw boundaries, and bend administrative discretion for partisan gain. Each act can be defended as technically permissible. The cumulative effect, however, is to transform constitutional government into a competition over how ruthlessly the rules can be gamed.

This is the domain of constitutional hardball. It occurs when political actors use lawful tools in ways that violate norms of restraint and mutual toleration. Democracies depend on more than enforceable rules. They also depend on the voluntary decision not to weaponize every available advantage. If one party begins to do so consistently, the other learns that restraint is strategically costly. It responds in kind. What begins as one-sided hardball becomes reciprocal escalation. Over time, the abnormal becomes routine. Practices that once caused outrage are now accepted features of the political landscape simply because they have been repeated enough times.

The public often struggles to recognize the danger because nothing dramatic has visibly happened. Elections are still scheduled. Parliamentary procedure is still invoked. Judicial opinions are still issued. Yet the deeper logic of the system has changed. Institutions no longer function as neutral arenas for processing conflict; they become arsenals for positional war. Judges are selected as partisan trophies. Procedural delay becomes a moral performance. Budgets become weapons. Investigations become rituals of humiliation. The cost of this legalized aggression is not merely inefficiency. It is the corrosion of legitimacy. Citizens begin to believe that law is no longer a shared framework, but a resource captured and deployed by whoever is temporarily strongest. Once that belief spreads, compliance becomes more conditional, distrust more general, and democracy more fragile.

V. The Monetization of Representation

Modern democratic politics is increasingly shaped by the monetization of representation. In principle, elected officials are agents of the public, accountable to citizens through elections and constrained by institutional checks. In practice, many become dependent on financial ecosystems that reshape what representation means. Campaigns require money. Visibility requires money. Staff require money. Party influence, media access, and organizational endurance all require money. Under such conditions, politicians become tied not only to voters but to donor networks, lobbying structures, patronage relationships, and industries that possess the resources to continuously shape agenda-setting.

The most damaging feature of this process is that overt bribery is not required for democratic distortion to occur. Dependence itself is enough. A politician who must constantly raise funds internalizes the preferences of the people most capable of giving them. He or she learns what proposals are too costly to advance, which interests are too dangerous to challenge, and which forms of rhetoric reliably unlock financial support. Even without explicit instruction, a narrowing of acceptable policy options takes place. Citizens are invited to vote, but the field of realistic political possibilities has already been filtered by concentrated influence.

This produces a widening gap between electoral ritual and substantive responsiveness. Voters hear grand promises while observing that core material problems remain stubbornly unsolved. Wages stagnate, housing becomes unaffordable, public services degrade, and yet political messaging grows ever more theatrical. That mismatch breeds disillusionment. Citizens start to suspect that the system is democratic in ceremony but oligarchic in operation. The tragedy is that this disillusionment then becomes politically useful to the very forces that produced it. Politicians who helped empty democracy of effectiveness can pivot and condemn "the establishment," presenting themselves as insurgents against a system they know intimately. In this way, the monetization of representation does not merely distort policy. It produces the emotional conditions under which demagogic anti-system politics can thrive.

VI. Governing by Performance, Not by Capacity

Another way politicians destroy democracy is by reducing governance to performance while neglecting state capacity. Democracies are not sustained by speeches alone. They require competent institutions capable of implementing laws, producing reliable information, coordinating across agencies, managing budgets, enforcing neutral standards, and delivering public goods. Yet many politicians now treat the state less as a structure to be maintained than as a stage on which narratives of strength, outrage, and symbolic loyalty can be performed.

This leads to a vicious cycle. Public institutions are politicized, underfunded, hollowed out, or staffed according to partisan allegiance rather than administrative competence. Predictably, performance suffers. Citizens experience frustration with delays, failures, and inconsistency. Politicians then point to these failures as proof that government itself is broken, using the resulting distrust to justify further attacks on the institutions they weakened. Deliberate degradation creates dysfunction; dysfunction creates cynicism; cynicism legitimizes deeper degradation. What appears to be an ideological conflict over the size of government is, in practice, often a struggle over whether the republic will retain the state capacity needed to govern at all.

The long-term effect is profound. Once citizens no longer expect neutral competence from public institutions, they become more dependent on factional intermediaries, personal networks, and charismatic patrons. Instead of relying on law, they seek access. Instead of trusting procedure, they cultivate proximity to power. This is a classic route from republican citizenship to clientelist dependency. The state ceases to function as an impersonal system of rules and becomes a prize to be captured. Politicians who prefer symbolic combat to administrative stewardship therefore do not merely make government less efficient. They erode one of the deepest preconditions of democratic legitimacy: the public belief that common institutions can act, however imperfectly, on behalf of everyone.

VII. Personalism and the Temptation of the Indispensable Leader

A constitutional democracy is designed to separate public authority from personal rule. Offices should matter more than occupants. Procedures should matter more than charisma. Leaders should be temporary trustees, not embodiments of the state. Yet personalism is one of the recurrent pathologies of democratic decline, and contemporary politicians often cultivate it deliberately. They present themselves as the singular voice of the nation, the authentic expression of "real" citizens, the one leader without whom the country will collapse. This is a potent political narrative because it offers emotional clarity in a complex world. Citizens exhausted by institutional drift may find reassurance in a leader who claims to cut through procedure and act decisively.

But the personalist logic is poison to constitutional order. Once loyalty shifts from the law to the individual, criticism becomes sacrilege. Internal party disagreement becomes betrayal. Succession becomes dangerous because the political coalition has fused its sense of purpose to a single figure. Under these conditions, parties cease to function as mediating institutions that discipline ambition and aggregate interests. They become protective shells around the leader. Appointments are made for loyalty, not merit. Narratives are crafted to preserve the leader's image, not public trust. Institutions exist increasingly to validate personal authority rather than to constrain it.

The transition from party politics to personalist politics also changes how citizens understand legitimacy. Instead of believing that power is legitimate when won through fair procedures, followers begin to believe it is legitimate when held by the right person. If that person loses, the result appears suspicious. This is why personalism and election denial are natural partners. A movement built around the myth of the indispensable leader will always struggle to accept ordinary democratic defeat. In that sense, personalist politicians do not merely strain democratic norms. They alter the emotional architecture of citizenship by teaching people to identify the fate of the republic with that of a single individual. That is among the clearest signs that a democracy is drifting toward plebiscitary authoritarian temptation.

VIII. Crisis as a Permanent Style of Rule

Democracies occasionally face genuine emergencies: war, financial collapse, terrorism, pandemics, ecological disaster, or episodes of serious civil unrest. Under such circumstances, temporary concentration of power may sometimes be unavoidable. The danger arises when politicians convert the language and psychology of crisis into a permanent style of rule. In that environment, everything becomes an emergency. Every election is the last chance to save the nation. Every legislative disagreement becomes proof of existential sabotage. Every legal constraint becomes an intolerable obstacle in a moment of supposed national peril.

Perpetual crisis is politically valuable because fear simplifies cognition. Frightened citizens often become more willing to excuse procedural shortcuts, tolerate broad assertions of power, and regard critics as reckless or disloyal. Leaders who govern through alarm therefore gain room to act outside normal democratic expectations. They can excuse secrecy, bypass consultation, pressure institutions, and rally supporters against oversight. The exception gradually becomes normalized. What should have been a temporary departure from ordinary rule becomes woven into the political culture.

In a complex democratic system, this matters enormously because the repeated use of emergency rhetoric alters future behavior even when no formal emergency exists. Citizens habituated to alarms become easier to mobilize and harder to persuade. Institutions forced into a constant reactive mode lose capacity for calm, long-term problem-solving. Opponents, expecting arbitrary uses of power, adopt more defensive and aggressive postures of their own. The system begins to live in an artificially heightened state, like a body trapped in a chronic fight-or-flight response. Politicians who cultivate this condition may gain a tactical advantage, but the republic pays the cost. A democracy that cannot distinguish between ordinary conflict and genuine emergency becomes vulnerable to leaders who find constitutional restraint inconvenient whenever ambition rises.

IX. THE DELEGITIMATION OF DEFEAT

No democracy can survive unless political defeat remains psychologically and institutionally survivable. Citizens and parties must believe that they can lose an election, regroup, and compete again under the same legitimate rules. Politicians destroy this principle when they systematically delegitimize outcomes that do not favor them. They may claim fraud without evidence, imply that only victory proves fairness, portray independent administrators as conspirators, or suggest that any loss proves national betrayal. These tactics are powerful because they flatter supporters: defeat is never the result of persuasion, changing public preferences, or strategic error; it is always theft.

Once this belief spreads, the entire logic of democratic competition changes. If losing means humiliation, exclusion, prosecution, or civilizational ruin, then every election becomes existential. Followers conclude that ordinary procedural commitments are luxuries they can no longer afford. Pressure on courts intensifies. Election officials are threatened. Routine certification becomes dangerous. Legislatures are treated as enemy citadels rather than representative bodies. The result is a regime in which formal democratic mechanisms continue to operate, but under conditions of chronic contested legitimacy.

This is one of the clearest pathways by which politicians convert constitutional competition into systemic instability. They consume reserves of trust accumulated over decades and replace them with suspicion that can be activated at will. In the short term, they preserve mobilization by ensuring that supporters never experience a clean defeat. In the long term, they teach a large share of the citizenry that democratic procedures are authoritative only when they produce the "correct" result. At that point, democracy becomes self-undermining. The very mechanism designed to allocate power peacefully becomes the occasion for heightened distrust, radicalization, and, sometimes, violence. Society can survive policy disagreement. It struggles to survive when significant actors cease to accept the legitimacy of losing.

X. THE PUBLIC DEMAND SIDE OF DEMOCRATIC EROSION

It would be comforting to imagine that politicians alone are responsible for democratic decline. But politicians thrive by exploiting real social conditions. They succeed because many citizens are already burdened by insecurity, resentment, mistrust, status anxiety, and the perception that institutions no longer respond to ordinary people. Extreme inequality worsens all of this. When citizens see wealth and influence concentrated at the top while everyday life becomes more precarious, the promise of democratic equality begins to feel fraudulent. The gap between formal rights and power becomes visible.

In such an environment, symbolic politics gains force. If the government seems unable or unwilling to address material frustration, citizens become more receptive to leaders who offer emotional compensation: a story of betrayal, a villain to blame, a promise of restored dignity, a spectacle of domination, or a pledge to punish cultural enemies. This does not solve structural problems, but it can satisfy the hunger for recognition. Politicians who understand this can weaponize social pain. They convert diffuse anxiety into targeted rage and rage into organized loyalty.

The danger is that this creates a mutually reinforcing loop between public grievance and elite manipulation. The more citizens feel abandoned, the more attractive, harsh, transgressive figures can seem. The more those figures intensify conflict and degrade institutions, the less capable institutions become of delivering competent relief. Failure deepens grievance, grievance strengthens demagogy, and demagogy deepens failure. In this sense, politicians are both cause and symptoms. They do not invent every democratic pathology, but they amplify existing fractures and organize them into a durable political economy of division. Any serious democratic repair effort must therefore address both elite incentives and the social conditions that make destructive leadership profitable.

XI. Why Party Structure Matters

The organization of party competition is one of the most important determinants of democratic strength. Party systems do not merely reflect social conflict; they structure it. They determine how interests are aggregated, how accountability is assigned, how moderation is rewarded or punished, and how citizens interpret the stakes of elections. The question of the optimal number of parties is therefore not abstract. It goes to the heart of whether a democracy can channel disagreement into governable outcomes without converting every contest into a regime crisis.

A one-party system is not meaningfully democratic, whatever its administrative discipline. Without genuine alternation, citizens cannot remove rulers through competition, and public accountability becomes largely internal to the ruling apparatus. Such systems may appear stable, but the stability they offer is brittle and coercive. Conflict is not processed democratically; it is suppressed, displaced, or absorbed into factional contests within the dominant organization.

A two-party system can, under certain conditions, function well. It can provide clarity of choice, simplify responsibility, and produce decisive outcomes. Large parties may incorporate many tendencies under one roof, forcing coalition-building before the election rather than after it. Where civic trust is strong and ideological sorting is limited, this can create stable competition. Yet under contemporary conditions of polarization, the rigid two-party model often imposes severe costs. It compresses complex societies into antagonistic binaries. It encourages citizens to see political life as a zero-sum war between two total camps. It leaves little room for defection, recombination, or coalition after the vote. If one party radicalizes, the entire system can become hostage to a stark civil conflict because there is not a sufficiently strong third force to absorb discontent or reorganize the field.

At the other extreme, highly fragmented multiparty systems can improve representation but weaken governability. When too many parties acquire bargaining leverage, coalition formation becomes unstable, small factions gain disproportionate influence, and accountability becomes difficult to assign. Voters may support a party for one set of promises only to watch it enter a coalition that produces the opposite. If fragmentation rises too far, democratic energy can drain into perpetual negotiation, public confusion, and policy paralysis. Under those conditions, citizens may become vulnerable to leaders who condemn pluralism itself as weakness.

XI.A. Party Gatekeeping and the Failure to Exclude Anti-System Actors

A democracy is stronger when parties behave as filters rather than merely as vessels. One of the least appreciated functions of a party is gatekeeping: the capacity to identify ambitious, charismatic, or electorally useful figures who are nevertheless dangerous to constitutional norms and to deny them access to full institutional legitimacy. When parties lose this capacity, they become transmission mechanisms for anti-system politics.

Failure usually begins with rationalization. A demagogic figure appears and is initially treated as useful because he or she can energize turnout, intimidate rivals, dominate media attention, or exploit public anger that traditional politicians have failed to address. Party elites tell themselves they can control the figure, contain the rhetoric, or harness the energy without absorbing the danger. But the logic of mass politics often reverses the relationship. Once the outsider figure demonstrates electoral potency, party leaders adapt to the new center of gravity. They stop disciplining the transgressive actor and begin imitating him. The party's threshold for unacceptable conduct rises. What would once have disqualified now becomes negotiable. What was once shocking becomes part of the brand.

When gatekeeping fails, the consequences extend beyond a single individual. Recruitments shift. Staff and candidates who demonstrate loyalty to the new style advance more rapidly than those who defend institutional norms. Internal critics are sidelined. Policy substance thins because the movement's cohesion rests less on a shared governing program than on emotional identification and a common set of enemies. In the short run, the party may gain energy. In the long run, it becomes less capable of self-correction. It can no longer expel behavior that threatens constitutional order because doing so would tear at the emotional core of the coalition itself.

This is why the optimal number of parties cannot be considered separately from party quality. A four-party system populated by organizations incapable of excluding anti-democratic actors may be less stable than a two-party system with strong gatekeeping norms. Party pluralism matters, but so does party discipline of the right kind: not discipline for ideological conformity alone, but discipline in defense of constitutional rules, peaceful alternation, and the legitimacy of lawful opposition.

XII. The Case for Three to Five Effective Parties

For most modern democracies, especially large and diverse ones, the strongest arrangement is usually neither a rigid duopoly nor an excessively fragmented party mosaic. The healthiest zone is often a plural but governable system characterized by roughly three to five effective parties and two to four plausible governing combinations. This is not a mechanistic law. It is a comparative judgment grounded in the balance between representation and settlement.

A three-to-five-party environment often yields several democratic advantages. First, it relaxes the suffocating binary logic of the two-party system. Citizens who are dissatisfied with one major bloc do not have to choose between loyalty and complete defection from democratic politics. They may support an alternative party that still operates within constitutional norms. Second, it makes coalition-building visible and explicit. In a two-party system, coalition-building still occurs, but it is internalized within giant parties and often hidden behind primary battles, donor bargaining, and opaque elite negotiation. In a moderate multiparty system, a coalition is a normal public act. Parties must explain why they can govern together. That visibility can make compromise more legible and less easily denounced as treachery.

Third, a moderate multiparty system can isolate extremes more effectively. If an anti-system faction emerges, other parties may be able to cooperate to prevent it from controlling the entire state. In a strict two-party system, by contrast, extremism within one major party can become unavoidable for half the electorate, because there is no alternative route to power of comparable scale. Fourth, a plural party ecology can reduce the apocalyptic character of elections. If power is likely to be shared, negotiated, or recomposed, defeat may feel less like total annihilation. That lowers the emotional temperature of democratic life.

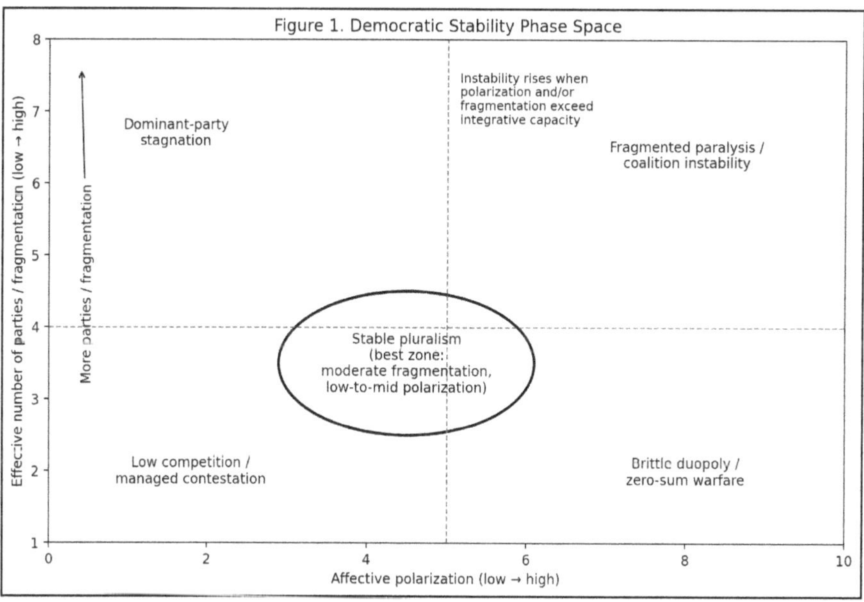

Figure 10.0: *Democratic Stability Phase Space*

The key qualifier is governability. More parties are not always better. The objective is not maximal diversity but functional diversity. A strong democracy requires enough variety to reflect real social complexity and enough concentration to make government possible. The middle range of three to five effective parties often best satisfies that requirement, particularly when coupled with electoral rules that discourage tiny transactional factions from holding the entire system hostage.

XIII. Electoral Design and Democratic Resilience

The number of parties is shaped by institutional design. Electoral systems do not determine outcomes with complete precision, but they strongly influence whether political competition consolidates into a few large camps or disperses across several parties. Winner-take-all systems with single-member districts tend to compress competition. Proportional systems tend to widen representation. Mixed systems can combine local accountability with broader fairness. Ranked-choice mechanisms, multi-member districts, open primaries, and reasonable thresholds for legislative entry can all alter the incentives parties face.

The practical democratic question is therefore not simply, "How many parties should we have?" It is, "What rules produce the right party ecology for this society?" A healthy design allows new entrants when major parties fail, but it does not make it effortless for every narrow personality vehicle to gain power to blackmail. It rewards coalition capacity and broad legitimacy, not just the ability to excite a hyper-intense niche. It enables citizens to express nuanced preferences without risking ungovernable fragmentation.

In a democracy already suffering from polarization, electoral reform can also serve a stabilizing function by reducing the all-or-nothing character of political competition. If citizens are given more than two viable avenues for participation, they may be less likely to interpret every election as a final showdown between existential enemies. If parties know they may need partners after the vote, they may have stronger incentives to avoid total rhetorical annihilation of all potential allies. If extreme actors can bypass the coalition rather than being indulged as necessary factional gatekeepers, constitutional actors gain room to defend the system from within.

Institutional design, however, is not magic. No voting rule can save a polity whose elites are committed to destroying trust for advantage. But design matters because it shapes which kinds of political behavior are rewarded. The essential democratic aim is to construct a system in which ambition is channeled through incentives that favor moderation, coalition, and accountability rather than panic, spectacle, and permanent siege mentality.

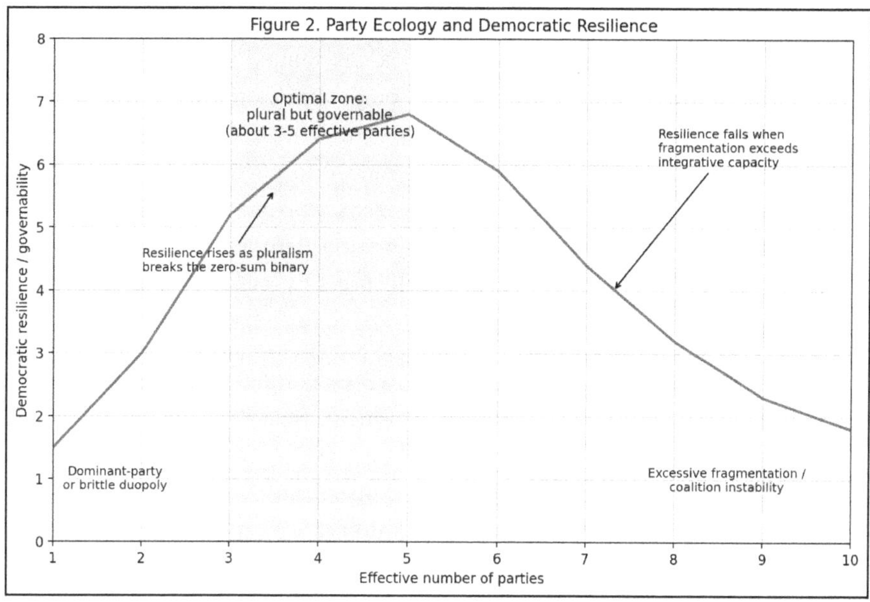

Figure 11.0: *Party Ecology and Democratic Resilience*

XIV. THE OPTIMAL PARTY ECOLOGY FOR A DEMOCRACY ON THE EDGE OF CHAOS

A democracy on the edge of chaos is one in which formal institutions still function but the reserves of legitimacy that once stabilized them are thinning. Polarization is high, trust is low, and public life is saturated with emotionally charged information flows. Under such conditions, the structure of party competition becomes even more consequential. A rigid two-party system may become brittle, forcing every division into a single zero-sum trench. A highly fragmented system may become too incoherent, dispersing authority so widely that coherent governance becomes elusive. The optimal ecology lies between monopoly and fragmentation.

The phrase "party ecology" is important. The health of democracy depends not only on the number of parties but on the relationships among them. Do they recognize one another as legitimate? Can they build coalitions without erasing programmatic differences? Can they exclude actors who reject democratic rules? Can they compete intensely without turning every contest into a moral apocalypse? Can voters clearly see both policy differences and plausible paths to govern? These ecological qualities matter more than raw arithmetic.

In practical terms, a strong democracy in the contemporary context is often best served by three to five effective parties, disciplined by rules that reward broad support and coalition viability. That range creates room for social complexity without multiplying veto points beyond governable limits. It allows moderate actors to reconfigure alliances when one party becomes captured by extremists. It creates alternatives for citizens who no longer trust one of the dominant blocs but do not wish to abandon democratic politics. And it can lower the psychic burden placed on elections by making outcomes more negotiable and less total.

What matters most is that the party system keeps conflict within constitutional bounds. Democracy requires real disagreement, but it cannot survive when disagreement becomes indistinguishable from war. A healthy party ecology, therefore, does not eliminate conflict. It domesticates conflict. It gives ambition a structure, opposition a future, and defeat a path back into legitimate competition.

XV. Rebuilding Democratic Incentives

If politicians are destroying democracy because present incentives reward them for doing so, then democratic repair must begin by changing those incentives. Moral appeals are not enough. Telling politicians to be more virtuous while leaving intact the structures that reward outrage, donor dependence, and norm-breaking is an invitation to disappointment. The republic must be designed so that constitutional stewardship is strategically viable.

Several broad reforms follow from this principle. Campaign finance systems should be restructured so that concentrated money has less power to narrow the policy agenda before citizens even vote. Parties should be strengthened as gatekeeping institutions, but only if they use that strength to discipline openly anti-democratic actors rather than shelter them. Electoral rules should expand representational flexibility without producing chaos, allowing citizens more than two meaningful options while keeping coalition formation governable. Legislative procedures should be revised to reduce the incentives for performative obstruction when the real goal is not oversight but perpetual mobilization. Administrative institutions should be protected from direct partisan capture so that state capacity is not continuously sacrificed to symbolic combat.

Equally important, democracies must address the material conditions that make destructive politics attractive. Extreme inequality, economic insecurity, social humiliation, and perceived elite impunity generate a public demand for transgressive leaders. A society in which millions feel unseen, precarious, and politically disposable will always provide fertile ground for politicians who offer revenge as a substitute for reform. Rebuilding democratic stability, therefore, requires more than institutional engineering. It requires restoring a sense that the political order can still produce fair, competent, and visible gains for ordinary people.

None of these guarantees success. Democracies remain contingent achievements. But institutional realism demands that we stop speaking as though the survival of self-government depends only on civic virtue. It also depends on the political reward structure. If destructive behavior is more profitable than constructive leadership, the destructive politician will keep winning. The question is not whether democracies can morally condemn such figures. The question is whether they can redesign themselves so that democratic arson is no longer the rational strategy of ambitious elites.

CONCLUSION: STEWARDSHIP OR EXTRACTION

The crisis of democracy in the present era is not simply that anti-democratic forces exist. It is that many politicians have learned to operate within democracy in a parasitic way. They draw authority from democratic forms while draining substance from democratic life. They exploit mistrust, accelerate polarization, monetize grievance, weaken institutions, personalize power, and teach citizens to treat constitutional defeat as illegitimate. None of these actions alone always destroys a republic. Taken together, they move the system toward a more volatile, brittle, and failure-prone equilibrium.

To say that politicians are destroying democracy is therefore not to claim that every officeholder is corrupt or that leadership itself is incompatible with liberty. It is to recognize that the governing class in many democracies now faces incentives that reward destabilization. When public office becomes a stage for spectacle rather than a duty of stewardship, when parties become machines for emotional warfare rather than institutions of aggregation, and when elections become rituals of mutually assured delegitimation, the constitutional order begins to consume its own foundations.

The answer is not to dream of a politics without conflict. Democracy requires conflict because free societies are plural, have unequal preferences, and face asymmetric information. The real task is to contain conflict within a structure that prevents rivalry from leading to regime breakdown. That means rebuilding norms of restraint, preserving neutral institutions, reducing material drivers of civic rage, and creating a party system that offers citizens genuine choice without making government impossible. In most contemporary democracies, this points toward a plural but governable party ecology: more flexible than a brittle duopoly, less chaotic than uncontrolled fragmentation, and structured to reward coalition, accountability, and moderation.

A strong democracy is one in which politicians gain more by preserving the republic than by setting it on fire. That is the benchmark. Where the opposite is true, democratic decay becomes not an accident but an emergent property of the system. The work of constitutional renewal, then, is to restore stewardship to rationality. Only then can democracy step back from the edge of chaos and recover the civic confidence required to endure.

The larger lesson is that democracy is never secured once and for all. It is a renewable political achievement that must be reproduced through habits, incentives, institutions, and material legitimacy. If citizens conclude that politics is nothing but performance, if parties become incapable of disciplining their own opportunists, and if leaders discover that rule-breaking consistently pays, the democratic order will not fail because people stopped speaking about freedom. It will fail because the practical routines that make freedom governable have disintegrated. That is why diagnosis must remain unsentimental. A republic cannot be preserved by nostalgia alone. It must be redesigned, defended, and made worthy of public loyalty in each generation.

Chapter 18

How Income and Wealth Inequality Will Bring Down Democracy

Democracy is often described as a political system, but it is just as much a social ecology. It depends on laws, elections, and constitutions, yes, but beneath those formal structures lies a deeper foundation: a broad belief that the system is fair enough to obey, open enough to influence, and responsive enough to be worth defending. That belief is not sustained by rhetoric alone. It rests on lived experience. Citizens must feel that effort and participation still matter, that the rules apply to the powerful as well as the weak, and that the future is not permanently closed to most people. When those conditions erode, democracy does not merely become unpopular. It becomes unstable.

Income and wealth inequality are among the most powerful forces that erode those conditions. Not because inequality is simply "unfair," though often it is, but because inequality changes how a society functions. It redistributes not just money, but time, risk, options, influence, and psychological security. It alters who can wait, who must panic, who can shape legislation, who can survive a crisis, and who is one missed paycheck away from despair. Over time, inequality becomes more than a distributional fact. It becomes an organizing principle of political life. The wealthy gain insulation from public failure, while everyone else becomes more vulnerable to it. The result is a democracy that still appears formally intact while its inner logic shifts from shared self-government to managed consent.

This is why inequality is so dangerous in nonlinear times. In a stable system, modest disparities can be moderated by mobility, trust, and institutional legitimacy. But in a stressed system—one marked by polarization, media fragmentation, institutional decay, and economic insecurity—inequality acts like an accelerant. It intensifies every other democratic weakness. It sharpens factionalism, magnifies elite capture, corrodes trust, and invites authoritarian solutions. It transforms ordinary political disagreement into a deeper crisis over whether the system itself still deserves loyalty. In this sense, inequality is not merely one problem among many. It is a master variable. It changes the behavior of the whole system.

The central claim of this essay is straightforward: severe income and wealth inequality do not simply coexist with democratic decline; they actively produce it. They hollow out the middle conditions required for democratic stability, translate economic power into political domination, fragment the citizenry into mutually distrustful camps, and push the polity toward a bad attractor in which formal elections persist but substantive self-government withers. Democracy falls not only when tanks arrive in the capital or constitutions are suspended. It also falls when citizens cease to experience the state as a common instrument and come instead to experience it as a machine serving others. Extreme inequality is one of the surest ways to create that condition.

Democracy Requires More Than Voting

A democracy is not secured simply because elections occur on schedule. Voting is a mechanism, not a civilization. The deeper requirements of democracy are social and moral before they are procedural. Citizens must accept losing some elections because they believe the system remains theirs even in defeat. They must tolerate opponents because they believe those opponents are adversaries within a shared order, not existential enemies feeding on a rigged game. They must comply with laws they did not write because they trust that the institutions enforcing them are, at least in principle, accountable and reciprocal.

All of this depends on a certain background level of inclusion. A society does not need perfect equality to remain democratic, but it does need a sufficiently broad distribution of dignity, security, and opportunity. Aristotle understood this long ago when he argued that stable political orders are often sustained by a strong middle class rather than by extremes of wealth and poverty. Tocqueville, too, saw that democratic life depends on habits of association and a rough social equality of condition. Modern constitutional design refines these insights, but it does not replace them. Where a society becomes sharply divided between those who own the future and those who merely endure the present, democracy becomes fragile.

This is because democracy is a regime of mutual recognition. It assumes that citizens encounter one another as co-equals in public life, even if their talents, occupations, and fortunes differ. Inequality, once it becomes severe, destroys that recognition. The rich no longer live under the same practical conditions as everyone else. They often do not use the same schools, hospitals, infrastructure, transportation systems, legal services, or neighborhoods. They can privatize security, insulate themselves from policy failure, and purchase alternatives to public provision. As this happens, they become less dependent on common institutions and less invested in maintaining them. The poor and the precarious, meanwhile, encounter those same institutions not as vehicles of shared citizenship but as sites of humiliation, scarcity, waiting, and arbitrary power. The state becomes bifurcated: a concierge for some, a maze for others.

Once this split deepens, democratic solidarity begins to fail. Citizens no longer believe they inhabit a common world. Politics ceases to be a negotiation over shared goods and becomes a struggle between socially distant populations with incompatible realities. The affluent speak the language of efficiency, investment, and "human capital," while the insecure speak the language of survival, betrayal, and abandonment. Neither vocabulary is wholly false. But when the gap becomes too large, democratic deliberation turns theatrical. There is no common floor of experience from which persuasion can begin.

That is why inequality is politically toxic even before it is economically catastrophic. A democracy can survive many policy errors if citizens still believe the system is fundamentally reciprocal. But when inequality makes reciprocity implausible, every policy dispute becomes a referendum on legitimacy itself. The question is no longer "What should we do?" but "Whose country is this, really?" Democracies seldom endure long once that question becomes chronic.

Inequality Converts Economic Power into Political Power

One of the great illusions of liberal democratic theory is the idea that market inequality and political equality can remain permanently separate. In theory, one person still gets one vote even if another person owns ten thousand times more wealth. In practice, however, concentrated wealth almost always finds pathways into concentrated power. Money purchases not only luxury but leverage. It buys access, expertise, lobbying capacity, media ownership, legal endurance, agenda-setting influence, and the ability to absorb risk while others cannot. As a result, economic inequality tends over time to harden into political inequality.

This conversion happens through both legal and informal channels. Wealth funds campaigns directly and indirectly. It shapes those who can run for office, who can afford to take time away from paid work, who gains elite endorsements, and who survives the donor gauntlet that structures modern electoral politics. It finances think tanks, policy networks, foundations, trade associations, litigation strategies, and revolving-door career paths that ensure certain interests are always represented in the rooms where decisions are made. Even when no explicit corruption occurs, the architecture of influence becomes skewed. The affluent do not need to buy every vote. They only need to saturate the ecosystem in which policy is formed.

The result is not usually a dramatic abolition of democracy. It is subtler and, in many ways, more dangerous. Legislatures continue to meet. Courts continue to issue rulings. Elections continue to occur. But policy responsiveness becomes asymmetrical. The preferences of the wealthy are heard earlier, taken more seriously, and encoded more consistently than the preferences of ordinary citizens. In such a system, formal equality masks substantive hierarchy. A citizen may retain the franchise while losing meaningful influence over the forces shaping their life.

As this pattern repeats, citizens begin to learn the system's true lesson: participation matters less than money. That lesson is devastating. Democracy depends on the belief that politics remains, however imperfectly, a domain in which organized citizens can still affect outcomes. But when wages stagnate, basic costs rise, and visible political decisions repeatedly benefit asset owners, large firms, and entrenched elites, cynicism becomes rational. People stop seeing the state as a contested public arena and start seeing it as a captured structure. Once that perception becomes widespread, democratic energy collapses in two opposite but equally dangerous directions: apathy and rage.

Apathy appears when people conclude that nothing can change. Rage appears when they conclude that change is possible only through rupture. Both reactions weaken democracy. The first empties institutions of participation. The second fills public life with punitive impulses that can be mobilized by demagogues. In this way, inequality does not merely distort policy. It changes the emotional chemistry of citizenship.

This is a key point. Democratic breakdown is not only institutional; it is affective. People must feel that politics is worth doing. Extreme inequality makes politics feel either futile or fraudulent. That is how economic concentration becomes regime fragility.

Wealth Inequality Is More Dangerous Than Income Inequality

Income inequality matters because it shapes daily life: rent burdens, debt stress, job insecurity, medical vulnerability, educational access, family strain. But wealth inequality is even more structurally dangerous because wealth is durable power. Income pays the bills. Wealth shapes the game.

A person with a high income can live comfortably. A person with large wealth holdings can shape markets, underwrite political projects, survive downturns, acquire distressed assets, finance narratives, and pass advantage across generations. Wealth compounds economically, but it also compounds institutionally. It provides time, insulation, and strategic patience. Those who possess it can wait out crises that would destroy everyone else. They can hire experts to navigate systems that confuse ordinary citizens. They can turn temporary disruptions into opportunities for acquisition. In a democracy under stress, that asymmetry becomes profound.

This matters because democracies often experience shock events: recessions, inflationary episodes, pandemics, wars, financial crises, technological dislocations. In such moments, wealth inequality determines who bears the pain and who emerges stronger. If repeated crises lead to asset consolidation at the top while insecurity spreads below, the population does not merely become poorer; it becomes more politically stratified. The wealthy gain even greater leverage over housing, labor markets, credit, media, and governance. Meanwhile, citizens with little or no wealth become less free in any meaningful sense. They cannot take risks, relocate easily, endure unemployment, leave bad jobs, challenge abusive institutions, or invest in long-term civic engagement. Their political choices narrow because their economic choices narrow first.

Wealth also turns democracy into inheritance. A child born into wealth inherits not only resources but networks, neighborhoods, educational pathways, legal buffers, and a different probability structure of life itself. A child born without wealth inherits greater exposure to instability, debt, poor public services, predatory markets, and civic marginalization. Over time, the ideal of democratic equality, however aspirational, becomes less believable because life chances are visibly pre-sorted. Citizens may still repeat democratic language, but they increasingly live in a quasi-feudal order dressed in meritocratic clothing.

That contradiction is fatal. Democracies can survive hardship more easily than they can survive visible hypocrisy. When public ideology says the system is open while lived reality says it is hereditary, resentment deepens. Not all resentment is noble; some of it curdles into cruelty or conspiracy. But its root is often intelligible: a sense that the social contract has become fictitious. Once people conclude that advantage reproduces itself by design, and that institutions are structured to ratify rather than correct that pattern, democratic faith begins to dissolve.

Wealth inequality, therefore, carries a unique political danger. It creates a class with the material ability to govern from outside public accountability and a larger population that experiences freedom as increasingly conditional. In the long run, that is not a democracy with unequal outcomes. It is an oligarchic order with democratic rituals.

Inequality Destroys the Material Basis of Citizenship

Citizenship is often spoken of in legal terms, but it also has material preconditions. To participate meaningfully in public life, people need more than formal rights. They need time, cognitive bandwidth, and a minimum level of stability. Someone working multiple jobs, carrying medical debt, juggling childcare, and living one emergency away from eviction is formally free to vote, attend meetings, organize, read, deliberate, and engage. But, in practice, that freedom is severely constrained.

Extreme inequality pushes more citizens into that condition of permanent compression. As wages fail to keep pace with essential costs, more of life becomes a scarcity problem. Scarcity is not only deprivation; it is attentional capture. It consumes focus. It shortens horizons. It encourages reactive decision-making. Under chronic economic stress, the future contracts. Political life, which often requires patience, abstraction, and deferred reward, becomes difficult to sustain.

This is one reason why inequality weakens democracy from below. It reduces the practical capacity of ordinary people to act as citizens. Elections are among the few moments when the system appears to solicit their presence, but even then, participation can feel symbolic if nothing fundamental changes. Outside election cycles, the machinery of governance is dominated by those with time, resources, and institutional fluency. Civic life then stratifies the same way the economy does. The affluent become repeat players; the insecure become episodic spectators.

The consequences extend beyond participation rates. Economic precarity alters the moral texture of social life. It increases humiliation, status anxiety, and fear of downward mobility. It intensifies competition over shrinking goods: affordable housing, school access, healthcare access, secure employment, and even basic public attention. In such an environment, solidarity becomes harder. Citizens who feel squeezed may begin to resent not only elites above them but also vulnerable groups beside them. This is one of inequality's cruelest political effects: it converts structural exclusion into lateral hostility.

Instead of directing anger upward toward the mechanisms that concentrate power, citizens are often encouraged to direct it sideways toward immigrants, urban residents, rural populations, welfare recipients, professionals, public employees, racial minorities, cultural minorities, or any group that can be framed as an immediate competitor. This fragmentation protects elite power. A divided public is easier to govern and easier to manipulate. But the cost is enormous. The demos—the "people" in whose name democracy rules—becomes psychologically incoherent.

A democracy cannot survive indefinitely if most citizens are too exhausted to participate, too insecure to plan, and too fragmented to trust one another. Material deprivation does not automatically produce authoritarianism. But prolonged precarity creates conditions in which democratic habits erode and anti-democratic appeals become more plausible. When citizens are stripped of stability, they become more vulnerable to anyone promising order, especially if that promise includes someone to blame.

Inequality Corrodes Trust, and Trust Is a Democratic Infrastructure

Trust is often treated as a soft cultural factor, but in a democracy, it functions as hard infrastructure. Societies run on millions of small acts of confidence: confidence that contracts will be honored, that tax burdens are not entirely one-sided, that institutions are not purely theatrical, that elections are meaningful, that the law is not simply a weapon of the powerful, that public sacrifice will not be exploited. Without these assumptions, social cooperation becomes brittle and costly.

Extreme inequality corrodes precisely these forms of trust. It signals that the rewards and burdens of society are not shared in any credible sense. Citizens begin to suspect—often correctly—that risk is socialized downward while gains are privatized upward. Losses are distributed broadly; protections are concentrated narrowly. In that environment, even reasonable public appeals for patience, sacrifice, or institutional deference are heard through a lens of distrust.

Why should they have precarious trust in fiscal discipline when they see bailouts for the already powerful? Why should ordinary citizens trust meritocracy when inheritance and elite networks so visibly structure success? Why should communities trust law enforcement, regulators, or courts when enforcement appears harsher for the weak and more negotiable for the wealthy? These are not abstract philosophical questions. They are daily political interpretations. And once they become widespread, they alter how citizens view every institution.

Trust decays at multiple levels. There is vertical trust between citizens and institutions. There is horizontal trust among citizens themselves. Inequality damages both. Vertically, it creates the perception that institutions answer to wealth. Horizontally, it produces status divisions so severe that citizens no longer experience one another as living under the same rules. The affluent seem insulated and alien; the poor seem abandoned and desperate. Each side becomes less legible to the other. Misrecognition grows.

The vacuum left by trust is typically filled by suspicion, irony, and conspiracy. When official explanations lose credibility, alternative narratives proliferate. Some are partially true; many are false; all compete in a context where public belief has already been destabilized by social inequality. That is why information disorder is easier to ignite in unequal societies. Citizens primed to believe the game is rigged are more likely to accept exaggerated or invented explanations because the core intuition—someone is cheating—feels broadly consistent with their experience.

Once trust collapses, governance becomes harder and harsher. Compliance drops. Institutions rely more on coercion and less on legitimacy. Political actors speak more in the language of enemies and less in the language of common purpose. In the long run, this can create a self-reinforcing cycle: inequality erodes trust, low trust weakens governance, weak governance worsens social outcomes, worsening outcomes deepen distrust, and deepened distrust makes reforms harder. This is a classic bad attractor. The system stabilizes, but around dysfunction.

Democracy requires a very different loop. It requires enough trust to make compromise possible, enough fairness to make trust rational, and enough reciprocity to keep disappointment from turning into permanent alienation. Extreme inequality makes all three progressively harder.

Inequality Produces Oligarchic Drift

Every democracy faces a recurring danger: that a temporary elite becomes a permanent governing class. This is not always a formal aristocracy. In modern societies, it more often appears as oligarchic drift—the gradual conversion of a formally open republic into a system substantively controlled by a narrow band of wealth holders, institutional insiders, and allied professionals.

Inequality accelerates that drift by centralizing the key inputs to durable power. Wealthy actors can shape the candidate pool, influence policy formation before issues reach public debate, fund legal strategies that outlast election cycles, and place people within the administrative, media, and intellectual organs that frame what counts as "serious" policy. This does not require secret cabals. It can arise through perfectly legal means. Indeed, that is what makes it so effective. Oligarchic drift often wears the costume of normalcy.

Over time, this changes the function of political parties. Rather than serving as vehicles for mass representation, parties can become brokerage platforms mediating between donors, consultants, media ecosystems, and increasingly cynical voters. The language of democracy remains, but the operational logic shifts to a managerial mode. Citizens are mobilized symbolically while policy is curated structurally. This gap between symbolic politics and structural power is one of the defining pathologies of unequal democracies.

As that gap widens, two linked developments occur. First, mainstream institutions lose credibility because they appear incapable of challenging the concentrated interests that shape outcomes. Second, anti-system figures gain appeal because they at least name the rot, even if they misdiagnose its causes or exploit it for authoritarian ends. This is why oligarchic drift often generates populist backlash. But not all populism is democratic. Some forms seek to reopen the system to broader participation. Others merely replace one elite faction with another while weakening constraints and amplifying personal rule.

Thus, inequality does not simply produce "too much elite influence." It destabilizes the balance between representation and restraint. Citizens become more willing to gamble on strongmen, not because they suddenly stop caring about liberty, but because procedural democracy has become associated with elite impunity and endless nonresponse. When lawful institutions are experienced as captured, extra-legal promises become seductive.

This is where democratic decline often becomes nonlinear. For years, citizens may tolerate rising inequality and obvious elite influence while still hoping the system can self-correct. Then a threshold is crossed—often during a crisis—and tolerance collapses rapidly. Trust evaporates. Norms weaken. A candidate or movement offers direct, punitive restoration. Institutions that once seemed resilient suddenly look brittle. Observers call the shift "sudden," but it was prepared slowly by decades of concentrated power.

In this sense, inequality is not only corrosive. It is cumulative. It stores instability inside the system until a trigger event releases it. By the time a visible democratic breakdown occurs, the structural conditions have usually been ripening for a long time.

Inequality Feeds Polarization and Identity Conflict

A healthy democracy can absorb disagreement. Indeed, disagreement is part of its strength. But severe inequality changes the character of disagreement. It turns normal policy conflict into a deeper conflict over distribution, status, and belonging. Once large parts of the population feel economically excluded, every political issue is refracted through the lens of insecurity. Cultural disputes intensify because material grievances seek language, while identity offers a readily available vocabulary.

This is not to say that all cultural conflicts are secretly economic. Human beings care about religion, ethnicity, gender, region, and moral order in ways that cannot be reduced to wages. But inequality raises the emotional temperature of every such conflict. When people are secure, they can often tolerate differences as one feature of a broader shared life. When they are insecure, differences are more easily perceived as threats. Economic scarcity narrows generosity.

Political entrepreneurs understand this. They exploit material anxiety by translating it into symbolic grievance. Instead of naming the structural concentration of wealth, they frame public anger around enemies who are more visible and less powerful: migrants, minorities, academics, journalists, bureaucrats, urban professionals, rural "backwardness," coastal "elites," or whatever target can be made to carry the system's tensions. In this way, inequality becomes a generator of polarization even when it is not discussed directly. It weakens the social middle and then invites identity-based narratives to occupy the space where class solidarity might otherwise form.

The consequence is not merely incivility. It is the destruction of cross-cutting ties. Democracies survive because citizens belong to multiple overlapping associations, workplaces, neighborhoods, schools, religious institutions, unions, voluntary groups, civic clubs, and professions—through which they encounter people unlike themselves in non-totalizing ways. These shared spaces soften political antagonism by reminding people that opponents are also co-workers, parents, neighbors, veterans, congregants, or fellow participants in local life. Extreme inequality tends to dissolve these shared spaces. Residential segregation rises. Educational pathways diverge. Private services replace public ones. Social worlds are sorted by class.

As shared spaces disappear, identities harden. Citizens encounter each other more as stereotypes than as participants in common institutions. The wealthy inhabit increasingly curated worlds. The insecure inhabit increasingly brittle ones. Each side consumes different media, trusts different authorities, and develops different expectations of the state. Politics then becomes more theatrical, more moralized, and less negotiable because there are fewer ordinary settings in which social repair can occur.

This is why polarization in unequal societies is often not just ideological but affective. People do not merely disagree; they dislike and distrust each other. That shift matters enormously. Ideological disagreement can sometimes be bargained over. Affective polarization turns opponents into enemies, and enemies are not compromised with—they are defeated, humiliated, or excluded.

That mentality is profoundly dangerous for democracy, which depends on the principle that today's loser remains tomorrow's legitimate participant.

Extreme inequality makes that principle harder to sustain because it transforms politics into a struggle over who gets left behind. As more citizens fear decline, democracy becomes less about self-government and more about defensive tribal positioning. That is not a stable democratic condition. It is a prelude to authoritarian sorting.

Inequality Makes Citizens Vulnerable to Demagogues

Demagogues do not arise in a vacuum. They flourish where institutions are mistrusted, elites are resented, and large numbers of citizens feel both humiliated and unheard. Severe inequality creates all three conditions.

The demagogue's basic promise is simple: the system is corrupt, the elite has betrayed you, and only a strong corrective force can restore justice. That promise is powerful because it contains a truth and a lie. The truth is that many unequal democracies are indeed marked by elite capture, asymmetrical responsiveness, and a widening gap between official ideals and lived reality. The lie is that these problems can be solved by concentrating power further in a single leader, faction, or movement unbound by democratic restraint.

Still, for citizens who have watched institutions fail repeatedly, the lie can feel plausible. Procedural caution begins to look like complicity. Checks and balances begin to look like excuses. Norms of restraint begin to look like protections for the already powerful. In that emotional landscape, calls for decisive action carry enormous appeal. The demagogue converts systemic frustration into personal loyalty. He offers not democratic renewal but an emotionally satisfying shortcut around institutional disappointment.

Inequality strengthens this dynamic in several ways. First, it increases the pool of citizens whose expectations have been broken. Second, it sharpens status humiliation, which is often more politically combustible than simple poverty. Third, it weakens intermediary institutions—unions, local associations, broadly trusted media, cross-class public schools, robust local newspapers—that might otherwise filter or moderate such appeals. Fourth, it teaches citizens that power already operates unequally, making anti-constitutional behavior easier to rationalize as merely a more honest version of what elites already do.

In other words, inequality does not make people abandon democracy because they suddenly become anti-liberty. It makes them susceptible to leaders who present anti-democratic concentration of power as the only realistic answer to an already captured order. The demagogue thrives by weaponizing the very legitimacy crisis inequality creates.

Once in motion, this process can feed on itself. Demagogic politics often intensify cronyism, reward loyal capital, punish independent institutions, and further erode universal public provision. That, in turn, can deepen both inequality and institutional distrust, making the regime both more authoritarian and more unstable. Here again, the system settles into a bad attractor: concentrated wealth, concentrated narrative control, concentrated political power, declining trust, and recurring manufactured enemies.

A democracy cannot indefinitely survive if large portions of its citizens come to believe that only an unbound ruler can overcome a bound and captured system. Extreme inequality is one of the most reliable ways to create that belief.

The Nonlinear Dynamics of Democratic Breakdown

The title of the book, Democracy on the Edge of Chaos, captures an essential truth: democratic decline is rarely linear. Systems of self-government often appear stable long after the forces undermining them have become severe. Then, suddenly, they do not.

This is why many observers are repeatedly surprised by the democratic crisis. They see continuity—elections, court hearings, legislative sessions, familiar party labels—and infer resilience. But complex systems can preserve outward form while accumulating internal stress. Feedback loops intensify beneath the surface. Thresholds approach silently. A triggering event—a recession, debt shock, contested election, corruption scandal, migration wave, inflationary spike, banking failure, or geopolitical conflict—can then push the system across a stability boundary. What looked durable turns out to be unstable and subject to regime shift.

Inequality is a central driver of this nonlinear behavior because it amplifies sensitivity across multiple domains at once. It increases household fragility, which makes economic shocks politically explosive. It increases elite insulation, making policy responses less reciprocal. It increases distrust, which makes crisis communication less credible. It increases polarization, which makes collective action harder. It increases status resentment, which makes scapegoating easier.

It weakens shared institutions, which reduces buffering capacity. In systems language, inequality reduces resilience while increasing coupling among failure points.

Once that happens, the polity can shift from a virtuous cycle to a vicious one. In a virtuous democratic loop, reasonably shared prosperity supports legitimacy; legitimacy supports compliance; compliance supports governability; governability supports investment in public goods; public goods support opportunity; and opportunity renews legitimacy. In a vicious loop, inequality erodes trust; low trust undermines governance; weak governance produces poor outcomes; poor outcomes intensify elite shielding and mass resentment; resentment fuels polarization and anti-system politics; anti-system politics further weakens institutions; and weakened institutions make redistributive or reconstructive reforms more difficult. The system does not merely decline. It begins reproducing its own decline.

This is the logic of the bad attractor. Once the political economy settles into a stable pattern of concentrated gains and diffuse losses, every institution begins to adapt to it. Parties recruit different candidates. The media reward different forms of outrage. Citizens make different assumptions. Bureaucracies become more cautious or more politicized. Courts become arenas of distributive struggle. The whole system reorients around mistrust and asymmetry. Reform becomes harder not because the problem is invisible, but because too many structures now depend on it.

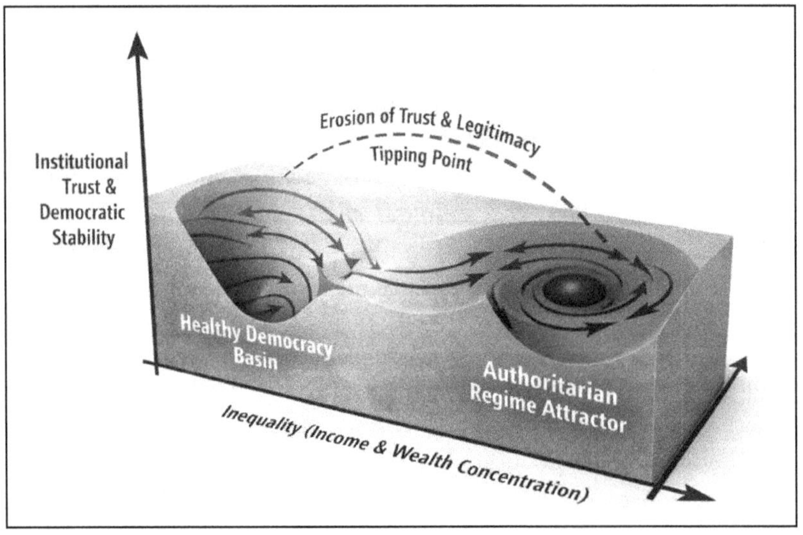

Figure 12.0: *Tipping Point of a Bad Attractor*

That is why inequality cannot be treated as one policy issue among others. It is not the same as adjusting a tax rate or regulating a sector. At high levels, it becomes a regime condition. It changes how democracy behaves.

Historical Echoes: When Republics Fray

History never repeats in simple form, but it often rhymes in structure. Across eras, republics and quasi-democratic orders have repeatedly shown vulnerability when wealth concentration outpaces institutional adaptation.

In the late Roman Republic, widening inequalities in land ownership, debt burdens, and elite competition contributed to repeated crises in representation and legitimacy. The problem was not only that some were richer than others. The deeper issue was that social and economic concentration destabilized the republic's political balance, intensified factional struggle, and made violence a more normal instrument of elite conflict.

In the industrial age, the Gilded Age in the United States revealed similar tensions in a different register. Vast fortunes, labor exploitation, financial speculation, machine politics, and extreme urban poverty generated enormous pressure on republican institutions. The system did not collapse, but only because countervailing reforms eventually emerged: antitrust efforts, labor organizing, progressive taxation, administrative reform, and a partial reconstruction of public authority. The lesson is important. High inequality does not always end democracy immediately. Sometimes it pushes a system toward reform. But that requires organized counter-power and institutional imagination. Without those, concentration hardens.

The crises of interwar Europe offer an even sharper warning. In several countries, economic dislocation, mass unemployment, class conflict, and institution al mistrust created conditions in which democracy appeared weak, divided, and incapable of governing. Authoritarian movements then presented themselves as solutions to paralysis, decay, and elite failure. The pathways varied by nation, but the broader pattern remains instructive: when economic insecurity becomes widespread and democratic institutions are seen as incapable of addressing it, the appetite for anti-democratic forces rises.

The relevance of such examples is not that today's democracies are identical to Rome, the Gilded Age, or interwar Europe. They are not. The relevance is structural. When wealth and power become excessively concentrated, when citizens lose faith in institutional reciprocity, when political representation grows visibly unequal, and when social fragmentation replaces common life, democracies enter dangerous territory. The outward symbols may remain modern and sophisticated, but the underlying dynamics are ancient.

History, therefore, does not tell us that collapse is inevitable. It tells us that inequality is one of the oldest solvents of republican life. A polity can ignore that lesson only at considerable risk.

Why the Middle Class Matters More Than Rhetoric

Political leaders often praise the middle class as a symbolic center of democracy, but the importance of a broad middle goes beyond symbolism. A durable middle class provides ballast. It moderates extremes of dependency and domination. It creates citizens with enough security to think beyond immediate survival but not enough insulation to detach from common institutions. It anchors tax legitimacy, supports local associations, sustains mass participation, and makes peaceful reform more plausible than revolutionary rupture.

When the middle class weakens, democracies become more erratic. A hollowed-out middle means more citizens slipping into precarity, while a smaller elite commands a larger share of the economy's gains. The political consequences are profound. The insecure become more volatile, more distrustful, and more open to anti-system appeals. The affluent become more influential, more insulated, and less dependent on the quality of public goods. The social center that makes democratic bargaining possible begins to erode.

This helps explain why democracies can become unstable even without mass destitution. If many citizens remain above absolute poverty but feel one shock away from falling into it, while a small upper tier accumulates enormous wealth and influence, the political system still enters a danger zone. People do not need to be starving to lose faith in democracy. They need only conclude that the system no longer offers reliable pathways to dignity, mobility, or fair representation.

Rhetoric cannot solve this. Leaders can celebrate national unity, constitutional values, and democratic norms as much as they wish. But if the underlying social structure keeps producing insecurity below and insulation above, rhetoric will eventually sound hollow. Democratic culture cannot float indefinitely above democratic political economy. The two must reinforce each other.

This is why economic reform is not separate from democratic reform. Policies that broaden asset ownership, strengthen wages, reduce extractive concentrations, lower precarity, and restore the credibility of common institutions are not merely "social policy." They are constitutional maintenance in economic form.

CAN DEMOCRACY SURVIVE INEQUALITY? ONLY UP TO A POINT

It would be simplistic to argue that any inequality destroys democracy. No complex society has ever achieved perfect equality, nor is absolute equality necessary for liberty. Differences in talent, risk preference, luck, innovation, and ambition will generate some unequal outcomes. The question is not whether inequality exists. The question is whether inequality has crossed the level at which democracy's core mechanisms begin to malfunction.

A modest degree of inequality can be politically compatible with democracy if three conditions hold. First, mobility remains plausible enough that advantage does not harden into caste. Second, public institutions remain universal enough that elites are still materially invested in common goods. Third, political influence remains broad enough that ordinary citizens can still organize effectively and secure meaningful reform. Once these conditions weaken, inequality ceases to be a tolerable background feature and becomes a destabilizing force.

The danger is not one magical threshold but a zone of compounding dysfunction. In that zone, policy increasingly favors asset holders over wage earners. Intergenerational mobility slows. Housing, education, and healthcare become major sorting mechanisms. Public systems deteriorate in ways the affluent can avoid. Civic trust declines. Political rhetoric grows harsher. Conspiracy and resentment spread. The wealthy become less dependent on democracy's ordinary performance, while the non-wealthy become more desperate for outcomes that democracy no longer seems able to provide. That is the point at which inequality becomes regime-threatening.

Seen this way, the real issue is not only the scale of inequality but its institutional embedding. A society may tolerate disparities in consumption while remaining democratic if those disparities do not convert into hereditary power and asymmetric influence. But once wealth concentration governs access to law, voice, knowledge, and security, democracy's equalizing premise is undone.

So yes, democracy can survive inequality—but only inequality that remains subordinate to democratic control. Once inequality begins to dictate the terms of politics, democracy no longer steers the economy. The economy is steering democracy.

What Would Prevent Collapse?

If inequality can bring down democracy, then defending democracy requires more than procedural piety. It requires rebuilding the material and institutional foundations of shared citizenship, or what I have called throughout this book Systems Humanism.

That begins with restoring the credibility of common life. A democracy needs public goods that are good enough for everyone to depend on: education, transportation, public health capacity, legal access, housing policy, and basic economic security. When affluent citizens can fully exit the public realm, democratic solidarity decays. Common institutions must be rebuilt not as poor substitutes for private privilege but as respected, capable, universal systems.

Second, democracies need countervailing power. Labor organizations, professional associations, civic groups, local journalism, and other intermediary institutions are not decorative features of pluralism. They are structural defenses against oligarchic drift. They organize citizens who would otherwise face concentrated wealth as isolated individuals. Without such institutions, politics becomes a direct encounter between atomized voters and massively capitalized interests—a contest democracy usually loses.

Third, wealth concentration must be politically bounded. That does not require hostility to markets or enterprises. It requires recognizing that democracy cannot survive if economic power is allowed to purchase endless political leverage. Campaign finance reform, antitrust enforcement, transparency, tax policy oriented toward limiting hereditary concentration, stronger enforcement against corruption and regulatory capture, and rules that reduce the revolving door between public office and private influence are not merely technocratic adjustments. They are a democratic self-defense.

Fourth, economic security must be widened. People who live in chronic precarity are less free, less civically engaged, and more vulnerable to demagogic manipulation. Stable wages, bargaining power, affordable essentials, and reduced exposure to catastrophic loss are not luxuries in a democracy. They are conditions under which citizens can think, participate, and resist authoritarian temptations.

Fifth, democratic societies must rebuild cross-cutting ties. Segregated social worlds intensify polarization. Schools, public spaces, service institutions, local associations, and civic projects that place unlike citizens in common frameworks are essential to democratic resilience. The goal is not sentimental unity. It is a practical coexistence. Democracies need settings in which disagreement occurs within shared membership rather than across sealed class and identity silos.

Finally, democracies must recover a moral language adequate to the problem. Inequality is not only a technical issue of taxation or productivity. It is a question about what a society believes citizens owe one another. If public life is reduced entirely to market metrics, then concentration will always be justified after the fact as the natural reward of efficiency. A democracy worthy of the name must insist that economic arrangements are subject to civic judgment. Wealth is a social creation as well as a private possession. It is produced within legal orders, infrastructures, and institutional heritages that no individual alone creates. To recognize this is not envy. It is realism.

The alternative is to continue allowing inequality to hollow out democratic life while hoping that constitutional forms alone will save the system. They will not. Institutions cannot remain healthy if the social order beneath them becomes too unequal to sustain reciprocal citizenship.

Conclusion: The Road from Inequality to Democratic Failure

Democracy does not usually die in a single dramatic moment. More often, it is slowly unmade by the cumulative erosion of the conditions that make self-government possible. Income and wealth inequality are among the most powerful engines of that erosion.

They weaken the social middle on which democratic stability depends. They convert economic leverage into political domination. They hollow out public institutions by allowing elites to exit common life. They reduce the practical capacity of ordinary citizens to participate meaningfully. They corrode trust, intensify humiliation, and fragment the public into rival camps. They fuel polarization, invite demagogic politics, and push the system toward authoritarian shortcuts. In nonlinear times, they amplify every other source of democratic fragility until a crisis arrives, revealing how little resilience remains.

At first, the system may still look normal. Elections continue. Courts function. Legislatures debate. Markets rise. But beneath the surface, democratic substance thins. The wealthy become less accountable. The insecure become less represented. The citizen becomes less a participant and more a managed audience. By the time the crisis becomes visible, the culture of democracy may already be deeply compromised.

This is why inequality must be understood not only as an economic or moral issue, but also as a constitutional issue. It determines whether citizens experience the republic as a shared project or as a staged performance hiding private rule. It determines whether politics remains a field of collective agency or collapses into cynicism, manipulation, and rage. It determines whether democratic institutions can absorb stress or whether they tip into a bad attractor from which recovery becomes difficult.

A democracy can survive disagreement. It can survive turnover. It can survive policy failure. It can even survive periods of hardship. What it cannot survive indefinitely is the widespread conviction that the system belongs to the wealthy, answers to the wealthy, and protects the wealthy while asking everyone else to keep believing. Once that conviction hardens, democracy becomes an empty shell vulnerable to capture from above and revolt from below.

That is the greatest danger of income and wealth inequality. It does not simply make society less fair. It makes democracy less real. And when democracy ceases to feel real enough to enough people, its collapse is no longer a distant possibility. It becomes a matter of physics and systemic time.

EPILOGUE

DEMOCRACY AT THE EDGE OF CHAOS: A MORAL ECOLOGY OF REPAIR

A DEMOCRACY IS a promise made to strangers.

It is the wager that we can live together—under rules we did not all choose, amid values we do not all share, under leaders we do not always admire—without turning political difference into civil war or civic life into humiliation. It is an audacious wager because it depends on a fragile miracle: that millions of people with competing interests and identities will accept a shared procedural frame as binding even when they lose. That acceptance is not natural. It is cultivated. It is maintained. It is constantly negotiated.

This book has argued that our era—what we have called nonlinear times—has changed the conditions under which that wager can hold. The republic is not simply facing more problems; it is facing problems that interact. Inequality raises stakes. Capture reshapes incentives. Information disorder accelerates contagion. Polarization becomes an identity threat. Institutions lose legitimacy. Once that happens, shocks no longer remain shocks. They become accelerants. And when a complex system is pushed near its critical thresholds, small events can produce regime shifts.

The language of chaos and complexity is not a metaphorical flourish. It is an analytic necessity. Democracies are complex adaptive systems. They can self-organize into stable cooperative equilibria, or they can fall into bad attractors—corruption, cynicism, permanent emergency, factional retaliation, and the collapse of shared reality. They can absorb stress or flip. And the most dangerous phase is not collapse itself but the period before it: when drift has not yet become rupture, when ordinary people sense instability but cannot name its mechanics, when elites feel the ground shifting but respond with extraction, and when every actor becomes tempted to play hardball "before the other side does."

This epilogue ties the themes of the book together as one integrated argument:

1. **Democratic stability is a systems property**, not a moral mood.
2. **Inequality and capture alter the system's physics**, raising stakes and shifting incentives toward extraction.
3. **Information disorder changes the speed of politics**, turning narratives into weapons and making shared reality scarce.
4. **Legitimacy is the binding constraint**: without visible fairness and rule consistency, democratic conflict becomes unstable, turbulent, and unmanageable.
5. **Nonlinear times demand institutional design**: we must build dampeners, constrain bad attractors, and widen the safe operating space.
6. **Repair is possible**, but only if it is sequenced, coalition-supported, legitimacy-engineered, and stress-tested.
7. **Systems Humanism provides the ethical operating system**: dignity, security, and meaning are not sentimental luxuries; they are stabilizers of the republic.

What follows is a synthesis, an attempt to show how these themes interlock into a single picture: a moral ecology of democratic repair.

I. The Republic as a Complex Adaptive System

The central intellectual movement of this book has been to treat democracy not as a static constitutional object but as a living dynamic system. That move changes everything.

A system is defined less by its parts than by its **relationships**: feedback loops, flows of information, incentives, thresholds, and emergent patterns. Democracies are made of citizens, parties, bureaucracies, courts, markets, media platforms, and civic institutions. But their stability is not located in any single component. Stability emerges from the interactions between components, from the degree to which the system can process conflict without losing legitimacy.

In Part I, we framed democracy as existing within a **safe operating space**. Inside that space, disagreements remain bounded by shared procedures; elections are accepted as legitimate; and institutions can correct themselves. Outside that space, conflict becomes existential; rumor replaces evidence; and institutions are treated as factional weapons. The system begins to behave like a high-gain amplifier: small provocations produce large reactions; small errors become scandals; small lies become mass beliefs. At the edge of chaos, the same interventions that would stabilize a healthy system can destabilize a fragile one.

Complexity theory holds that systems do not always respond in proportion. They can drift gradually and then flip suddenly. They can show warning signs—rising variance, slower recovery after shocks, increasing sensitivity to perturbations—before crossing thresholds. Democracies show those signs too: increasing polarization, declining trust, growing corruption perceptions, widening inequality, information fragmentation, and intensifying procedural hardball.

Once you see democracy as a complex system, you stop asking only, "What policy is right?" and begin asking, "What interventions reduce cascade risk? What strengthens dampeners? What shifts incentives away from extraction and toward cooperation?" The moral question remains, but it is joined by a physics question. And in nonlinear times, the physics question often determines whether the moral goal is achievable.

II. Inequality as a System Parameter

Part II insisted on a hard truth: inequality is not merely unjust; it is dynamically destabilizing. It changes the system's operating conditions and the way temperature affects chemical reactions. When inequality rises:

- **stakes rise**: losing political battles becomes materially catastrophic for many;
- **fear rises**: insecurity narrows horizons and reduces tolerance for compromise;
- **status resentment rises**: humiliation becomes political fuel;
- **capture becomes easier**: concentrated wealth purchases influence and shape rules;
- **trust collapses**: citizens conclude the system is rigged;
- **polarization intensifies**: politics becomes a battle over survival and recognition.

The chapter on inequality as a system parameter argued that high inequality raises the system's sensitivity to shocks and increases the probability that elites and factions will adopt hardball tactics. It also generates a moral ecology in which solidarity becomes harder to sustain as the lived worlds of citizens diverge. People begin to inhabit different material realities, and that divergence becomes epistemic divergence: different fears, different experiences of institutions, different narratives that feel plausible.

This is why reforms aimed only at "growth" without security and dignity can fail. Growth can coexist with despair if the distribution of risk and respect is broken. A society can be rich and unstable if it concentrates wealth, humiliates segments of its population, and allows capture to hollow out equal citizenship. The question is not only how much the system produces, but how it distributes security, dignity, and meaning—the stabilizers that keep democratic conflict within stable basins.

III. The Fragility Stack: Polarization and Information Disorder as Nonlinear Contagion

Polarization is not new. Democracies have always had factions. What is new is the way modern information systems turn polarization into **contagion**.

Part II described the "fragility stack": polarization layered atop information disorder. In a fragmented media environment, political identity becomes both shield and weapon. Social platforms reward outrage and certainty. Algorithms amplify content that triggers high arousal. Narratives travel faster than verification. And because attention is monetized, there is always a supply of entrepreneurs who profit from escalating conflict.

This changes the tempo of politics. It turns governance into an attention contest. It turns policy disputes into moral battles. It turns uncertainty into vulnerability. And it turns procedural mistakes—inevitable in any human system—into viral proof of conspiracy.

Information disorder is thus not simply a cultural problem; it is an institutional and incentive problem. It is the consequence of a system that rewards virality over truth, humiliation over deliberation, and tribal allegiance over epistemic humility. In such an environment, a democracy's most precious asset—shared reality—becomes scarce.

When shared reality collapses, accountability collapses. Without accountability, capture deepens. With capture, inequality rises. With inequality, fear and resentment intensify. And the system's gain increases. This is how a democracy can enter a self-reinforcing loop in which each pathology strengthens the next.

The book's argument is not that technology causes collapse deterministically. In nonlinear times, the information environment functions as a multiplier. It amplifies existing vulnerabilities. It accelerates drift. It raises the likelihood that a shock will trigger a regime shift.

IV. Dampeners, Bad Attractors, and Tipping Points

The conceptual heart of the book has been the triad of **dampeners**, **bad attractors**, and **tipping points**.

Dampeners

Dampeners are the stabilizers that reduce the amplitude of conflict:

- trust
- legitimacy
- rule consistency
- competence
- fairness that is visible
- social cohesion and bridging ties

Dampeners do not eliminate conflict. They make conflict survivable. They keep the system inside its safe operating space.

Bad attractors

Bad attractors are stable failure regimes:

- corruption that becomes normal
- capture that becomes profitable and defended
- permanent emergency governance
- factional retaliation cycles
- delegitimation spirals
- epistemic collapse

Attractors are "stable" not because they are good, but because once the system enters them, feedback loops reinforce them. This is why corruption becomes stable: it creates networks of mutual protection, narrative defenses, and incentive structures that make exit costly. It becomes a self-organizing equilibrium.

Tipping points

Tipping points are thresholds beyond which small shocks produce large changes:

- contested elections that trigger mass refusal
- economic shocks that trigger scapegoating and violence
- scandal cascades that collapse institutional credibility
- sudden disinformation waves that provoke emergency overreaction
- localized unrest that spreads through network contagion

A key insight about complexity is that systems often exhibit warning signs before tipping: rising variance, slower recovery, and greater sensitivity. Democracies show those signs too: greater volatility in public trust, more frequent legitimacy crises, intensifying hardball tactics, and a growing willingness to deny procedural outcomes.

This triad gives the book its architecture: build dampeners, avoid bad attractors, and prevent tipping points by widening the safe operating space.

V. Designing Institutions for Nonlinear Times

Part III argued that moral aspiration is insufficient without institutional design. Good intentions cannot overcome bad payoffs. Civic virtue cannot carry a polity whose incentive gradients reward extraction, humiliation, and narrative warfare.

Nonlinear times require institutions that are:

- resilient to bad faith
- transparent and auditable
- capable of learning
- constrained in emergencies
- designed to reduce capture
- and aligned with human flourishing

This is where the book's practical program emerged.

The anti-capture state

The anti-capture state is the structural core: rules that change payoffs, so extraction becomes costly and visible. It is not merely anti-corruption rhetoric. It is procurement firewalls, transparency of influence pathways, beneficial ownership disclosure, independent oversight, competition policy, and enforcement symmetry.

The anti-capture state is the answer to the central stability question: who controls the rules? If capture dominates, democracy becomes theater. If capture is constrained, equal citizenship becomes plausible.

The prosperity architecture

Prosperity architecture is the stabilizer core: policies that distribute security, dignity, and meaning broadly enough that politics is no longer existential. It is automatic stabilizers, healthcare cost containment, housing stability, portable benefits, and service delivery that avoid humiliation.

This is the Systems Humanist insight: security is not paternalism; it is freedom. Dignity is not sentiment; it is a legitimacy infrastructure. Meaning is not a luxury; it is a civic immune function.

Systems Humanism

Systems Humanism is an ethical operating system. It says that flourishing is emergent, that moral ecology shapes behavior, and that institutions must be designed so that humane behavior is stable. It refuses the false choice between technocracy and moralism. It insists on structure and spirit: payoffs and values, constraints and meaning.

Systems Humanism does not demand saints. It demands systems that do not punish decency and reward predation. It aims for stable freedom: a democracy whose stability is rooted in dignity and fairness rather than repression and fear.

VI. Implementation Is the Battlefield

Part IV confronted the hardest truth: implementation is where reform dies or survives. Democracies do not fail because they lack ideas. They fail because they cannot install ideas under adversarial conditions.

Sequencing the repair

Chapter 11 argued that repair must be staged. In low-trust environments, you do not begin with maximal transformation. You begin with **keystone reforms** that raise minimum viable legitimacy: election integrity audits, procurement transparency, conflict-of-interest rules, independent oversight, and competence upgrades. These reforms produce visible fairness and rule consistency. They lower the system's gain. They create the platform for bigger change.

Sequencing is not cowardice. It is systems realism. Without credibility, ambitious reforms are interpreted as domination and trigger backlash cascades.

Coalitions for nonlinear times

Chapter 12 argued that repair requires a coalition that is not simply ideological but procedural and moral: a new democratic majority organized around rule consistency, anti-capture fairness, security, and dignity floors, and a rebuilt epistemic commons. Coalition-building must avoid humiliation dynamics, emphasize shared wins, and build bridging institutions that make demonization harder.

Legitimacy engineering

Chapter 13 argued that legitimacy is not a mood. It is a condition produced by procedural fairness, competence, and moral respect. In nonlinear times, legitimacy must be engineered through auditability, transparency, routine evidence, and disciplined communication that treats uncertainty honestly and links claims to verification.

The core rule: do not ask citizens to trust; give them visible reasons.

Stress tests and crisis protocols

Chapter 14 argued that crises determine regime continuity. Democracies must stress-test their vulnerabilities and pre-commit to protocols that allow for speed with constraint. Emergency governance must have triggers, time limits, oversight, procurement firewalls, and evidence-linked communication cadence. Shocks are inevitable; regime shifts are not.

Measuring what matters

Chapter 15 argued that drift is invisible without measurement. A Democratic Stability Scorecard and Flourishing Index provide early warning, guide sequencing, and create a shared evidence layer that reduces the risk of rumor-driven accountability collapse. Measurement is not a replacement for politics; it is an instrument of democratic self-correction.

Chapters 16-18 address the roadmap for "pulling back from the edge."

VII. The Moral Ecology of Democratic Life

The book's deepest claim is that democracies do not survive on procedures alone. They survive on **moral ecology**, the environment that shapes civic character and makes cooperation rational.

A moral ecology is formed by:

- the distribution of risk (security)
- the distribution of respect (dignity)
- the availability of contribution pathways (meaning)
- the integrity of information flows (shared reality)
- the fairness and consistency of enforcement (rule consistency)
- and the visibility of constraint (legitimacy)

When the moral ecology is healthy, democracy feels livable. People can disagree without feeling annihilated. They can lose elections without fearing ruin. They can criticize institutions without believing the entire system is fraudulent. They can compromise without humiliation.

When the moral ecology is degraded, democracy becomes unbearable. Cynicism becomes adaptive. Outrage becomes currency. Hardball becomes rational. And people begin to seek meaning in domination—because domination feels like the only reliable source of recognition.

This is why Systems Humanism is not a philosophical ornament. It is a diagnostic of what makes a repair durable. You cannot repair democracy by tinkering with procedures while leaving humiliation, insecurity, inequality, and meaninglessness intact. Those conditions will reproduce instability even if formal rules improve.

VIII. A Practical Theory of Hope

In a book that takes instability seriously, hope must be disciplined. The goal is not to reassure. The goal is to explain why repair is possible.

Repair is possible because complex systems can reorganize. They can move from bad attractors to better basins if incentives change, if dampeners thicken, if legitimacy becomes visible, and if citizens experience dignity and security.

History shows that democratic societies have reinvented themselves under stress. They did not do so through purity or perfect consensus. They did so through:

- building constraints on power
- reducing extreme insecurity
- increasing fairness and predictability
- and expanding the sense of shared belonging

The challenge today is that the information environment punishes these efforts, while capture networks resist them. But those constraints do not eliminate the possibility. They clarify strategy. They make sequencing and legitimacy engineering essential. They make evidence and auditability decisive. They make coalition-building a craft. They make stress testing a necessity.

Hope becomes practical when it is translated into mechanisms:

- **We can reduce capture** by changing payoffs and increasing detection.
- **We can reduce existential politics** by building security and dignity floors.
- **We can restore shared reality** by strengthening verification infrastructure.
- **We can widen the safe operating space** by stress testing and crisis protocols.
- **We can prevent drift** by measuring stability and flourishing indicators.

- **We can rebuild civic immune function** by expanding pathways of contribution and meaning.

This is not utopia. It is repair work and architectural reform.

IX. A Closing Synthesis: The Edge of Chaos as a Choice Point

The phrase "edge of chaos" describes a zone where systems are neither rigid nor collapsing—capable of adaptation but vulnerable to rupture. Democracies at the edge of chaos face a choice point: either adapt by redesigning institutions and moral ecology, or drift into bad attractors where emergency governance, capture, and factional resentment become stable.

This book has tried to make that choice point intelligible.

It has insisted that the republic is not only a legal architecture but a living moral ecosystem. It has argued that inequality, capture, and information disorder alter the system's dynamics, raising the gain on conflict and increasing sensitivity to shocks. It has been proposed that stability must be designed through dampeners—trust, legitimacy, rule consistency—and defended against tipping points through crisis protocols and stress tests. It has been argued that repair must be sequenced, coalition-supported, legitimacy-engineered, and measurable. And it has insisted that human flourishing—security, dignity, meaning—is not secondary to stability but constitutive of it.

If democracy is a promise made to strangers, then the work of repair is the work of making that promise believable again.

Believability is not produced by speeches. It is produced by procedures that bind, services that work, enforcement that is symmetric, money flows that are transparent, crises handled with constraint, and a civic culture that offers meaning beyond humiliation warfare.

We may not be able to eliminate conflict. We should not want to. Pluralism is the point. But we can design a republic where conflict is not annihilating. We can build a moral ecology where people do not need to dominate to feel seen, where they do not need to lie to belong, where they do not need to burn the system down to make the system listen.

That is the ambition of Systems Humanism: to build institutions that make decency stable and humane.

X. Final Word: Repair as a Civic Practice

Democratic repair is not a single law, a single election, or a single leader. It is a practice. It is the repeated choice to prefer constraint over conquest, evidence over rumor, dignity over humiliation, and long horizons over short-term extraction.

In nonlinear times, the most radical act may be restraint, the willingness to build rules that bind your own side, to accept audits that might embarrass you, to defend procedures even when they limit your advantage, and to treat opponents as citizens rather than enemies.

Restraint is not weakness. It is the price of legitimacy. And legitimacy is the basis of stability.

If the republic is to endure, it will endure not because we finally agree on everything, but because we rebuild the conditions under which disagreement is survivable. That is the physics of democratic stability. That is the moral ecology of repair.

The edge of chaos is not only a danger zone. It is also an opportunity zone—where systems can reconfigure. The future is not predetermined. But it will not be delivered by hope alone. It will be built, step by step, through the hard craft of institutional design, the discipline of legitimacy engineering, the courage of coalition-building, the humility of stress testing, the clarity of measurement, and the moral insistence that human dignity is not negotiable.

A democracy is a promise made to strangers. Repair and reform are how we keep it.

REFERENCES

A

Acemoglu, Daron, and James A. Robinson. 2012. *Why Nations Fail: The Origins of Power, Prosperity, and Poverty*. New York: Crown.

Acemoglu, Daron, and James A. Robinson. 2019. *The Narrow Corridor: States, Societies, and the Fate of Liberty*. New York: Penguin Press.

Achen, Christopher H., and Larry M. Bartels. 2016. *Democracy for Realists: Why Elections Do Not Produce Responsive Government*. Princeton, NJ: Princeton University Press.

Akerlof, George A., and Robert J. Shiller. 2015. *Phishing for Phools: The Economics of Manipulation and Deception*. Princeton, NJ: Princeton University Press.

Alesina, Alberto, and Edward L. Glaeser. 2004. *Fighting Poverty in the US and Europe: A World of Difference*. Oxford: Oxford University Press.

Allen, Danielle. 2014. *Our Declaration: A Reading of the Declaration of Independence in Defense of Equality*. New York: Liveright.

Anderson, Elizabeth. 1999. "What Is the Point of Equality?" *Ethics* 109 (2): 287–337.

Anderson, Elizabeth. 2017. *Private Government: How Employers Rule Our Lives (and Why We Don't Talk about It)*. Princeton, NJ: Princeton University Press.

Appadurai, Arjun. 2006. *Fear of Small Numbers: An Essay on the Geography of Anger.* Durham, NC: Duke University Press.

Arendt, Hannah. 1951. *The Origins of Totalitarianism.* New York: Harcourt, Brace.

Arendt, Hannah. 1963. *On Revolution.* New York: Viking.

Arendt, Hannah. 1972. *Crises of the Republic.* New York: Harcourt Brace Jovanovich.

Arrow, Kenneth J. 1951. *Social Choice and Individual Values.* New York: Wiley.

Arthur, W. Brian. 1994. *Increasing Returns and Path Dependence in the Economy.* Ann Arbor: University of Michigan Press.

Atkinson, Anthony B. 2015. *Inequality: What Can Be Done?* Cambridge, MA: Harvard University Press.

Axelrod, Robert. 1984. *The Evolution of Cooperation.* New York: Basic Books.

B

Bail, Christopher A. 2021. *Breaking the Social Media Prism: How to Make Our Platforms Less Polarizing.* Princeton, NJ: Princeton University Press.

Baldwin, Robert, Martin Cave, and Martin Lodge. 2012. *Understanding Regulation: Theory, Strategy, and Practice.* 2nd ed. Oxford: Oxford University Press.

Banerjee, Abhijit V., and Esther Duflo. 2019. *Good Economics for Hard Times.* New York: PublicAffairs.

Barabási, Albert-László. 2002. *Linked: The New Science of Networks.* Cambridge, MA: Perseus.

Bateson, Gregory. 1972. *Steps to an Ecology of Mind.* Chicago: University of Chicago Press.

Baumol, William J. 1990. "Entrepreneurship: Productive, Unproductive, and Destructive." *Journal of Political Economy* 98 (5): 893–921.

Beetham, David. 1991. *The Legitimation of Power.* Atlantic Highlands, NJ: Humanities Press International.

Beinhocker, Eric D. 2006. *The Origin of Wealth: Evolution, Complexity, and the Radical Remaking of Economics*. Boston: Harvard Business School Press.

Benkler, Yochai, Robert Faris, and Hal Roberts. 2018. *Network Propaganda: Manipulation, Disinformation, and Radicalization in American Politics*. New York: Oxford University Press.

Bermeo, Nancy. 2016. "On Democratic Backsliding." *Journal of Democracy* 27 (1): 5–19.

Bernays, Edward L. 1928. *Propaganda*. New York: Horace Liveright.

Bishop, Bill. 2008. *The Big Sort: Why the Clustering of Like-Minded America Is Tearing Us Apart*. Boston: Houghton Mifflin.

Bourdieu, Pierre. 1998. *Acts of Resistance: Against the Tyranny of the Market*. New York: New Press.

Brennan, Jason. 2016. *Against Democracy*. Princeton, NJ: Princeton University Press.

Buchanan, James M., and Gordon Tullock. 1962. *The Calculus of Consent: Logical Foundations of Constitutional Democracy*. Ann Arbor: University of Michigan Press.

C

Caplan, Bryan. 2007. *The Myth of the Rational Voter: Why Democracies Choose Bad Policies*. Princeton, NJ: Princeton University Press.

Carpenter, Daniel, and David A. Moss, eds. 2014. *Preventing Regulatory Capture: Special Interest Influence and How to Limit It*. New York: Cambridge University Press.

Castells, Manuel. 2009. *Communication Power*. New York: Oxford University Press.

Centola, Damon. 2018. *How Behavior Spreads: The Science of Complex Contagions*. Princeton, NJ: Princeton University Press.

Cialdini, Robert B. 2006. *Influence: The Psychology of Persuasion*. Rev. ed. New York: Harper Business.

Cohen, Joshua. 1989. "Deliberation and Democratic Legitimacy." In *The Good Polity*, edited by Alan Hamlin and Philip Pettit, 17–34. Oxford: Blackwell.

Coleman, James S. 1990. *Foundations of Social Theory*. Cambridge, MA: Harvard University Press.

Coase, Ronald H. 1960. "The Problem of Social Cost." *Journal of Law and Economics* 3: 1–44.

Collier, Paul. 2018. *The Future of Capitalism: Facing the New Anxieties*. New York: Harper.

Cox, Gary W. 1997. *Making Votes Count: Strategic Coordination in the World's Electoral Systems*. New York: Cambridge University Press.

D

Dahl, Robert A. 1971. *Polyarchy: Participation and Opposition*. New Haven, CT: Yale University Press.

Dahl, Robert A. 1989. *Democracy and Its Critics*. New Haven, CT: Yale University Press.

Diamond, Larry. 2019. *Ill Winds: Saving Democracy from Russian Rage, Chinese Ambition, and American Complacency*. New York: Penguin Press.

Dixit, Avinash K. 2004. *Lawlessness and Economics: Alternative Modes of Governance*. Princeton, NJ: Princeton University Press.

Downs, Anthony. 1957. *An Economic Theory of Democracy*. New York: Harper.

E

Easton, David. 1965. *A Systems Analysis of Political Life*. New York: Wiley.

Edelman, Murray. 1964. *The Symbolic Uses of Politics*. Urbana: University of Illinois Press.

Elster, Jon. 1998. *Deliberative Democracy*. Cambridge: Cambridge University Press.

Evans, Peter. 1995. *Embedded Autonomy: States and Industrial Transformation*. Princeton, NJ: Princeton University Press.

F

Farmer, J. Doyne. 2019. *Fluctuations and Finance: A History of the Future*. Oxford: Oxford University Press.

Foa, Roberto Stefan, and Yascha Mounk. 2016. "The Democratic Disconnect." *Journal of Democracy* 27 (3): 5–17.

Fukuyama, Francis. 2011. *The Origins of Political Order: From Prehuman Times to the French Revolution*. New York: Farrar, Straus and Giroux.

Fukuyama, Francis. 2014. *Political Order and Political Decay: From the Industrial Revolution to the Globalization of Democracy*. New York: Farrar, Straus and Giroux.

G

Galston, William A. 2020. *Anti-Pluralism: The Populist Threat to Liberal Democracy*. New Haven, CT: Yale University Press.

Gell-Mann, Murray. 1994. *The Quark and the Jaguar: Adventures in the Simple and the Complex*. New York: W. H. Freeman.

Gerring, John. 2005. "Causation: A Unified Framework for the Social Sciences." *Journal of Theoretical Politics* 17 (2): 163–98.

Gleick, James. 1987. *Chaos: Making a New Science*. New York: Viking.

Goldin, Claudia, and Lawrence F. Katz. 2008. *The Race between Education and Technology*. Cambridge, MA: Harvard University Press.

Granovetter, Mark. 1973. "The Strength of Weak Ties." *American Journal of Sociology* 78 (6): 1360–80.

Greif, Avner. 2006. *Institutions and the Path to the Modern Economy: Lessons from Medieval Trade*. New York: Cambridge University Press.

Guriev, Sergei, and Daniel Treisman. 2022. *Spin Dictators: The Changing Face of Tyranny in the 21st Century*. Princeton, NJ: Princeton University Press.

H

Habermas, Jürgen. 1996. *Between Facts and Norms: Contributions to a Discourse Theory of Law and Democracy*. Cambridge, MA: MIT Press.

Haidt, Jonathan. 2012. *The Righteous Mind: Why Good People Are Divided by Politics and Religion*. New York: Pantheon.

Hall, Peter A., and David Soskice, eds. 2001. *Varieties of Capitalism: The Institutional Foundations of Comparative Advantage*. New York: Oxford University Press.

Hardin, Russell. 2002. *Trust and Trustworthiness*. New York: Russell Sage Foundation.

Hasen, Richard L. 2016. *Plutocrats United: Campaign Money, the Supreme Court, and the Distortion of American Elections*. New Haven, CT: Yale University Press.

Herd, Pamela, and Donald P. Moynihan. 2018. *Administrative Burden: Policymaking by Other Means*. New York: Russell Sage Foundation.

Hirschman, Albert O. 1970. *Exit, Voice, and Loyalty: Responses to Decline in Firms, Organizations, and States*. Cambridge, MA: Harvard University Press.

Holling, C. S. 1973. "Resilience and Stability of Ecological Systems." *Annual Review of Ecology and Systematics* 4: 1–23.

Hollnagel, Erik. 2014. *Safety-I and Safety-II: The Past and Future of Safety Management*. Farnham, UK: Ashgate.

Holland, John H. 1992. *Adaptation in Natural and Artificial Systems*. Cambridge, MA: MIT Press.

Huntington, Samuel P. 1968. *Political Order in Changing Societies*. New Haven, CT: Yale University Press.

I

Inglehart, Ronald, and Pippa Norris. 2019. *Cultural Backlash: Trump, Brexit, and Authoritarian Populism*. New York: Cambridge University Press.

Iyengar, Shanto, and Masha Krupenkin. 2018. "The Strengthening of Partisan Affect." *Political Psychology* 39 (S1): 201–18.

J

Johnston, Michael. 2005. *Syndromes of Corruption: Wealth, Power, and Democracy.* New York: Cambridge University Press.

Judt, Tony. 2010. *Ill Fares the Land.* New York: Penguin Press.

K

Kahneman, Daniel. 2011. *Thinking, Fast and Slow.* New York: Farrar, Straus and Giroux.

Kahneman, Daniel, and Amos Tversky. 1979. "Prospect Theory: An Analysis of Decision under Risk." *Econometrica* 47 (2): 263–91.

Kauffman, Stuart A. 1993. *The Origins of Order: Self-Organization and Selection in Evolution.* New York: Oxford University Press.

Kauffman, Stuart A. 1995. *At Home in the Universe: The Search for the Laws of Self-Organization and Complexity.* New York: Oxford University Press.

Keynes, John Maynard. 1936. *The General Theory of Employment, Interest and Money.* London: Macmillan.

Klein, Ezra. 2020. *Why We're Polarized.* New York: Avid Reader Press.

Kunkel, Lawrence R. 2026. *The Moral Ecology of Collapse: Essays on Inequality, Complexity, and the Instability of Democratic Societies.* New York: Moral Ecology Press

Kuran, Timur. 1995. *Private Truths, Public Lies: The Social Consequences of Preference Falsification.* Cambridge, MA: Harvard University Press.

L

Landemore, Hélène. 2020. *Open Democracy: Reinventing Popular Rule for the Twenty-First Century.* Princeton, NJ: Princeton University Press.

Lessig, Lawrence. 2011. *Republic, Lost: How Money Corrupts Congress—and a Plan to Stop It.* New York: Twelve.

Levitsky, Steven, and Daniel Ziblatt. 2018. *How Democracies Die*. New York: Crown.

Levi, Margaret. 1997. *Consent, Dissent, and Patriotism*. New York: Cambridge University Press.

Lijphart, Arend. 1999. *Patterns of Democracy: Government Forms and Performance in Thirty-Six Countries*. New Haven, CT: Yale University Press.

Lipset, Seymour Martin. 1959. "Some Social Requisites of Democracy: Economic Development and Political Legitimacy." *American Political Science Review* 53 (1): 69–105.

Linz, Juan J., and Alfred Stepan. 1996. *Problems of Democratic Transition and Consolidation*. Baltimore: Johns Hopkins University Press.

Lorenz, Edward N. 1963. "Deterministic Nonperiodic Flow." *Journal of the Atmospheric Sciences* 20 (2): 130–41.

M

Machiavelli, Niccolò. 1998. *The Prince*. Translated by Harvey C. Mansfield. 2nd ed. Chicago: University of Chicago Press.

Mansbridge, Jane. 1983. *Beyond Adversary Democracy*. New York: Basic Books.

Mansbridge, Jane, and Cathie Jo Martin, eds. 2013. *Negotiating Agreement in Politics*. Washington, DC: American Political Science Association.

Mason, Lilliana. 2018. *Uncivil Agreement: How Politics Became Our Identity*. Chicago: University of Chicago Press.

May, Robert M. 1976. "Simple Mathematical Models with Very Complicated Dynamics." *Nature* 261: 459–67.

Meadows, Donella H. 2008. *Thinking in Systems: A Primer*. Edited by Diana Wright. White River Junction, VT: Chelsea Green.

Meadows, Donella H., Dennis L. Meadows, Jørgen Randers, and William W. Behrens III. 1972. *The Limits to Growth*. New York: Universe Books.

Mettler, Suzanne, and Robert C. Lieberman. 2020. *Four Threats: The Recurring Crises of American Democracy*. New York: St. Martin's Press.

Michels, Robert. 1911. *Political Parties: A Sociological Study of the Oligarchical Tendencies of Modern Democracy*. New York: Free Press (later editions).

Milanovic, Branko. 2016. *Global Inequality: A New Approach for the Age of Globalization*. Cambridge, MA: Harvard University Press.

Mitchell, Melanie. 2009. *Complexity: A Guided Tour*. New York: Oxford University Press.

Mounk, Yascha. 2018. *The People vs. Democracy: Why Our Freedom Is in Danger and How to Save It*. Cambridge, MA: Harvard University Press.

Müller, Jan-Werner. 2016. *What Is Populism?* Philadelphia: University of Pennsylvania Press.

Myerson, Roger B. 1991. *Game Theory: Analysis of Conflict*. Cambridge, MA: Harvard University Press.

N

Nash, John F. 1950. "Equilibrium Points in N-Person Games." *Proceedings of the National Academy of Sciences* 36 (1): 48–49.

Neumann, John von, and Oskar Morgenstern. 1944. *Theory of Games and Economic Behavior*. Princeton, NJ: Princeton University Press.

Newman, M. E. J. 2010. *Networks: An Introduction*. New York: Oxford University Press.

North, Douglass C. 1990. *Institutions, Institutional Change, and Economic Performance*. New York: Cambridge University Press.

North, Douglass C., John Joseph Wallis, and Barry R. Weingast. 2009. *Violence and Social Orders: A Conceptual Framework for Interpreting Recorded Human History*. New York: Cambridge University Press.

Nyhan, Brendan, and Jason Reifler. 2010. "When Corrections Fail: The Persistence of Political Misperceptions." *Political Behavior* 32 (2): 303–30.

O

Ober, Josiah. 2008. *Democracy and Knowledge: Innovation and Learning in Classical Athens*. Princeton, NJ: Princeton University Press.

OECD. 2017. *Trust and Public Policy: How Better Governance Can Help Rebuild Public Trust*. Paris: OECD Publishing.

OECD. 2020. *How's Life? 2020: Measuring Well-Being*. Paris: OECD Publishing.

Olson, Mancur. 1965. *The Logic of Collective Action: Public Goods and the Theory of Groups*. Cambridge, MA: Harvard University Press.

Olson, Mancur. 1982. *The Rise and Decline of Nations: Economic Growth, Stagflation, and Social Rigidities*. New Haven, CT: Yale University Press.

Osborne, Martin J., and Ariel Rubinstein. 1994. *A Course in Game Theory*. Cambridge, MA: MIT Press.

Ostrom, Elinor. 1990. *Governing the Commons: The Evolution of Institutions for Collective Action*. New York: Cambridge University Press.

P

Pariser, Eli. 2011. *The Filter Bubble: What the Internet Is Hiding from You*. New York: Penguin Press.

Perrow, Charles. 1984. *Normal Accidents: Living with High-Risk Technologies*. New York: Basic Books.

Pettit, Philip. 1997. *Republicanism: A Theory of Freedom and Government*. New York: Oxford University Press.

Piketty, Thomas. 2014. *Capital in the Twenty-First Century*. Cambridge, MA: Harvard University Press.

Polanyi, Karl. 1944. *The Great Transformation: The Political and Economic Origins of Our Time*. New York: Farrar & Rinehart.

Popper, Karl. 1945. *The Open Society and Its Enemies*. London: Routledge.

Posner, Richard A. 1976. *Antitrust Law: An Economic Perspective*. Chicago: University of Chicago Press.

Putnam, Robert D. 1993. *Making Democracy Work: Civic Traditions in Modern Italy.* Princeton, NJ: Princeton University Press.

Putnam, Robert D. 2000. *Bowling Alone: The Collapse and Revival of American Community.* New York: Simon & Schuster.

R

Rawls, John. 1971. *A Theory of Justice.* Cambridge, MA: Harvard University Press.

Rawls, John. 1993. *Political Liberalism.* New York: Columbia University Press.

Rose-Ackerman, Susan. 1999. *Corruption and Government: Causes, Consequences, and Reform.* New York: Cambridge University Press.

Rosen, Michael. 2012. *Dignity: Its History and Meaning.* Cambridge, MA: Harvard University Press.

Runciman, David. 2018. *How Democracy Ends.* New York: Basic Books.

S

Schelling, Thomas C. 1978. *Micromotives and Macrobehavior.* New York: W. W. Norton.

Scheffer, Marten. 2009. *Critical Transitions in Nature and Society.* Princeton, NJ: Princeton University Press.

Schumpeter, Joseph A. 1942. *Capitalism, Socialism and Democracy.* New York: Harper.

Scott, James C. 1998. *Seeing Like a State: How Certain Schemes to Improve the Human Condition Have Failed.* New Haven, CT: Yale University Press.

Sen, Amartya. 1999. *Development as Freedom.* New York: Knopf.

Solnit, Rebecca. 2009. *A Paradise Built in Hell: The Extraordinary Communities That Arise in Disaster.* New York: Viking.

Sterman, John D. 2000. *Business Dynamics: Systems Thinking and Modeling for a Complex World.* Boston: Irwin/McGraw-Hill.

Stigler, George J. 1971. "The Theory of Economic Regulation." *Bell Journal of Economics and Management Science* 2 (1): 3–21.

Stiglitz, Joseph E. 2012. *The Price of Inequality: How Today's Divided Society Endangers Our Future.* New York: W. W. Norton.

Stiglitz, Joseph E., Amartya Sen, and Jean-Paul Fitoussi. 2009. *Report by the Commission on the Measurement of Economic Performance and Social Progress.* Paris.

Strogatz, Steven H. 2003. *Sync: The Emerging Science of Spontaneous Order.* New York: Hyperion.

Suchman, Mark C. 1995. "Managing Legitimacy: Strategic and Institutional Approaches." *Academy of Management Review* 20 (3): 571–610.

Sunstein, Cass R. 2001. *Republic.com.* Princeton, NJ: Princeton University Press.

Sunstein, Cass R. 2017. *#Republic: Divided Democracy in the Age of Social Media.* Princeton, NJ: Princeton University Press.

Snyder, Timothy. 2017. *On Tyranny: Twenty Lessons from the Twentieth Century.* New York: Tim Duggan Books.

T

Taleb, Nassim Nicholas. 2012. *Antifragile: Things That Gain from Disorder.* New York: Random House.

Tilly, Charles. 2007. *Democracy.* New York: Cambridge University Press.

Tocqueville, Alexis de. 2000. *Democracy in America.* Translated by Harvey C. Mansfield and Delba Winthrop. Chicago: University of Chicago Press.

Tufekci, Zeynep. 2017. *Twitter and Tear Gas: The Power and Fragility of Networked Protest.* New Haven, CT: Yale University Press.

Tyler, Tom R. 1990. *Why People Obey the Law.* New Haven, CT: Yale University Press.

Tushnet, Mark. 2004. *The New Constitutional Order.* Princeton, NJ: Princeton University Press.

Tushnet, Mark. 2014. *The Constitution of the United States of America: A Contextual Analysis.* Oxford: Hart Publishing.

V

Varshney, Ashutosh. 2002. *Ethnic Conflict and Civic Life: Hindus and Muslims in India.* New Haven, CT: Yale University Press.

V-Dem Institute. 2023. *Democracy Report 2023: Defiance in the Face of Autocratization.* Gothenburg: University of Gothenburg.

W

Waldrop, M. Mitchell. 1992. *Complexity: The Emerging Science at the Edge of Order and Chaos.* New York: Simon & Schuster.

Wardle, Claire, and Hossein Derakhshan. 2017. *Information Disorder: Toward an Interdisciplinary Framework for Research and Policymaking.* Strasbourg: Council of Europe.

Watts, Duncan J. 2003. *Six Degrees: The Science of a Connected Age.* New York: W. W. Norton.

Weber, Max. 1946. "Politics as a Vocation." In *From Max Weber: Essays in Sociology*, edited by H. H. Gerth and C. Wright Mills, 77–128. New York: Oxford University Press. (Original lecture 1919.)

Weick, Karl E., and Kathleen M. Sutcliffe. 2007. *Managing the Unexpected: Resilient Performance in an Age of Uncertainty.* 2nd ed. San Francisco: Jossey-Bass.

Winters, Jeffrey A. 2011. *Oligarchy.* New York: Cambridge University Press.

World Bank. 2020. *Worldwide Governance Indicators.* Washington, DC: World Bank.

Z

Zuboff, Shoshana. 2019. *The Age of Surveillance Capitalism: The Fight for a Human Future at the New Frontier of Power.* New York: PublicAffairs.

www.ingramcontent.com/pod-product-compliance
Lightning Source LLC
LaVergne TN
LVHW050526160826
845677LV00011B/1964
* 9 7 9 8 9 9 5 3 8 5 7 1 4 *